Analecta Gregoriana
Cura Pontificiae Universitatis Gregorianae edita
Vol. 252, Series Facultatis Iuris Canonici: sectio B, n. 50

JOSEPH BAJADA

SEXUAL IMPOTENCE

THE CONTRIBUTION OF PAOLO ZACCHIA
(1584-1659)

EDITRICE PONTIFICIA UNIVERSITÀ GREGORIANA

ROMA 1988

IMPRIMI POTEST

Romae die 12 maii 1988

R. P. GILLES PELLAND, S.J.
Rector Universitatis

IMPRIMATUR

✠ GIOVANNI MARRA, *Ausiliare*
Dal Vicariato di Roma, 8 novembre 1988

© 1988 - E.P.U.G. - ROMA

EDITRICE PONTIFICIA UNIVERSITÀ GREGORIANA
EDITRICE PONTIFICIO ISTITUTO BIBLICO
Piazza della Pilotta 35 - 00187 Roma, Italia

ACKNOWLEDGEMENTS

I wish to express my gratitude to all who have encouraged and assisted me during the past years of studies. I am particularly grateful to the Most Reverend Joseph Mercieca, the Archbishop of Malta, for giving me the assignment of post-graduate studies in Canon Law, as well as for his constant assistance.

I sincerely thank the Faculty of Canon Law of the Pontifical Gregorian University and in particular the Dean of the Faculty, Father Urbano Navarrete, S.J., and Fr. Ignacio Gordon, S.J., for his dedicated guidance and direction all throughout my research and writing of this work.

Finally, I wish to express heartfelt gratitude to my parents, my first teachers, for their unwavering example, constant love and prayers, and to all my family and friends in Malta.

For the tiresome work of typing the drafts, I am indebted to Mrs. Valerie Briffa.

May the good Lord bless them all.

9th May, 1988

ABBREVIATIONS

QML	= Paolo Zacchia, *Quaestiones medico-legales*, Lyon 1661. Unless otherwise indicated, all references will be to this edition.
QML, 3.1.1.5.	= Idem. The numbers indicate: 1°: Liber, 2°: Titulus, 3°: Quaestio, and 4°: Paragraphus/Articulus, in this order.
QML, 10 cons. 49.	= Idem, Liber 10, Consilium 49.
QML, 10 dec. XX	= Idem, Liber 10, Decisio XX.
SRRD	= Sacrae Romanae Rotae Decisiones seu Sententiae.
Thesaurus	= Sacra Congregatio Concilii, *Thesaurus Resolutionum S.C. Concilii quae consentanee ad Tridentinorum Patrum decreta aliasque canonici iuris sanctiones prodierunt in causis ab anno 1° (1718) ad annum 168° (1909-1910)*, voll. 1-5, Urbino 1739-1740; voll. 6 ff., Rome 1741 ff.
Volantes	= P.U.G. collection of Rotal Decisions, covering the period 1640-1870 (cfr. chapter One, note 58, p. 39).

CONTENTS

INTRODUCTION

The canonical concept of sexual impotence has undergone a process of development. Although the *ius in corpus* has always been considered as an essential constituent of the object of consent to marriage[1], yet its understanding has evolved through the ages. And it must be admitted that this process was not always a sufficiently clear one.[2] For one thing, canonical doctrine and jurisprudence had to wait for medicine to provide the required

---

[1] "In questa essenza del matrimonio vi è la *deditio* dello *ius in corpus*, a prescindere dall'effettivo esercizio di tale *ius*. Ora, qual'è il contenuto specifico di questo *ius in corpus,* che certamente non esaurisce il matrimonio, ma ne è un aspetto essenziale, senza il quale non vi è matrimonio? Il contenuto di esso è lo scambio tra gli sposi — che avviene nel *matrimonium in fieri* e si concreterà poi nel rapporto dato dal *matrimonium in facto esse* — del diritto ed insieme del dovere aventi per oggetto certi atti fisici. Questi atti fisici, se debbono constituire gli atti mediante i quali si realizza la *una caro* secondo natura, non possono che essere gli atti stessi con i quali l'*actio naturae* arriva alla procreazione": O. GIACCHI, *Relazione*, in *Quaderni Romani di Diritto Canonico*, P. Fedele (dir.), Roma 1978, pp. 13-14.

[2] "The reference to impotency in the Code of Canon Law is very brief and direct. To all appearances, it would give the impression that the entire matter was very clear, provided no difficulties or problems, and gave rise to no controversies. However, before this study is completed, the reader realizes that beneath and in the back of the rather innocent wording of the statute lies a long history of conceptual and notional evolution, which has included many difficulties, controversies, divergent opinions and contradictory statements": HARRINGTON, P., *The impediment of impotency and the notion of male impotency*, in *The Jurist*, 19 (1959) 29-30. About the history of this impediment of impotence in the law of the Church, cfr.: D'AVACK, P.A., *Cause di nullità e di divorzio nel diritto matrimoniale canonico*, Florence 1952, pp. 426-449; CAPPELLO, F.M., *Tractatus canonico-moralis de Sacramentis iuxta Codicem Iuris Canonici*, vol. V: *De matrimonio*, 6th edit., Rome 1950, pp. 386-388; ESMEIN-GENESTAL, *Le mariage en droit canonique*, vol. I, 2nd edit., Paris 1929, pp. 259-270; OESTERLE, G., *Impuissance*, in *D.D.C.*, coll. 1262-1268; WERNZ-VIDAL, *Ius canonicum ad codicis normam exactum*, vol. V: *Ius matrimoniale*, ed. altera, Rome 1928, n. 222, pp. 247-250.

scientific foundations on which to base itself, given that impotence is a biological concept.[3]

For centuries the problem of what really constitutes the canonical impediment of sexual impotence has been at the center of attention and the theme of innumerable studies and never-ending discussions. One such study was provided as far back as the early 17th century by a well-known pioneer of forensic medicine in Italy: PAOLO ZACCHIA (1584-1659). A doctor by profession, who also possessed a sound basis of philosophy, theology and canon law, Zacchia set out his expert thinking on the problem of sexual impotence in his monumental treatise — the *Quaestiones medico-legales* — in which he also examined a variety of other arguments.

One would perhaps approach yet another work on this problem with some scepticism, since it would seem just a superfluous addition to the long list of studies available on impotence. But this is not so. A careful study of Zacchia's treatise as well as of the related sources and ecclesiastical jurisprudence would immediately prove such an approach to be quite unjustified. His *Quaestiones*, in fact, provide a fine example of professional reflection, in which medicine and law found a peaceful and harmonious coexistence, because of which Zacchia soon proved to be an unequalled authority, especially in ecclesiastical tribunals, for more than two centuries.

One of Zacchia's great merits and important contributions to law lies in his extensive and detailed, though at times understandably limited, exposition of the subjects he treated, as well as in the rather accurate reflection which he offered from a canonical point of view. One can readily understand, therefore, the great interest canonists showed in his work, especially when one considers that there existed as yet no such complete and systematical treatment from the medico-legal point of view. And it was precisely this which soon turned Zacchia's *Quaestiones medico-legales* into a constant point of reference and a very useful tool for judges and advocates alike. The most tangible proof of this lies not only in the frequency with which in the past the name of Zacchia appeared in manuals of canon law and collections of ecclesiastical jurisprudence, but most of all in the respect he was shown as an authority in legal matters.

In matters of impotence and non-consummation of marriage, Paolo Zacchia was time and again hailed by ecclesiastical Judges as

---

[3] Cfr. FEDELE, P., *Problemi di diritto canonico. L'impotenza*, Rome 1962, pp. 76-80.

inter veteres et recentes peritos facile princeps doctissimus. This remark is not without significance, when one considers the fact that the period in which Zacchia wrote his treatise was particularly important to the whole problem of sexual impotence, since it immediately followed on the publication of the Brief *Cum Frequenter* of Pope Sixtus V, on the 27th June 1587. Besides, Thomas Sánchez had just died, leaving behind him one of the greatest classical works on marriage. Nor is there any doubt about the influence which Sánchez's interpretation of and proposed doctrine on the notion of impotence had on the following generations.

THE PROBLEM OF SEXUAL IMPOTENCE.

Impotence may be defined as the inability to perform the sexual act: *impotentia coeundi*, which both jurisprudence and canonical doctrine clearly distinguish from the other type of impotence, namely *impotentia generandi* or sterility. Only the former carries juridical relevance[4], in that such impotence would *ex ipsa eius natura* render a marriage null.[5]

As far as *potentia coeundi* is concerned, the physical elements that are juridically required for the conjugal copula are: on the part of man, erection of the genital organ, penetration inside the woman's vagina and ejaculation therein. On the other hand, the woman must possess a vagina that is capable of receiving the male's genital organ inside it as well as ejaculation therein.[6] This is today quite peacefully admitted by almost everyone, but in the past things were somewhat different.

Undoubtedly, the most thorny question of all regarded the nature of the ejaculated semen. The actual problem started in the

---

[4] The motive behind the actual formula *impotentia coeundi* in the new law is that "plures dantur species impotentiae (coeundi, generandi, moralis) et etiam quia conceptus canonisticus impotentiae organicae (impotentia coeundi) non coincidit cum conceptu impotentiae legum civilium, quae generatim impotentiam generandi considerant": *Communicationes*, 7 (1975) 53; cfr. Ibid., 15 (1983) 228.

[5] Code of Canon Law, canon 1084#1; cfr. *Communicationes*, 7 (1975) 54-56.

[6] To the query whether a definition of a perfect copula was to be introduced in the Code, "omnes consultores negative respondent. Nulla definitio neque descriptio copulae perfectae facienda est. Sufficit ut in normis quae attinent sive ad consummationem sive ad impedimentum impotentiae, saltem oblique illa elementa appareant quae sint necessaria ad copulam, super quae versari debeat consensus et sine quibus aliquis impotens dici debeat". However, the necessity of penetration as an element of the perfect copula was retained: *Communicationes*, 6 (1974) 184-186.

latter half of the 16th century when doubts were raised concerning the validity of the marriage of men who, though they lacked both testicles, nevertheless retained the ability to have an erection and even to penetrate inside the wife's vagina.[7] There were then three different opinions: some authors maintained that such persons could validly marry even if they could not emit any semen at all, since through their copula they could still achieve one of the ends of marriage, namely the *remedium concupiscentiae*; others, however, claimed that some form of semination was required, and consequently such persons could only marry validly if they were capable of some sort of ejaculation inside the vagina; finally, there were those authors who insisted that such persons were indeed impotent, since they could not ejaculate *verum semen*.[8]

Since such a situation was creating pastoral and moral problems, the Apostolic Nuncio in Spain turned to the Supreme Authority enquiring "quid de huiusmodi connubiis sit statuendum". Pope Sixtus V gave a twofold answer: in the first place, he noted that

> "secundum canonicas sanctiones et naturae rationem, qui frigidae naturae sunt et impotentes, iidem minime apti ad contrahenda matrimonia reputantur";

and such frigid men could only pretend to be potent, for in reality they are not at all capable of erection, penetration and ejaculation of any sort of semen. In the second place, added the Pope, from the marriage of such men "nulla utilitas provenit", in other words, no end of marriage could be achieved. And the Pope made no reference to the *verum semen* or to the *humorem forsan quemdam similem semini* about which there was express reference in the doubt raised by the Nuncio![9]

It is common knowledge that after the promulgation of this document, a new element was introduced to define the concept of *potentia coeundi*: the ejaculation of the *verum semen* by the man

---

[7] CASTAÑEDA DELGADO, E., *Una sentencia española en el siglo XVI. La validez del matrimonio de los eunucos y espadones*, in *Revista Española de Derecho Canónico*, 12 (1957) 259-287.

[8] Cfr. GORDON, I., *Adnotationes quaedam de valore matrimonii virorum qui ex toto secti sunt a tempore Gratiani usque ad Breve "Cum Frequenter"*, in *Periodica*, 66 (1977) 171-247; DEL AMO, L., *La impotencia que dirime el matrimonio. Comentario al Decreto de 13 de mayo de 1977*, in *Revista Española de Derecho Canónico*, 33 (1977) 462.

[9] SIXTUS V., Epist. *Cum Frequenter*, 27th June 1587, in *Fontes Codicis Iuris Canonici*, vol. I, n. 169, pp. 298 ff.

inside the female's vagina. And in this, Thomas Sánchez played a very influential role. During the last century then, Cardinal Gasparri identified this *verum semen* with the *semen in testiculis elaboratum*.

This line of interpretation was taken up by the Tribunals of the Roman Rota and remained constant until our own days. Rotal jurisprudence unanimously required for the perfect copula on the part of man the possibility for the semen elaborated in the testicles to pass into the vagina of the woman, and this through erection and penetration inside it. Thus, for example, a decision coram Wynen, stated:

> "Iurisprudentia igitur Rotalis, quae innititur sana doctrina communi probatorum Auctorum, tenet tantum, ad copulam perfectam statuendam necessarium esse ut vir praeditus sit testiculis qui, neque difformes neque atrophizati, semen elaborare *possint*, et ut habeat canales communicantes pervios per quos semen ad extra eiaculari *possit*".[10]

On the other hand, however, and despite this common opinion, a minority of authors still considered that for the natural copula, the ejaculation of the semen elaborated in the testicles was not necessary. They did not consider such semen as an essential element of the perfect copula. If a man could perform a *copula satiativa*, he could not be considered impotent.[11]

Such doubts were not confined to authors alone. In fact, the whole problem rose again towards the end of the last century, when sterilisation as a preventive measure against the transmission of certain illnesses started to be practised in some countries.[12] It was only, however, in the thirties of this century that such a practice constituted grave concern when it became legally enforced in Germany. Given the circumstances, some German Ordinaries

---

[10] Decision of the 25*10*45, in *SRRD*, 37 (1945) 583, n. 12. Cfr. c. BONET, 24*4*67, in *SRRD*, 59 (1967) 223, n. 3: "Cum tamen coitus tria complectatur, nempe erectionem veretri virilis, penetrationem in vaginam mulieris ac eiaculationem in eam seminis in testiculis elaboratum. Hinc trita est iurisprudentia quae docet uti verum semen habendum non esse liquidum emissum ab illis qui testiculis omnino careant, vel eos plene atrophicos habeant, vel occlusam viam qua liquidum in testiculis elaboratum defertur per urethram emittendum, habeant."

[11] Cfr. VERMEERSCH, A., *Theologia Moralis*, vol. IV, Rome 1954, n. 47, pp. 48-49; AREND, R.D., *De genuina notione impedimenti . impotentiae*, in *Ephemerides Theologicae Lovanienses*, IX (1932) 67-69; VLAMING-BENDER, *Praelectiones iuris matrimonii*, ed. Busum, Holland 1950.

[12] Cfr. DE SMET, A., *Tractatus theologico-canonicus de sponsalibus et matrimonio*, Bruges 1927, p. 382.

consulted the Holy Office, the present-day S.C. for the Doctrine of the Faith, and asked whether a person who had undergone double vasectomy could be permitted to marry, "cum verum semen emittere non valeat atque de hoc extrinsecus certe constet". The reply of the Holy Office was always a constant one, to the effect that in line with paragraph 2 of canon 1068, the marriage was not to be impeded.[13]

Such a praxis was clearly in open contradiction with the position taken by the Roman Rota as well as by the Congregation for the Sacraments, which likewise expressed itself in favour of a dispensation *super rato* when the perpetuity of such an inability to ejaculate *verum semen* could not be proved in a given case.[14]

Gradually, however, and in spite of the authority of ecclesiastical jurisprudence in favour of the necessity of the *verum semen*, the position of the Congregation of the Doctrine of the Faith gathered more momentum and in the early seventies, it could be stated that:

> "iamvero, non obstante auctoritate iurisprudentiae tribunalium ecclesiasticorum et praxis S. Sedis, progredientibus scientiis anthropologicis atque doctrina catholica de matrimonio, probabilior fit in dies sententia quae tenet semen in testiculis elaboratum non esse elementum essentiale copulae coniugalis ideoque potentes ad matrimonium exsistere posse, qui semen in testiculis elaboratum emittere nequeant, itemque matrimonium consummari posse copula carnali in qua semen testiculare non emittatur".[15]

And in fact, during the process for the revision of the Code of Canon Law, the Pontifical Commission took up the question "de impotentia organica et speciatim de vasectomia viri, an sit retinenda tamquam impotentia viri matrimonium dirimens".[16] Almost in their unanimity, those consulted expressed themselves in favour of the *copula satiativa libidinis*, as required and sufficient for the validity of marriage. It was also pointed out that in reality that

---

[13] S.C.S. Officii, Resp. to the Ordinary of Aachen, 16*2*1935: Ochoa, X., *Leges Ecclesiae post Codicem Iuris Canonici editae*, vol. I, Rome 1966, n. 1262; cfr. Silvestrelli, A., *Circa l'impotenza e l'inconsumazione nella giurisprudenza canonica anche del S. Ufficio*, in Monitor Ecclesiasticus, 98 (1973) 114-117.

[14] Cfr. Gómez López, A., *Revisión del concepto de impotencia a la luz del Decreto de la Sagrada Congregación para la Doctrina de la Fe, del 13.5.77*, in Ius Canonicum, 17 (1977) 33: 163-180.

[15] Navarrete, U., *De notione et effectibus consummationis matrimonii*, in Periodica, 59 (1970) 628.

[16] *Communicationes*, 6 (1974) 177.

doctrine and jurisprudence which through the ages had insisted on the necessity of the *verum semen in testiculis elaboratum* and on a *copula apta ad generationem* had exaggerated the notion of *impotentia coeundi* to such a point as to cause confusion in the distinction between both types of impotence, that is, *coeundi* and *generandi*.[17] In the end, save for some exceptions of minor importance, all the consultors were of the opinion that

> "valde expedit ... ut reditus fiat ad doctrinam antiquorum secundum quos illa copula habebatur perfecta quae sit satiativa libidinis, sine respectu ad naturam veri seminis"[18];

and consequently, while insisting on the necessity of penetration as an essential element of *potentia coeundi*, "omnes consultores negant necessitatem seminis prout a iurisprudentia rotali requiritur".[19] For the perfect copula therefore, the *semen in testiculis elaboratum* is not to be considered as an essential element.

Finally, in line with the new orientation of Vatican Council II[20] and with this position of the Pontifical Commission for the Revision of the Code of Canon Law, on the 13th May 1977, the Congregation for the Doctrine of the Faith published a decree *circa impotentiam quae matrimonium dirimit*, in which it authentically set

---

[17] "Doctrina et iurisprudentia, quae asseruerunt necessitatem seminis in testiculis elaborati copulaeque per se aptae ad prolis generationem, ita notionem impotentiae coeundi exaggeraverunt ut distinctio ipsam inter et generandi impotentiam confusa facta sit. Immo notio ipsa matrimonii ita strictiorem habuit sensum ut eius finis, qui primarius dicebatur et in prole ponebatur, quasi tota esset unaque coniugii causa. Ex qua exaggeratione nata est illa gravissima discrepantia quae deprehenditur in decisionibus S. Sedis: viro qui vasectomiam subiit matrimonium non prohibetur; viri autem, qui accusatur apud Tribunalia de incapacitate emittendi semen in testiculis elaboratum, matrimonium nullum dicitur propter impotentiam. Et quidem in recentioribus sententiis quorundam tribunalium remota est clausula de non transeundo ad alias nuptias, quae viro ita impotenti antea dabatur. Confusio crescit in dies": *Communicationes*, 6 (1974) 179.

[18] *Ibid.*, p. 179.

[19] *Ibid.*, p. 179. "In tota traditione usque ad Epist. *Cum Frequenter* Sixti V, 22 iunii 1587, videtur historice certum Ecclesiam numquam exegisse capacitatem emittendi semen in testiculis elaboratum ut quis potens haberetur ad matrimonium contrahendum. A matrimonio excludebantur uti impotentes tantum illi qui seminationem ordinariam habere nequibant. Seminatio vero ordinaria reputabatur illa qua libidinis sedatio seu naturae resolutio obtinebatur": *Communicationes*, 6 (1974) 186-187. This position has been proved right by GORDON, I., art. cit., supra note 8, and by McGRATH, A., *A controversy concerning male impotence.* Analecta Gregoriana, vol. 247, Rome 1988.

[20] Cfr. *Communicationes*, cit., p. 187; NAVARRETE, U., loc. cit., pp. 628-629.

forth the actual doctrine of the Church.[21] This decree resolved in a
definite way the long-lasting problem, by declaring that the *verum
semen* understood in the sense of the *semen in testiculis elaboratum*
is not a necessary element of the perfect copula; and consequently,
in conformity with its long-standing praxis, "a matrimonio non esse
impediendos eos qui vasectomiam passi sunt aliosque in similibus
conditionibus versantes."

THE CONTRIBUTION OF PAOLO ZACCHIA.

In this wider perspective, Zacchia's expert opinion on what
really constitutes the sexual copula that is required for the canonical validity of a marriage can be better appreciated.
Zacchia readily admitted the opinion which held that for the
validity of marriage, one had to be free of any "vitium quo
impeditur alteri carnaliter commisceri".[22] On the part of man, this
meant that he could achieve an erection, sufficient to penetrate the
wife's vagina and ejaculate therein. Zacchia considered all three
elements as essential for a perfect copula. Besides, it is only
through such a copula that a marriage can be truly consummated.
Still this position of the author, both as a doctor and as a legal
expert, differed substantially from the opinion which was then
current among other authors and canonists, and this in the way he
understood the terms of this description of the copula.
Zacchia was fully aware of the trend that had established itself
after Sixtus' Brief and which required, as an essential element of
the copula, the ejaculation of the *verum semen*. But he evidently
did not share such a view! Strictly linking the function of the
testicles with the elaboration of the seminal liquid "ut generationis
materia fiat", Zacchia concluded that the absence or anomalous
condition of these organs as such only affected the person's ability
to procreate, while it usually left him capable of an otherwise
normal sexual act through which the other ends of marriage could
be achieved. The strict relation between testicles, *verum semen* and
generation is very evident in Zacchia, so that his position was
definitely in favour of the opinion that held that the *copula satiativa
libidinis* is all that is truly required for the validity of marriage. In
reality, argued Zacchia, those men who lacked both testicles

---

[21] S.C. pro DOCTRINA FIDEI, *Decretum circa impotentiam quae matrimonium
dirimit*, 13 maii 1977, in *AAS*, 69 (1977) 426.
[22] ZACCHIA, P., *QML*, 3.1.1.6.

"apti sunt ad coeundum, non tamen apti sunt ad generandum, ob seminis absentiam aut imperfectionem".[23]

Nor did the author share what then appeared to be another current opinion among canonists regarding the necessity of penetration for the consummation of marriage. Canonists readily admitted that a *copula appositiva* consummates marriage. Zacchia himself literally quoted Thomas Sánchez to the effect that a joining of bodies is not required and provided that the husband's semen *quacumque arte* enters the wife's vagina, the marriage was to be considered as consummated.[24] But this position was untenable for Zacchia: "a canonistarum determinatione recedere cogor". He insisted that effective insertion of the male's genital organ inside the vagina and ejaculation therein are both equally essential for the true concept of consummation:

> "absque ulla haesitantia firmandum est, matrimonium consummari ubi per membra generationis coniuges commixti fuerint prout natura exposcit".[25]

Zacchia's contribution to the true understanding of sexual impotence was indeed a valid one; and the importance of its study is evidently not merely of a purely historical nature. It is true that for many years, his position regarding the ability of vasectomised men to contract a valid marriage was not taken up. In the end, however, if the praxis and the decree of the Sacred Congregation for the Doctrine of the Faith proved him right, he in turn provided incontestable proof that, contrary to all authoritative allegations, Sixtus' *Cum Frequenter* did not really resolve the question in the sense it was claimed to do and that all along there was indeed much reason to doubt the wisdom of the opinion that was actually followed.

THE OBJECT OF THIS STUDY.

For all these reasons, the object of this study is to present the thought and doctrine of Paolo Zacchia on *impotentia coeundi*, its definition, classification, causes, its forensic implications for the validity of marriage, and above all, to find out where his original

---

[23] *Ibid.*, 9.3.7.1; cfr. 3.1.5.19; 3.1.9.13; 9.3.2.16.
[24] Cfr. SÁNCHEZ, T., *De sancto matrimonii sacramento disputationum*, Lyon 1654, 2.21.5.
[25] ZACCHIA, P., *QML*, 9.10.1.8.

contribution towards the right understanding of sexual impotence lay.

To do this, we shall first present the author, his socio-cultural environment and his contribution to forensic medicine in general. To provide the basis for an assessment of the real nature of sexual impotence as understood by this author, we shall then pass on to see some aspects that are particularly related to the question of generation, and the knowledge which his times afforded to Zacchia in this regard. This will be followed by Zacchia's doctrine on the role of sexual relations in marriage and his definition and distinctions of sexual impotence. The last four chapters are dedicated to Zacchia's treatment of the different causes of organic and functional impotence, both in man and in woman.

In every case, Zacchia's opinion is evaluated not only against the background of the then current medical knowledge and canonical doctrine, but also in the light of modern medical science. In this way, both the limitations and the true worth of Zacchia's contribution can be appreciated.

Three appendices are added to this study. The first contains a complete catalogue of all the published and unpublished works of the author. The second contains some of the more important tributes paid to Zacchia by his contemporaries; while the third reproduces the complete index to his *Quaestiones medico-legales*. This last index is in itself further proof of the author's vast forensic knowledge, while at the same time it shows the extensive treatment he gave to all the arguments he presented.

CHAPTER ONE

THE AUTHOR AND HIS WORK

1. INTRODUCTION.

The seventeenth century can well be described as the age that saw experimental science in its infancy; an infancy that was to grow and reach its maturity in the following centuries. This was the time that marked both an achievement in itself and a starting point for science in general, and perhaps for medicine in particular. It was a point of arrival for the preceding so-called "dark" ages, for it did provide some really useful and enlightened observations, which due to a lack of mature experience were left isolated and unreflected upon. Important works belonging to this period were produced by Redi in the field of helminthology[1] and by Ramazzini who contributed to social medicine with his *Diatriba de morbis artificum*.[2] Other no lesser important contributions were made by Théophile Bonet and Jean Jacques Manget with their respective *Sepulcretum*[3] and *Teatrum Anatomicum*[4], which marked a step forward in the study of anatomy.

This period, however, was also a starting point for science. It was during this century that solid foundations were laid, upon which later discoveries and verifications were eventually based. In

---

[1] REDI, F., *Osservazioni intorno agli animali viventi che si trovano negli animali viventi*, Florence 1684.

[2] RAMAZZINI, B., *Diatriba de morbis artificum*, Modena 1679.

[3] BONET, T., *Sepulcretum sive anatomica pratica*, Geneve 1679.

[4] MANGET, J.J., *Teatrum anatomicum*, 1717.

the field of medicine the seventeenth century marked a true scientific renaissance. It was the century of consolidating previous scientific thinking and a great step forward in enriching the knowledge inherited up to that time. It was during that century that light was shed on many of the physiological and pathological phenomena of the human organism.

The seventeenth century has been called the "golden age" of medicine. It was the century in which Galileo invented the microscope and opened new horizons to the scientist of his time. Such a discovery was to revolutionize all the ideas concerning the process of fecundation and generation, which is not without special interest for the theme under discussion. In fact the century of Galileo was also the time in which the problem of generation was actually tackled with new vigour, marking a glorious page in the history of embriology with such names as Fabrizi, Aromatari, Harvey, Stenson, Redi, Malpighi, Swammerdam, De Graaf, Ham, Leeowenhoek, Bonelli: all milestones in this field.[5]

This was "the century of genius", as the seventeenth century has been called. And it is among these respectable architects of science that we find one of the great names of that century, Paolo Zacchia, who made a valid contribution to the field of forensic medicine.

2. PAOLO ZACCHIA: HIS LIFE.

Paolo Zacchia was born in Rome in 1584. He received his general education under the Jesuits, and afterwards dedicated himself to the study of Medicine. He proved to be a man of great talents and at an early age he received his doctorate degree at the "Archiginnasio Romano della Sapienza". In 1644 he was designated "General Proto-Physician of the entire Ecclesiastical State" by Pope Innocent X.

Although very little is known about the life of this "notissimus, doctissimusque Philosophus et Medicus"[6], we do know that Zacchia had a versatile mind and was a man of vast knowledge. Possessing a profound humanistic culture, he was also both a lover

---

[5] Cfr. FRANCESCHINI, P., *Il secolo di Galileo e il problema della generazione*, in *Physis*, 4 (1964) 141, 148.

[6] MANDOSIO, P., *Theatron in quo maximorum Christiani orbis pontificum archiatros Prosper Mandosius inspectandos exhibet*, in MARINI, G., *Degli Archiatri pontifici*, vol. II, Rome 1784, p. 119.

and a composer of music. He likewise delighted himself in painting and poetry.

Besides being one of the most eminent doctors of his time, Paolo Zacchia was also well versed in philosophy, theology and jurisprudence.[7] As a medical practitioner he exercised his profession with great ability and conscientious responsibility, earning himself both fame and fortune.[8]

Paolo Zacchia died in Rome in 1659, at the age of seventy-five. He was buried in the Church of Santa Maria in Vallicella, commonly known as La Chiesa Nuova.

3. HIS WORKS.

Zacchia's acute sense of observation is well shown in his many writings dealing with the most varied arguments, which bear witness to his vast culture and to his medical, philosophical and literary knowledge.[9]

Among the more important of these writings, one can mention *Il Vitto Quaresimale*, a small booklet published in 1637 in which the author explained how one was to regulate oneself in matters of diet and of fasting during Lent, without causing harm to one's health. In this book, Zacchia gave details about the food to be used, the mistakes to be avoided in its preparation and use; the time when certain food was not to be used, the harms it might cause and the remedies for any indispositions it might cause.[10]

Another much more important work by Zacchia was his *De' Mali Hipochondriaci*. First published in Rome in 1639, the book was several times corrected and revised by Zacchia himself.[11] It

[7] *Ibid.*, pp. 119-120; cfr. CAPPARONI, P., *Profili bio-bibliografici di medici e naturalisti celebri italiani dal secolo XV al secolo XVIII*, vol. II, Rome 1926, pp. 134-136.

[8] KARPLUS, H., *Medical ethics in Paolo Zacchia's "Quaestiones medico-legales"*, in *International Symposium on Society, Medicine and Law, Jerusalem, March 1972*, ed. KARPLUS, H.,Amsterdam 1973, pp. 125-134. Cfr. DEFFENU, G., *Invito a Zacchia*, in *Castalia*, 9 (1953) 101-106.

[9] Cfr. infra, Appendix One, p. 165 for a complete list of Zacchia's works.

[10] *Il Vitto Quaresimale* di Paolo Zacchia medico romano. Ove insegnasi, come senza offender la sanità si possa viver nella Quaresima. Si discorre de' cibi in essa usati, degli errori che si commettono nell'usargli, dell'indisposizioni ch'il loro uso impediscono, de gli accidenti, che soglion cagionare e del modo di rimediarvi, Rome 1637.

[11] *De' Mali Hipochondriaci* libri due di Paolo Zacchia, medico romano. Nel primo s'insegna quanto appartiene alla cognitione, e alla cura di questi mali. Nel secondo si discorre degli accidenti di essi, e de' loro rimedii, Rome 1639.

immediately met with success not only in Italy, but in other
countries as well. Stimulated by "the strange and marvellous effects
of such sickness", as he himself pointed out in his preface to the
book[12], Zacchia explained its various definitions, gave a list of its
symptoms and treated its pathogenesis and prognosis, at the same
time also suggesting the necessary therapy. Once again, this work
bears the mark of a great learned scholar, as the many detailed
references clearly show.

But the work that was to bring immortal fame to our author
was undoubtedly his treatise entitled *Quaestiones medico-legales in
quibus omnes eae materiae medicae, quae ad legales facultates
pertinere videntur, pertractantur et resolvuntur.* This was a work
which for its vastness of thought, its copious doctrine, and the
technical know-how of its exposition, was to become the classical
text of undiscussed authority for the next two centuries.[13] The
work, made up of nine books, was published gradually over a
period of time, taking about twenty-nine years to be entirely
published. Book I was published in Rome in 1621, whereas the
ninth book was first published in Amsterdam in 1650. The first
complete edition, consisting of the nine books, was published in
Lyon in 1654. After the author's death, his nephew Lanfranco
added a tenth book containing a series of eighty-five cases ("consilia"), all previously written by Zacchia, as well as a hundred
decisions of the Roman Rota.[14]

These cases and Rotal decisions deal with various arguments,
which Zacchia had already treated in the first nine books. According to Pazzini, it is this collection of Rotal Decisions, which extends
from 1569-1657, that gives an experimental dimension to Zacchia's
work. By experimental it is here meant that the author's doctrine
and conclusions did not merely rely on the undiscussed authority of
dogma, but rather on his own counterproof. To experiment means
to ascertain at practical level that which theory affirms, to control
that which has already been stated, at the same time adding
something that has not as yet been suggested, and which is the fruit
of personal research.[15]

As the text of Zacchia gradually found itself in the hands of

---

[12] *Ibid.*, pp. 1-2.
[13] Cfr. PALMIERI, V.M., *Medicina Forense*, Naples 1964, p. 10; PALAZZINI,
A., *Storia della medicina*, Milan 1949, p. 93.
[14] Cfr. infra, Appendix One, p. 165.
[15] Cfr. PALAZZINI, A., *Elogio di Paolo Zacchia*, in *Pagine di storia della
medicina*, 4 (1960) 136.

doctors and jurists, it immediately became apparent that it constituted a singular contribution in which medicine and law found a
peaceful coexistence. The tributes paid to Zacchia clearly show the
impact that the work had from its earliest publications. Hailed as
"the Mercury of doctors and jurists" and "the Italian Hermes"[16] by
his contemporary scholars, Zacchia was described even in the
twentieth century as "the most learned exponent in medico-legal
matters of the 17th century"[17], "the illustrious representative of
forensic medicine whose universal prestige surpassed that of his
predecessors" and as "the uncontestable master of forensic
medicine".[18] With this contribution, Paolo Zacchia earned himself
a place with G.F. Ingrassia, G.B. Codronchi and F. Fedele as one
of the four great pioneers in the history of forensic medicine in Italy
during the sixteenth and seventeenth centuries.[19]

4. THE *Quaestiones medico-legales*.

Zacchia divided each of the nine books in chapters or "tituli",
the number of which goes from a minimum of two to a maximum of
five for each book. Each chapter treats a different argument and
there is generally no connection between the contents of one
"titulus" and another in the same book. Every "titulus" is in turn
subdivided in "quaestiones" (extending from a single "quaestio" to
twenty-four for each chapter). Each one of these "quaestiones" is
further subdivided in paragraphs, every one of which is headed by
an enumerated brief summary of the contents according to the
order in which it is treated.

A quick review of the various "tituli" immediately shows the
vast perspective and the laborious work that our author set himself.
The arguments he treated dealt with all the topics that today form
the subject matter of forensic medicine. They range from the most

---

[16] Cfr. DEFFENU, G., cit., p. 104; infra, Appendix Two, p. 167, for the
tributes paid to Zacchia.

[17] ZIINO, G., *Medicina legale e giurisprudenza medica*, vol. I, Milan 1906, pp.
13-14.

[18] LAIGNEL LAVASTINE, M., *Histoire générale de la médicine*, vol. II, Paris
1938, p. 228; vol. III, Paris 1949, pp. 464-465.

[19] RANDONE, M., *Le origini della medicina legale*, in *Minerva Medica*, 57
(1966) 1532; cfr. DEFFENU, G., cit., in note 8, p. 101; PAZZINI, A., *Paolo Zacchia e
l'opera sua massima*, in *Zacchia*, 23 (1960) 529; GERIN, C., *La medicina legale nei
suoi momenti storici e nel suo sistema*, ibid., 12 (1949) 15-16; LAIGNEL LAVASTINE,
M., cit., vol. II, p. 228.

classical ones related to sexual matters (virginity, rape, impotence, marital relations), to forensic obstetrics (pregnancy, childbirth), to traumatology (wounds) and toxicology (poison); to those most modern of forensic psychology and psychiatry; to anthropology (age, irregularities, monsters), to crime and punishment. To all this, Zacchia added other themes dealing with miracles, monastic life and stigmata.[20]

Perhaps what first attracts one's attention on reading Zacchia's work is the fact that while he proposes to address himself primarily to the jurist, he does so in the shoes of a doctor, who is well acquainted with human physiology as well as with the different maladies — both physical and psychiatric — to which man is subject. As a doctor, Zacchia set himself the task to study the various maladies in order to offer the legal institutions new elements that would help to avoid erroneous decisions. His aim was therefore to make clear the juridical implications and consequences of medical questions. Accordingly one can see his constant preoccupation to offer the word of a medical expert to the legal forum. By doing so, he was able to provide the legal background for the common Courts and for the Ecclesiastical Tribunals: impediments, irregularities, matrimonial matters; as well as queries connected with illnesses, death and its causes.[21]

If one were to grade or create a scale of the sciences, there is no doubt that for Zacchia, medicine is a step higher than law. According to Amerio, "Zacchia, the restorer of forensic medicine was a doctor and he felt himself to be above all a doctor; nor did he hesitate to defend medicine openly against the criticisms that were directed against this discipline"[22], although he also held the jurist in great esteem.[23] Zacchia considered medicine a part of philosophy,

---

[20] Cfr. infra, Appendix Three, p. 173, for the Index to the *QML*.

[21] ZACCHIA, P., Preface to "Lectori Legumperito", in *QML*, Lyon 1661, on page 16 of the unnumbered pages at the beginning of vol. I: "Bona igitur spe stimulatus ad operis finem propositum assequendum totis nervis contendi, qui talis fuit, ut iurisperitis primo, ac dehinc etiam medicis ipsis scriberem, ac utrisque quoad fieri poterat, satisfacerem ... Neque enim ut iurisperitis rem gratam facerem sat habui, eas materias, quae ad propositum argumentum pertinebant, nostro, medico nimirum more, pertractare, sed omnino me in iurisperitum transformare tentavi, ac in omnibus, et per omnia legaliter agere". Cfr. *ibid.*, 2.1.1.1-3.

[22] AMERIO, A., *La preminenza della medicina sul diritto nel pensiero di Paolo Zacchia*, in *Medicina nei Secoli*, 8 (1971) 4: 53-54; cfr. *QML*, 2.2.13.1; 3.1.1.5; 3.1.3.6; 3.2.2.4; 5.1.1.7; 6.3.8 per totam; 9.10.1.7.

[23] *QML*, 6.3.1.1-4. According to Zacchia, the jurist is he who "in constitutarum legum recta perceptione insistit, ut quam maxime fieri potest, secundum

as the science of natural things.[24] As a science, it considers the natural elements in relation to the health of the human body. He argued that the doctor, as a doctor, occupies a higher position than the jurist, because he offers the human community a greater good, that is health. Zacchia considered medicine as a social, and therefore, a collective reality. When speaking of law, he distinguished jurists from judges and it is to the former, and not to the latter, that he attributed what has been stated above. The jurist furnishes the proper interpretation of laws to the judges, just as those who gather medicinal herbs provide the doctor with the means with which he effects cure. Both doctors and judges are, therefore, a step higher than the herbalist and the jurist.[25]

Zacchia's medico-legal treatise was therefore of a great social import, and it has always been considered as such. Of its very nature, forensic medicine has its very roots in the social vision of the art and science of medicine. The intimate connection between the doctor and the legislator clearly demostrates the close link that exists between medicine and law. Laws are the norms, the canons that regulate the life of society. Therefore their medical aspect cannot but be likewise social. It was with this intuition that Zacchia probed deeper into the precincts of law. The legislator himself could not dare to make such a step, nor was he equipped to do it, since he did not have the required medical competence. For this reason, our author sought, found and studied new points of contact where medicine could contribute to the social life of the human community and there, he authoritatively suggested what the legislator had to keep in mind and follow when formulating new laws, and how the judge was to interpret and apply the norms.

Zacchia's success in establishing this harmonious relation between medicine and law was recognised and appreciated by his contemporary scholars.[26] And it was precisely for this reason that Paolo Zacchia came to be considered as the renewer and cofounder of forensic medicine, as an independent discipline in all its ramifications. Zacchia could very well say that he had reached his aim, namely that of presenting both doctors and judges with a scientific text based on medical, juridical, philosophical, social, moral and religious foundations.[27]

---

earum mentem et dispositionem, particularium casuum decisionem, a iudice reportet", 6.3.7.12.

[24] *Ibid.*, 6.3.7.13-14.
[25] *Ibid.*, 6.3.8.24; cfr. AMERIO, A., cit., pp. 52-53.
[26] Cfr. infra, Appendix Two, p. 167.
[27] OTTOLENGHI, S., *Il nuovo Istituto di Medicina Legale della R. Università di*

Zacchia had at hand the works of about 270 doctors, 200 jurists and theologians, as well as 90 other authors from which he abundantly quoted to corroborate his conclusions.[28] From all of them he drew all the available information he wanted. All throughout, Zacchia offered a clear intuition that only later was to be better understood.[29]

Zacchia was grateful to the great thinkers of all times, and he recognised and paid tribute to their greatness and the contribution they had made to society. This is evident from his frequent references to their works. But he also realised and pointed out the limits that their own times imposed on them. He knew his own times and the progress that had been made; but he also realised that new problems faced the man of his own era. He likewise knew what means his own times afforded him to meet and cater for these problems. Above all, he wanted to use his mind and his means. To do this he was even ready to contradict what the great masters had said. What mattered was the truth; what was said, not who said it. And the truth was to be his only guide. He made this point very clear in his writings. For example, in his preface to *De' Mali Hipochondriaci* Zacchia wrote:

> "chi vorrà raffrontare, quanto io son per dirne con quanto n'han detto gli altri, ch'avanti di me hanno scritto, vi troverà delle cose non mica di niun momento di più di quelle, ch'appresso gli altri si ritrovano; ancorchè, se vogliamo dar fede ad un dottissimo scrittore moderno, e gli antichi e i moderni autori in trattar di questi mali siano stati manchevoli havendo tralasciate le più importanti e necessarie cose per conoscergli, e per curargli ancora".[30]

And in his address to the members of the medical profession who were to read the *Quaestiones medico-legales*, Zacchia asked:

> "Num tantum posse debet personarum acceptio ut magis attendendum, ducatur, quod quisquis sic loquatur, quam quid loquatur? ... ego praeceptores summo honore afficiendos esse sentio, caeterum quemlibet philosophari etiam contra eorum dogmata non solum non improbandum sed laudandum, nec modo non negligendum, sed

---

Roma. Discorso inaugurale, in *Zacchia*, 3 (1924) 4-5; cfr. GERIN, G., cit., pp. 15-16.

[28] A complete list of all the authors quoted or referred to by Zacchia is given on pp. 22-24 (unnumbered) at the beginning of *QML*, Avignon 1655.

[29] PAZZINI, A., *L'opera medico-sociale di Paolo Zacchia*, Rome 1964, p. 7; cfr. OTTOLENGHI, S., cit., pp. 4-5.

[30] ZACCHIA, P., *De' Mali Hipochondriaci*, Rome 1637, p. 3.

optandum, neque enim aliter in dies magis magisque veritas
elucescit, etiam ex his, que contra ipsam veritatem pronunciantur.
Quod ergo hic me tantopere in multis medicinae, ac philosophiae
praeceptoribus primariis contrariari comperias, scito, Deum
hominesque testor, nonnisi rerum veritatem indagandi avidum, id
me patrasse; et licet potuerit vana veritatis species me decipere,
tamen non ob id accusandum me erroris existimes, quisquis es qui
veritatem prae omnibus amandam ac recolendam censes".[31]

Zacchia seemed convinced. He was not afraid to embark and
continue on the road of progress!

5. ZACCHIA'S CONTRIBUTION TO LEGAL MEDICINE.

Legal medicine was a new medical discipline that naturally
followed the anatomical and surgical progress of the period. It is
here that Zacchia's *Quaestiones medico-legales* constitute a land-
mark in the early history of the subject. Few physicians enjoyed
more universal respect from their contemporaries than did Zacchia,
who thereby came to enjoy an authoritative position in the legal
profession as well as among physicians. The *Quaestiones* came to be
considered as a classic text throughout Europe. It is a fact that his
work, despite its shortcomings, surpassed those of his reknowned
predecessors and contemporaries[32]; and this not only in the number
of arguments treated but also, and perhaps above all, in the learned
exposition of every subject he treated.
    Zacchia's major contribution consisted in his ability to collect,
organise, evaluate and draw to a logical conclusion what previous
great thinkers had written about, but which they had left dispersed
and disorganised. On his part, Zacchia succeeded in producing the
first systematic treatise which contains an extraordinary amount of
legal information.[33] In all the arguments he treated, Zacchia
showed a great sense of objectivity in his investigation and inde-

---

[31] Idem, Preface to "Lectori Medico", in *QML*, page 15 (unnumbered) at the
beginning of vol. I.
[32] By way of example, one can perhaps mention: CODRONCHI, G.B., *De
christiana ac tuta medendi ratione*, Ferrara 1591; Idem, *Methodus testificandi*,
Ferrara 1597; FEDELE, F., *Contemplationum medicarum*, Palermo 1621; SEVERINO,
M.A., *Therapeuta neapolitanus seu veni mecum consultor*, Naples 1653; CARDANO,
J., *Opera omnia*, Lyon 1663.
[33] Cfr. PAZZINI, A., *Paolo Zacchia e l'opera sua massima*, in *Zacchia*, Serie
2a, 23 (1960) 529; CARRARA, M.-ROMANESE, R.-CANUTO, G.-TOVO, C., *Manuale di
medicina legale*, vol. I, Turin 1937, p. 6.

pendence of judgement. What adds to his original value is therefore
the precision of his analysis and the prudence projected in his
conclusion.[34] It is evident that Zacchia's main preoccupation was to
give the most complete treatment he could of every argument he
examined.

It has been said above that Zacchia also offered a rare intuition
in some of the arguments which he treated. With a great sense of
modern feeling, Zacchia was the first doctor to treat about the
matter of life insurance and to suggest the medico-legal implications that had to be taken into consideration.[35] As a doctor he
designated himself as the arbiter in deciding the questions which
arose from current legislation. He treated in detail the causes,
natural or otherwise, of death, speaking at length about contagious
diseases and concluding that epidemics were to be considered
among the causes of an unnatural death. In each case he suggested
when contractual stipulations should be considered binding or
not.[36]

Zacchia also showed a great sense of intuition regarding
diabolical possession. It is clear that, notwithstanding his intention
to reject all mistaken views yet, in practice he could not openly
challenge some, at least, of the current laws of his time. Indeed,
had he indiscriminately applied a criterion of judgement totally
contrary to that of the period in which he lived, he would have had
difficulty not only in having his views accepted by his contemporaries, but also, and this would have been graver still, in preparing
and opening the way to true progress. On the other hand, Zacchia
did not completely refrain from manifesting his views and making a
daring step forward. He was well aware of the possible reaction that
his intellectual courage and faith in the truth clarified by his
scientific study would have to face. In fact, diabolical possession
and witchcraft constituted a true social calamity in those times.
Naturally the social importance of all this was great.[37] Zacchia
sought a medical explanation of the phenomenon, which up till that
time had always been viewed "in an atmosphere of satanic

---

[34] Cfr. LAIGNEL LAVASTINE, M., *Histoire générale de la médicine*, vol. III,
Paris 1949, p. 298; OTTOLENGHI, S., cit., p. 6.

[35] *QML*, 2.3.1-15.

[36] Cfr. FRACHE, G., *Elementi di medicina legale della assicurazione vita negli
scritti di Paolo Zacchia*, in *Atti del III Congresso Internazionale di Medicina
dell'Assicurazione Vita*, Rome 1949.

[37] Cfr. PAZZINI, A., *Storia della medicina*, vol. III, Milan 1947, pp. 89-93;
CASTIGLIONI, A., *A history of medicine*, New York 1947, pp. 498-500.

surrealism".[38] He set himself the task of presenting a systematic study of mental illnesses in relation to the legal forum, suggesting a terminology that, more than was customary during his times, was nearer to that used in clinical psychiatry today. Up till then, this branch of medicine had received only occasional and cursory attention. With sufficient clarity, Zacchia expressed his views and intuitions in what was to be a true and proper treatise of psychiatry, giving a full treatment of the subject.[39]

So important was his contribution in this regard, that modern scholars do not hesitate to divide the history of psychiatry in two periods: the pre-Zacchia and the post-Zacchia.[40]

Contact with the people led the author to conclude that diabolical possession was in fact an illness, a distortion of the mind. Zacchia noted that in common parlance the majority of persons suffering from any sort of mental deficiency were called *daemoniaci*. On his part, however, he retained that such a term was to be reserved only to those

> "qui ex malincholiae vitio, quo tanquam instrumento utitur daemonium eos obsidens, in insaniam aguntur... Licet enim causa insaniae in his supernaturalis semper existat, hoc est, daemonium corpus obsidens, tamen praecedit semper corporis dispositio quaedam ex malincholia ... quae hominem ad insaniam concinnat".[41]

The devil, Zacchia argued, delights himself in the melancholic condition of those suffering from depression. Such a conclusion was not without importance, since it shows that according to Zacchia the ultimate cause of some mental illness was not to be attributed to the devil but to a pathological reason. In other words, medical science had another, more reliable explanation of the phenomenon. One proof of this, said Zacchia, was that even in the case where one was freed of diabolical possession through exorcism and other religious means, the patient was still helped along by other natural (medical) remedies.[42]

---

[38] PAZZINI, A., op. cit., in note 29, pp. 7-8.

[39] QML, 2.1.1-23.

[40] Cfr. PAZZINI, A., *Storia della medicina*, cit., p. 89; LAIGNEL LAVASTINE, M., *Histoire générale...*, cit., vol. III, pp. 297-298.

[41] QML, 2.1.18.1-14.

[42] QML, 2.1.18.13-18: "Licet enim causa insaniae in his supernaturalis semper existat, hoc est, daemonium corpus obsidens, tamen praecedit semper corporis dispositio quaedam ex melancholia, ... quae hominem ad insaniam concinnat ...; etiam daemoniaci, et a malo spiritu obsessi post exorcismos, et Ecclesiae ceremonias, naturalibus auxiliis, et remediis iuvantur...; quod reme-

Sometimes, claimed our doctor, an illness appeared to be so grave, its symptoms so rare and its course so abnormal, that being unable to explain all this, one would quickly attribute it to some supernatural factor and often to the devil. Zacchia warned that one should not let himself be perplexed by some situations that were difficult to explain, nor be misled by rumors which very often were started by incompetent persons. Rather than hurriedly attributing the causes of some mental illness (no matter how odd) to some supernatural or malign spirit Zacchia counselled that one had to look for its natural cause.

> "An non ob eam causam, plurimas earum, ut alias dixi, a daemonibus obsessas existimamus, et tandem tamen naturalibus remediis eas curatas conspicimus, quod in illis naturalis tantum causa suam vim exerceret? ... Non ita ergo nos moveat symptomatum insuetorum frequentia, ut supernaturalibus causis tribuamus, quod a naturalibus originem habet".[43]

Zacchia therefore believed that "diabolical possession" was only the result of a natural condition having a medical explanation. In spite of the views held in his times, he nevertheless succeeded in reconciling science and religious faith even in this field.

6. ZACCHIA'S ROLE AS COURT EXPERT.

In elaborating the theme under discussion, namely Zacchia's teaching on sexual impotence, we can see the author at his best. His aim was quite a modest one, and he had no false pretences. Marriage is among the prior interests of canonists, and the doctor is very often called upon to give a helping hand with the problems that face the Judge:

> "In contrahendis matrimoniis multae causae interveniunt, ex quibus aut ea dissolvi contingit, aut divortium inter coniuges fieri, vel torum separari, inter quos causas non postremae considerationis nonnullae sunt, quae ad medicam speculationem pertinent; et idcirco a medico discutiendae, et examinandae".[44]

Among such causes that lead to the breakdown of marriage, the principal one is *impotentia coeundi,* and here the doctor has a very

---

dium, etiamsi supernaturale pie existimandum sit, tamen naturalem habet causam". Cfr. *QML*, 2.1.23.5; 4.1.8.25-30.

[43] *QML*, 10 cons. 49.9-10; cfr. 4.1.4.8-9; 7.4.4.1; 10 cons. 49.4.

[44] *QML*, 9.10.1.1.

important contribution to give, a fact which Rotal Jurisprudence repeatedly stressed.[45]

Zacchia did not deal "ex professo" with the doctor's role as an expert in legal matters in one place, but his ideas can easily be gathered. His aim was always to offer expert counsel to jurists and to tribunal personnel who were often faced with many doubts. Zacchia argued that in making decisions, the judge had to realise that he was in need of the prudent counsel of the doctor, since he was dealing with matters that were not, or could not be defined by law.[46] Zacchia did not usurp the jurist's right and duty to interpret laws, nor the judge's exclusive right and competence to apply them. On the contrary, he even praised them for the scientific mastery of their profession. But, he argued, in medical matters their knowledge was necessarily limited and they could not competently make certain decisions. Zacchia had this to say about the advice provided by the expert to the judge:

> "Communis autem iurisconsultorum opinio, de qua ille, est eam rem iudicis arbitrio decidendam esse. Quam tamen opinionem prudenter quidem moderatur Farinaccius, volens in hoc iudicem debere sequi medicorum aut chirurgorum sententiam. Et iure quidem optimo. Quomodo enim arbitrabitur iudex ex se in re, quam prorsus ignorat? Quanquam enim scientissimus legum fuerit, et exquisite, quantum ad iurisconsultum pertinet, de ea temporis conditione determinare sciverit, naturam tamen particularium individuorum, cuius respectus habendus in sententia ferenda, nunquam ut medicus callere poterit ... Quod quanam ratione per se determinare absque medicorum ope iudex possit, ego quidem non video".[47]

Time and again, Zacchia repeated that "in particularibus ad medici iudicium recurrendum omnino est", for only in this way could the judge acquire a complete knowledge of the situation and give a just decision.[48] The medical expert's advice was not only welcome, but

---

[45] A number of Rotal decisions reproduced in Book 10 of the *QML* clearly affirm this practice. Cfr. for example: c. COCCINO, Toletana Nullitatis Matrimonii, 18 februarii 1639, n. 4: 10 dec. LXXX; c. SERAPHINO, Favetana Matrimonii, 1 februarii 1585, n. 5: 10 dec. VII; c. BUBALO, Calaguritana Divortii, 13 iunii 1584, n. 8: 10 dec. VI; c. MANTICA, Romana Donationis annuli, 10 maii 1589, n. 2: 10 dec. IX; c. LUDOVISIO, Pampilonensis Abbatiae de Azara, 20 iunii 1603, n. 10: 10 dec. XXIII; c. PENIA, Virdunensis Fructum, 5 iulii 1604, n. 3: 10 dec. XXV; c. VEROSPIO, Melvitana Antianitatis, 1 iulii 1643, n. 12: 10 dec. LXXXIII; etc.
[46] *QML*, 2.2.4.19: "... adhibito prudentium medicorum iudicio; nam arbitrium iudicis intrat in rebus minime a iure definitis, vel quae definiri non possunt".
[47] *QML*, 5.2.5.8-9; cfr. 3.3.1.1.
[48] *QML*, 3.1.6.41; cfr. 2.1.1.1-3; 2.2.1.1-4; 3.1.7.32; 3.1.9.11-12; 3.2.1.4; 4.1.1.1; 4.2.1.1; 4.2.5.1; 5.1.1.1-7; 5.3.1.4; 5.4.1.1; 5.4.6.1; 6.3.7.14-15; 7.1.1.4; 7.3.2.3.

essential, and jurisprudence itself insisted on this, since in such cases the right solution "ex medica solummodo officina depromere iurisconsultis licet".[49]

For this reason, when giving his contribution, the expert must be conscious of his responsibilities, and "arti suae fidere et eius praecepta solertissime exequi"; he must be diligent in his preparation and let justice be the sole guide that enlightens his way. Nor should such an expert simply be content with the usual means that medical science provides him with. On the contrary, he should strive to find all the elements that can help him arrive at the right solution.[50]

The expert's intervention was as necessary as it was indispensable also in matters related to the conjugal relationship: from the exchange of the marital right to problems of impotence and non-consummation of marriage. With regards to impotence, Zacchia noted that where doubts arose as to a person's ability or otherwise to have intercourse, doctors were to be consulted[51].

Speaking of the great confusion and the many fables that were in circulation regarding this problem in marriage, Zacchia was rather ironical when he referred to whole chapters written by jurists and canonists about "de frigidis et maleficiatis". He noted that authors massed up all cases of people who were unable to perform the sexual act for any reason whatsoever, even when such impotence resulted neither from frigidity nor from any "maleficium". He also referred to the confusion that existed regarding the two types of impotence, namely *impotentia coeundi* and *impotentia generandi.*[52]

At this stage, one should perhaps note that in spite of his being so sure of himself, Zacchia did commit certain mistakes, which will be discussed in greater detail further on in this study. Some of these mistakes he could not completely avoid, since medicine had not as yet evolved to such a point that could permit him a clear knowledge of the nature of things. A case in point is Zacchia's teaching on the "semen" produced by the female. But on other occasions, Zacchia erred in spite of the fact that the point in question had already been

---

[49] *QML*, 2.1.1.3.

[50] *QML*, 6.1.6.14; cfr. 3.2.2.3; 6.1.5.26; 6.1.6.15.

[51] *QML*, 3.1.1.5: "Hinc patet multoties de sufficientia, aut insufficientia coeundi dubitari posse, quo in casu, ut in aliis multis, qui circa hanc materiam iurisconsultos exercent, medici in iudices, tamquam periti adhibentur". Cfr. 3.1.5.41; 3.1.7.32; 3.2.7.2; 7.3.1.1-4; 7.3.2.3; 4.2.1.1.

[52] Cfr. infra, chapter 3, Art. 3, pp. 75 f; chapter 5, Art. 2, pp. 115 f.

clarified and proved. Thus, for example, his theory — inspired by Aristotle — on the nature and fragility of the "seminis spiritus", which could not survive "ne per momentum quidem" outside the vagina, led him to deny any possibility whatsoever of conception, unless this was preceded by penetration and ejaculation of the semen inside the vagina. In other words, Zacchia stubbornly denied that the vagina could absorb inside it any semen that might have been ejaculated "ante portas", or that might have come in contact with the external genital organs.[53]

On his part, Zacchia readily excused canonists for their limited knowledge of certain things. Since canonists were not doctors, they did not have the necessary knowledge and intuition to achieve a true insight into the nature of medical factors. Consequently they based their conclusions on external appearances thereby risking, and in fact sometimes even making the wrong conclusions.

He therefore invited them to search for the truth from the right persons:

> "Adeant canonistae medicos in operationibus naturalibus expertissimos; hi enim ipsos a veritate pueriliter aberrantes sensu ipso, non effictis quibusdam historiolis, ac nugis ad eius semitam manuducent; non enim canonistae ab aliis canonistis, aut aliis professoribus ediscere debent, quid in rei veritate evenire inter generantes naturaliter possit, quid non".[54]

Following this advice, the canonist would avoid committing puerile mistakes or making certain statements that lack any solid basis or are destitute of any truth.

There is therefore no doubt that Zacchia assumed the role of an expert in legal matters. This role as he saw it, was to clarify doubtful cases and to help the judge understand the nature of a particular illness or impediment, and accordingly decide on the sufficiency or otherwise of proof and gravity in case. As an expert,

---

[53] Cfr. infra, chapter 2, Art. 2, # 3, pp. 54 f; chapter 4, Art. 1, pp. 81 ff. To do justice to Zacchia, however, it must also be said that such doubts were still possible since the discovery of the spermatozoon was still a long way off; and therefore its true nature was still shrouded in mystery. Future discoveries would show that the spermatozoon was not as fragile as Aristotle, and Zacchia himself, would have it.

One may perhaps also mention some other obvious shortcomings of Zacchia's work, such as references which are not sufficiently corroborated with the necessary details and abbreviations of titles or books and names of authors, without providing a key list of such abbreviations. Cfr. PALMIERI, V.M., *Medicina Forense*, Naples 1964, pp. 10-14; DEFFENU, G., cit. in note 8, pp. 105-106.

[54] *QML*, 9.10.1.7; cfr. 7.3.1.54; 9.3.5.5.

Zacchia only wanted to say that which was considered medically certain. Furthermore, he limited himself to give his opinion from a medical point of view, without trespassing the limits that were beyond his medical profession and competence.[55]

In fact, he felt it his duty to make this point clear to his reader:

> "Illud ante omnia lectorem commonendo, me semper tanquam medicum loqui, nolens, ut haec quae assero, vim legis habeant, sed ea potius canonistarum iudicio submittens illud unum satis superque mihi esse testatus, si secundum artem quam profiteor, ea quae sese mihi offerunt discutienda, determinavero".[56]

In all the matters which he treated, he followed the same pattern sticking to his profession, yet, at the same time drawing the attention of canonists to certain queries to which they had to provide an answer. When treating impediments and irregularities, Zacchia noted that the method he used there, was the same as that he used throughout his work:

> "In quibus pertractandis, a consueto, et mihi alias familiari modo non recedam, qui semper is fuit, ut ea tantum quae ad meam professionem spectant, assertive doceam, caetera vero, quae ad alios pertinent professores, proponam tantum, aut nonnisi conditionaliter, et quatenus non aliter iisdem professoribus visum fuerit, decidere ambigam. Quod tanto curiosius et in aliis argumentis praestiti, et in iis praestabo, quanto ad theologos, et canonistas ea spectare magis noverim, cum nonnisi, prout hi edocere ex Catholicae fidei documentis me debent, omnia ac singula a me proferri desiderem".[57]

The conclusion is not only clear but also very important: Zacchia did not intend to establish laws or question canonical norms, but to offer the necessary medical knowledge and insight in the light of which the legislator was to establish laws and canonists and judges to interpret and apply them correctly. If one is to interpret Zacchia correctly and to do justice to him, it is essential that this premise be kept constantly in mind.

In view of all this, it is interesting to see how Zacchia's treatise was greeted by canonists, particularly in the environment of ecclesiastical tribunals. Among the various sources studied to answer this question, there is one of the collections of Rotal

---

[55] *Ibid.*, 3.1.8.20; 8.1.2.17; 8.1.13.4; etc.
[56] *Ibid.*, 7.2.1.17.
[57] *Ibid.*, 8.1.1.1.

decisions known as *Volantes*.[58] However, Zacchia's authority in the Tribunal of the Rota is not restricted to his time alone. It is very indicative to note that he is still quoted in the twentieth century.[59] Another important source which sheds further light on the role of Zacchia as court expert, is the collection of decisions published by the Sacred Congregation of the Council, *Thesaurus Resolutionum S. Congregationis Concilii*.[60] The decisions contained therein cover a period that extends from 1718 to 1910.

The conclusion that one draws from such a study leaves no doubt as to the respect and authority that Zacchia enjoyed in forensic circles. He was hailed by the Rota as "nostri aevi alter Hippocrates"[61] and by the Congregation of the Council as "non minus in utroque iure quam in arte medica excellens".[62] In the judgement of this Congregation, Zacchia was a true "peritissimus"[63], who dealt "aptissime et acutissime" with the

---

[58] The term *Volantes* refers to those "decisiones quas vel Cameralis Impressor, vel aliquae privatae et innominatae personae in complures tomos religarunt, a Camerali Typographo acquirendo exemplaria decisionum, quae dietim cameralis typographia excudebat pro litigantibus" — CERCHIARI E., *Cappellani Papae et Apostolicae Sedis Auditores causarum sacri palatii Apostolici seu Sacra Romana Rota*, vol. I, Rome 1921, pp. 255-257, n. 11.

In this study, we have used the collection held at the Pontifical Gregorian University, "quae constat 321 voluminibus, et comprehendit 'Volantes' impressas in typographia Camerae Apostolicae ab anno 1640 ad annum 1870. Decisiones distribuuntur intra singulos annos secundum dioeceses (quae procedunt ordine alphabetico et intra dioeceses secundum ordinem chronologicum; praeterea plura volumina pollent foliatione et indice manuscriptis" - GORDON, I., *Decisio Signaturae Iustitiae diei 19 iunii 1834 qua nova forma contentiosi-administrativi in statu Pontificio introducta est*, in *Investigationes Theologico-Canonicae*, Rome 1978, p. 186, note 5.

[59] Cfr. *SRRD*: 13 (1921), dec. 12, nn. 2-3; 14 (1922), dec. 13, n. 3; 16 (1924), dec. 4, n. 11; 19 (1927), dec. 11, n. 2; *ibid.*, dec. 30, n. 3; 22 (1930), dec. 10, n. 6; 23 (1931), dec. 36, n. 2; 25 (1933), dec. 24, n. 2; 33 (1941), dec. 89, n. 6; 34 (1942), dec. 27, n. 2; *ibid.*, dec. 38, n. 2; dec. 69, n. 2; c. MASALA, Romana Nullit. Matrim., ob impotentiam viri, 7 octobris 1980, in *Monitor Ecclesiasticus*, 106 (1981) 326, n. 18.

[60] S. CONGREGATIO CONCILII, *Thesaurus Resolutionum S. Congregationis Concilii*, quae consentanee ad Tridentinorum Patrum decreta aliasque canonici iuris sanctiones prodierunt in causis ab anno 1° (1718) ad annum 168° (1909-1910). Voll. 1-5, Urbino 1739-1740; voll. 6ff., Rome 1741ff.

[61] Coram ZARATE, Bononien. Fideicommissi de Buccaferris, 24 maii 1655, n. 2, in *QML*, 10 dec. XCVIII.

[62] Bonearen. Matrimonii, 23 iunii 1900, in *Thesaurus*, vol. 159, p. 466.

[63] Panormitana Matrimonii, 12 iulii 1890, *Ibid.*, vol. 149, p. 635, n. 5; Cameracen. Dispensat. Matrimonii, 20 ianuarii 1894, *ibid.*, vol. 153, p. 29; Parisien. Dispensat. Matrimonii, 17 decembris 1898, *ibid.*, p. 898; Cameracen. Matrimonii, 31 iulii 1897, *ibid.*, vol. 156, p. 342; Seinen. Matrimonii, 16 februarii

arguments he studied.[64] In matters of impotence and non-consummation of marriage as well as of mental illness, Zacchia was time and again referred to as "inter veteres et recentes peritos facile princeps doctissimus"[65] and as "scientiae Magister et Nestor".[66]

In these matrimonial decisions, one very frequently finds the name of Paolo Zacchia side by side with that of other doctors and jurists whose medical and forensic treatises were to appear many decades, even centuries later — Mahon, Schuring, Vannet, Filippi, Garnier, Bartholin, Laura, etc., side by side with Capelmann, Teuchmeyer, Antonelli and Eschbach. Canonists like Schmier[67], Pichler[68], Schmalzgrueber[69] and Cosci[70] considered Zacchia as a major source of information, in matters of impotence, non-consummation and nullity of marriage. This is not astonishing when one considers how Zacchia was still at the centre of attention in the discussions that raged about the true understanding of *impotentia coeundi* and *impotentia generandi* (with special reference to the female side) at the turn of the twentieth century.[71] Indeed, even

---

1884, *ibid.*,vol. 143, p. 150; Pragen. Dispensat. Matrimonii, 29 maii 1869, *ibid.*, vol. 128, p. 409; etc.

[64] Curien. Matrimonii, 26 ianuarii 1878, *ibid.*, vol. 137, p. 52, n. 22.

[65] Lycien. Matrimonii, 30 iunii 1877, *ibid.*, vol. 136, p. 323, n. 13; Neapolit. Matrimonii, 15 decembris 1888, *ibid.*, vol. 147, pp. 808-819; Parisien. Matrimonii, 23 ianuarii 1892, *ibid.*, vol. 151, p. 3; Scepusien. Dispensat. Matrimonii, 18 martii 1893, *ibid.*, vol. 152, p. 131; Toloson. Dispensat. Matrimonii, 25 maii 1895, *ibid.*, vol. 154, p. 392.

[66] Curien. Matrimonii, 20 iulii 1878, *ibid.*, vol. 137, p. 367, n. 12.

[67] SCHMIER, F., *Iurisprudentia canonico-civilis seu Jus Canonicum universum iuxta V libros Decretalium*, lib. IV, *De matrimonio*, Salzburg 1729, pp. 58-61, 104-110, 125.

[68] PICHLER, V., *Ius Canonicum secundum quinque decretalium titulos Gregorii Papae IX explicatum*, lib. IV, *De sponsalibus et matrimonio*, Venice 1758, pp. 485, 504.

[69] SCHMALZGRUEBER, F., *Ius ecclesiasticum universum*, lib. IV, pars II, *Sponsalia et matrimonium*, Rome 1845, pp. 9, 151f.

[70] COSCI, C., *De separatione tori coniugalis*, lib. II, cap. XII, Florence 1856, pp. 375-383.

[71] Cfr. ESCHBACH, A., *Disputationes physiologico-theologicae*, Rome 1901, pp. 22-184; Idem, *De novo quodam sterilitatis conceptu*, Rome 1902, pp. 9-16, 34-39; ANTONELLI, J., *De conceptu impotentiae et sterilitatis relate ad matrimonium*, Rome, 1900, pp. 24-45, 100-102; Idem, *Pro conceptu impotentiae et sterilitatis relate ad matrimonium. Animadversiones in opus P. Eschbach "Disputationes" etc.*, Rome 1901, pp. 18-22, 35-38, 44-46, 83-86; Idem, *De mulieris excisae impotentia ad matrimonium*, Rome 1903, pp. 21-3, 73-79; ARENDT, G., *Relectio analitica super controversia de impotentia feminae ad generandum*, Rome 1913, passim; Idem, *Circa controversiam validitatis matrimonii feminae excisae*, Rome 1923, pp. 10-13; DE LUCA, M., *Summa praelectionum in libris decretalium*

well into the present century, canonists still referred to Zacchia as a major source of their doctrine. One may quote Cappello, Oesterle, and Gasparri in this respect.[72]

commentarii in Libro IV seu de sponsalibus et matrimonio, Prato 1904, pp. 232-255.

[72] CAPPELLO, F.M., *Tractatus canonico-moralis de sacramentis,* vol. V, *De matrimonio,* Rome 1947, pp. 348ff; OESTERLE, D.G., *De hermaphrodismo in sua relatione ad canonem 1068 CIC,* in *Il Diritto Ecclesiastico,* 1948, pp. 5-25; GASPARRI, P., *Tractatus canonicus de matrimonio,* Rome 1932, pp. 313ff.

CHAPTER TWO

PARTICULAR ASPECTS RELATED TO THE PROBLEM OF GENERATION

Introduction — Art. 1. The concept of generation in the great doctors and philosophers preceding Zacchia. # 1. Hippocrates, Aristotle and Galen. # 2. From Galen to the Renaissance — Art. 2. Zacchia's theory of generation. # 1. The function of the testicles. # 2. The female's role. # 3. The process of generation. — Art. 3. New discoveries and critique of Zacchia's theory. # 1. Important discoveries. # 2. The generative system in the light of modern science. 1. A basic outline. 2. The testicles, the spermatozoon and its iter. 3. The ovary, the ovum and its iter.

INTRODUCTION.

It has been said in the first chapter that although Zacchia was well versed in theology and canon law, among other sciences, it was primarily as an experienced doctor of medicine, that he wrote his *Quaestiones medico-legales*. It is therefore important, in view of the theme that forms the subject of this study, to see what knowledge he had of the anatomical, biological and physiological elements and functions that come into play in the process of generation. Such an approach is all the more warranted by the fact that the concepts of *impotentia coeundi* and *impotentia generandi* were, in the past, always considered in strict relation.[1] For this reason, if one is to appreciate Zacchia's contribution to the complex question of sexual impotence, the insights which his times afforded him must be kept well in view.

Even a cursory reading of the *Quaestiones* immediately shows that notwithstanding his frequent references to his contemporary and immediately preceding anatomists and biologists, Zacchia's

---

[1] Such a strict treatment of both types of impotence often gave rise to confusion, which was caused by the different terminology used in canon law, civil law and medicine. Cfr. FEDELE, P., *L'impotenza*, Rome 1962, p. 78.

medical foundation stones were the writings of Hippocrates, Aristotle and Galen. In this chapter we shall therefore start by giving a very brief exposition of the theories of generation propagated by the great doctors and philosophers that preceded Zacchia. Zacchia's own theory is then presented against this general background and from the merely medical point of view. Lastly the discoveries that were made in the period following the publication of his treatise are presented; for it is against objective facts that the true worth of Zacchia's theory must be evaluated. All along, we shall limit ourselves to those particular aspects of generation that are strictly connected with the functional aspect of sex.

Art. 1.   THE CONCEPT OF GENERATION IN THE GREAT DOCTORS AND PHILOSOPHERS PRECEDING ZACCHIA

1. *Hippocrates, Aristotle and Galen*

The problem of generation has always aroused man's interest. Scholars of medicine and philosophers never abandoned their search to penetrate into this mysterious world. But the first detailed and clear-cut treatment of this problem is associated with the name of *Hippocrates* (c. 460-c. 375 B.C.). Although Hippocrates had only an elementary knowledge of anatomy and physiology, yet it is generally agreed that he set medicine in the direction of scientific thought.[2]

When treating the argument of generation, Hippocrates took his point of departure from the premise that both sexes are equal as regards the functional aspect of sex in generation. Although he had no knowledge of the female ovaries and held that the testicles in man serve only as a passage for the sperm yet, Hippocrates also affirmed that both the male and the female produce their own sperm which, when they unite, generate a new being.[3] According to

---

[2] Is is held that some, at least, of the writings attributed to Hippocrates were in fact written by Polybus, his son-in-law. Cfr. LITTRÉ, *Oeuvres complètes d'Hippocrate, traduction nouvelle avec le teste grec en regard*, Paris 1839; NEEDHAM, J., *History of Embriology*, Cambridge 1934, p. 31; STROPPIANA, L. *Il concetto di generazione nel "Corpus Hippocraticum"*, in *Atti e Memorie dell'Accademia di Storia dell'Arte Sanitaria*, 4 (1964) 122. P. ZACCHIA himself noted: "Hippocrates ipse, vel quisquis sit eorum libellorum auctor", 9.2. qu. un. 6.

[3] HIPPOCRATES, *De genitura liber*, in the series "Medicorum graecorum opera quae extant", edited by GOTTLOB KÜHN, C., vol. 21, Leipzig 1825, p. 379.

Hippocrates, this semen is the product of the whole body, though it is the brain which mostly contributes to its formation.[4] At the moment of sexual intercourse, the humidity in the body becomes like effervescent foam, the semen is carried through the veins to the spinal cord and the kidneys, whence it makes its way to the testicles en route to the genital organ. The semen serves not only as a matter for the formation of the foetus, but also as a stimulant for sexual intercourse.[5]

At the moment of intercourse, the female too ejaculates her own semen, sometimes inside the vagina (which is why it is moistened) and sometimes outside.[6] If the female's semen is deposited inside the vagina, both semina mix together and unite to start the process of generation. Hippocrates thought that in both semina there is a male and a female sperm, of which the former is the stronger, although it is not always the male who produces the stronger sperm.[7]

Aristotle (384-322 B.C.) was the first biologist who tackled the issue of generation as a fundamental philosophical problem. He distinguished four ways of generation, among which the most common is through sexual intercourse.[8] To Aristotle, the male is that which generates in another, the female that which generates in herself.[9]

Aristotle gave rather precise and detailed descriptions of the male and female genital organs. He retained that the seminal ducts elaborate the semen, and consequently the testicles play no active part in its formation. As such, they are not necessary for generation. Their function is merely physical, mechanical, serving as two weights to lengthen the seminal ducts, thereby slowing down the course of the semen to allow it to achieve a more complete elaboration or digestion. This stretching causes the spermatic secretion to take more time as well as a not so violent sexual desire and a sexual act that is less rapid.[10]

Aristotle refused the widely held view that the semen takes its

---

[4] *Ibid.*, p. 374; cfr. also, *De aere, locis et acquis liber, ibid.*, p. 551.
[5] *Ibid.*, pp. 371-373.
[6] *Ibid.*, pp. 373, 375-376.
[7] *Ibid.*, pp. 376-377.
[8] ARISTOTLE, *De generatione animalium*, 1.3; in *Opera Omnia*, ed. F. DIDOT, vol. 3, Paris 1854, pp. 370-392.
[9] *Ibid.*, 1.1, c. 2; p. 320.
[10] *Ibid.*, 1.1. c. 4; p. 323. Cfr. MEINERI, P.A., *Le correlazioni fra ghiandole genitali ed organismo nelle opere di Ippocrate, Aristotele e Galeno*, in *Minerva Medica*, 7 (1927) 8.

origin from all the parts of the body in order to reproduce the same part in the offspring. He considered the semen as "a true secretion, and not a homogeneous natural part (a tissue), nor a heterogeneous natural part (an organ), nor an unnatural part such as growth, nor mere nutriment, nor yet a waste product".[11] Accordingly, the semen is a secretion of the most pure and elaborated nourishment. Such nourishment in fact receives its first digestion in the stomach and intestines to pass into the veins and liver where it is digested for a second time and transformed into blood. Still in an impure form, it passes into the heart where it is given a vital warmth and the capacity to set the process of generation in motion. There it also becomes true blood. This is the most useful and perfect nourishment from which the seminal secretion is produced. On its course through the spermatic ducts, it is further digested into the semen.

Treating the nature of the semen, Aristotle noted that such semen is dense and white at the moment of ejaculation. This is because it contains a great deal of hot "pneuma" owing to the internal bodily heat. It is this pneuma which causes the semen to be fertile. However, on leaving the body, the exposed semen gradually loses its heat by evaporation, and consequently it also loses its generative power.

Aristotle also considered the active nature of the male and the passive nature of the female in the process of generation. In his view, the female does not produce any semen, but only the menstrual blood. When sexual intercourse takes place, the male semen comes into contact with the female menstrual blood and acts as a principle of motion, thereby starting the process of generation. It also causes the blood produced by the female to coagulate. This female matter is thus purified and a germ is formed that gradually develops into an embryo. It is therefore the dynamic element contained in the male semen that gives form to the inert matter (the menstrual blood) of the female and which sets in motion the formation of flesh and bone.[12]

Galen (130-200 A.D.). With this last great doctor of antiquity, who lived almost six centuries after Hippocrates and five after

---

[11] NEEDHAM, J., *History of embriology*, Cambridge 1934, p. 39.

[12] ARISTOTELE, *De generatione animalium*, l.1, cc. 2, 20; *ibid.*, pp. 320, 340; l.2, c. 1; *ibid.*, p. 347; l.2, c. 2; *ibid.*, pp. 348-349: l.2, c. 4; *ibid.*, pp. 356, 358; *De anima; ibid.*, vol. 3, p. 444. Cfr. also MONTALENTI, G., *Il sistema aristotelico della generazione degli animali*, in *Quaderni di Storia della Scienza*, Rome 1926, pp. 14-18; CASTELLANI, C., *Il problema della generazione da Ippocrate al XX secolo*, in *Bollettino delle Riunioni medico-chirurgiche*, 46 (1963) 9.

Aristotle, human anatomy received a more organic and ordered expression in the scientific medicine of the West.[13] Galen's anatomical and physiological knowledge of the genital organs was greater than that possessed by his predecessors. Throughout his works, he gave detailed and at times complete anatomical descriptions of the internal genital organs, both of the male and of the female. Here, Galen's finalistic approach must be noted: every part of the body is structured in view of the function it is to fulfil.[14]

Galen stressed the importance of the testicles. Observing the effects brought about by the removal of such glands in animals of both sexes, he attributed to them a much more complex function than the mere formation of the semen. There is something which these glands diffuse throughout the whole body and gives virility to the male and femininity to the female, arousing in them the sexual urge and producing exterior characteristic notes which differentiate them from each other.[15] The sexual appetite is therefore connected to the presence and normal functioning of such glands. Their removal would make itself felt on the whole personality; the male would become effeminate, whereas the female would take on the characteristics of the castrated male.[16] According to Galen, these glands create a kind of force, a particular heat, which they rapidly diffuse throughout the whole body. When a certain fluid passes into them from the kidneys, the sexual instinct is aroused.[17]

Notwithstanding all this, Galen did not attribute to the testicles an exclusive role in the formation of the semen. He was sure that the arteries and veins produce the semen. As the blood approaches the testicles, it is continuously purified to acquire the characteristics of the seminal liquid. Galen noted that together with this blood there is also a vital spirit. This spirit is the vehicle of a special formative power that is almost a synthesis of the other powers of the soul. For Galen, the testicles do not, therefore, generate the

---

[13] Born at Bergamo, where he also studied medicine, Galen later continued his studies at Corinth and Alexandria, from where he later moved to Rome. Cfr. BALLESTER, L.G., Galeno. En la sociedad y en la ciencia de su tiempo, Madrid 1972; Idem, Aproximación genética a la obra anatómica de Galeno, in Asclepio, 23 (1971) 191-208.

[14] Cfr. GALEN, C., De usu partium corporis humani, 1. 17; in the series "Medicorum graecorum opera quae extant", edited by GOTTLOB KÜHN, C., Claudii Galeni opera omnia, vol. 4, Leipzig 1822, pp. 346-366.

[15] Idem, De semine, 1.1, c. 15; ibid., pp. 570, 572-573; 1.1, c. 16; ibid., pp. 582, 585.

[16] Idem, De semine, 1.2, c. 6; ibid., pp. 642-644.

[17] Idem, De semine, 1.1, c. 15; ibid., p. 574.

sperm, but rather serve as a laboratory where the already existing
semen arrives. Herein thanks to the spirit that is contained in the
semen, a last digestion takes place, whereby the semen changes
colour and becomes foamy, as it acquires its generative power.
From this moment, the semen is mature and only waits to be
ejaculated.[18]

Contrary to Aristotle, Galen asserted that even the female
produces her own semen, and therefore she too participates
actively in the dynamics of generation. He also distinguished the
menstrual fluid from what Hippocrates called the female semen,
which is secreted by her testicles. To these testicles and spermatic
glands, Galen attributed an essential function in the process of
reproduction. According to him, during the sexual act, the woman
secretes a liquid that is similar to that secreted by the male.
Moreover, just like the male semen, it possesses that active,
formative power on which the development of the embryo depends. The only difference that exists between the two semina is
that in the female semen this formative capacity is not as powerful
as that in the male's, and therefore it needs the concurrence of the
latter.[19] Galen also noted that the female semen has a triple
function. It stimulates the female to sexual intercourse, it widens
the neck of the vagina so that the semen can move upwards into the
womb more easily and it also contributes to the formation of the
new being.[20] The process of generation starts when the male and
the female semina mix together and unite inside the vagina.[21]

2.   From Galen to the Renaissance

After Galen, starting from the fourth century, medicine en-
tered a period of stagnation. Centuries had to pass before renewed

[18] Idem, *De semine*, 1.1, cc. 12, 15; *ibid.*, pp. 555-557; 563-581; 1.1, c. 16;
ibid., p. 582; 1.2, c. 6; *ibid.*, pp. 648-649; *De usu partium corporis humani*, 1.15, cc.
7, 10; *ibid.*, pp. 165-175, 183-188; *De formatione foetui*, c. 3; *ibid.*, pp. 660-674.
Cfr. DE MARTINI, V., *Considerazioni sulla dottrina dello pneuma in Galeno*, in
Pagine di Storia della Medicina, 8 (1964) 44; BALLESTER, L.G. *Galeno*, cit., pp.
105-106.
[19] GALEN, *De usu partium corporis humani*, 1.14, c. 7; *ibid.*, pp. 165-175; *De
semine*, 1.1, c. 7; *ibid.*, pp. 535-539. Cfr. NARDI, M.G., *Il problema della
generazione umana nel pensiero di alcuni medici e filosofi medievali*, in *Castalia*, 15
(1959) 103-104.
[20] GALEN, *De usu partium corporis humani*, 1.14, c. 11; *ibid.*, p. 188.
[21] Idem, *De usu partium corporis humani*, 1.14, c. 9; *ibid.*, p. 183; cfr. also *De
semine*, 1.1, c. 4; *ibid.*, p. 562.

scientific interest started to sprout once more in the West which, devastated by the barbaric invasions, rapidly lost its Greek traditions. In the meantime, the Arab culture brought to the West the Aristotelic doctrine.[22] Medieval doctors, on their part, searched for a solution to the complicated problem of generation and in their efforts they constantly turned to the works of Aristotle and Galen.

One of the salient, extraordinarily gifted figures in the field of medicine and philosophy was undoubtedly Abou 'Ali al Hosain ibn 'Abdullah ibn Sina, more commonly known as *Avicenna* (980-1037 A.D.). Closely following Galen, Avicenna defined the semen as that substance which remains after the fourth digestion, once the food has been distilled through the veins. It is in the testicles that this blood undergoes its final elaboration, where it also becomes impregnated with a vital spirit that is likewise passed into the testicles from the arteries.[23] This view was commonly followed by medieval doctors.[24] Once again, it was Galen's formative power that gave the semen the power to form a new organism.

Regarding the female, Avicenna stated that just like the male, she too has testicles, although there is a difference in size, shape and position between them. Women have also spermatic ducts situated between the testicles.[25] Avicenna also accepted the theory of the two sperms. However, he seemed to rule out identical equality between the male and the female sperm, reserving only to the former the generative power, although he agreed that the female too contributes to the process of generation. Doctors following Avicenna continued to speak of the *semen muliebre*, which they too distinguished from the menstrual blood.

With the approach of the fifteenth century, a gradual revival in the anatomical and biological sciences started to gain momentum.

---

[22] One of the greatest physicians of the Eastern Caliphate was 'Ali ibn al-'Abbas al-Majusi, known in the West as Haly-Abbas. He was a Persian doctor at Bagdad's hospital. His *Kitab al-Malaki* was first translated in Latin between 1070 and 1085 by Constantine the African, under the title of *Liber de humana natura*. It reappeared in Venice, in 1492 under the title of *Regalis dispositio*. Cfr. MEYERHOF, M. - JOANNIDES, D., *La gynécologie et l'obstétrique chez Avicenne (Ibn Sina) et leurs rapports avec celles des Grecs*, Cairo 1938, p. 7.

[23] AVICENNA, *Canon medicinae*, l.3, sect. 20, tr. I, c. 1, Venice 1595, p. 899; ibid., c. 2, pp. 900-901.

[24] Cfr. Nardi, M.G., *Il problema della generazione umana nel pensiero di alcuni medici e filosofi medievali*, cit., p. 102.

[25] AVICENNA, ibid., l. 3, sect. 21, tr. I, c. 1, p. 919; cfr. l.3, sect. 20, tr. I, c. 3, p. 901.

Gradually too, Galen's theory attracted more followers, although Aristotle's was not completely abandoned. This was probably due to the fact that it was then becoming more possible to study anatomy on human corpses.[26]

The sixteenth century saw the birth of four great embriologists, Ulisse Aldovrandi, Gabriele Falloppia, Giulio Cesare Aranzi and Volcher Coiter, as well as of a great anatomist, Andrea Vesalio. During this same century, Realdo Colombo made detailed studies of the female genitalia, paying particular attention to the ovaries which nevertheless he still considered as testicles. Falloppia described the female's tubes, to which he ascribed the role of carrying the woman's semen elaborated in her testicles to the uterus. In 1578, Jean Fernel published a treatise in which he wrote about the procreation of man. Called "the Galen of France", he held that the semen is derived not from the whole body but from the main parts, namely, from the liver and the brain. It is then carried by the arteries into the testicles, where it is digested.[27]

In the meantime, the sixteenth century was also producing remarkable obstetrical and gynaecological works, which were based either on a careful study of Aristotle and Galen or upon the results of dissections made. One such work was that of Jacob Rueff which was published in 1554 and entitled *De conceptu et generatione hominis*. This work can shed much light as to what was passing through the minds of such writers like André du Laurens, Jean Riolan senior, Geronimo Mercuriali, Saxonia, Guillaume Rondelet, Verrusti, Holler, Vallesio, Saverin Pineau, Ludovico Buonaccioli, Felix Platter, as well as Girolamo Capivaccio, Fortunato Liceti, Jean Costeau, Emilio Parisano and Jean Riolan junior — to mention only some of the names that are frequently quoted by Paolo Zacchia to corroborate his medical assertions in this field of science.

In 1621, the work of Girolamo Fabrizi, *De formatione ovi et pulli* was published at Padova. Here for the first time, the term "ovarium" was used to refer to the female gonads. This was followed in 1625 by *Epistola de generatione plantarum* of Giuseppe Degli Aromatari, in which he stated that "principia animalium esse in ovo, et plantarum in semine ... sed maximam inter semina

---

[26] Cfr. CASTELLANI, C., *Della generazione*, in *Castalia*, 19 (1963) 20; Idem, *Intuizioni endocrinologiche nelle opere di alcuni autori italiani del '600*, in *Castalia*, 18 (1962) 19.

[27] Cfr. FERNEL, J., *De universa medicina*, Lyon 1578, chapter 7.

vegetabilium et ova animalium intercedere analogiam, utraque continere futuri foetus rudimenta".[28] Still there are no elements in the *Quaestiones* to show that Zacchia in any way took up this line of thought.

Art. 2. ZACCHIA'S THEORY OF GENERATION

1. *The function of the testicles*

The early seventeenth century was also the period when Zacchia started publishing his treatise. Closely following Galen, Zacchia strictly linked the function of the male's testicles with the "elaboration" of the semen:

> "Testes habere distinctam operationem, atque illam quidem insignem, ac perfectissimam seminis scilicet conficiendi".[29]

He was careful to note, however, that in its original state, the semen is produced by the brain, kidneys and liver, and it reaches the testicles as a crude "materia sanguinea". It is the function of the testicles, noted Zacchia, to digest this crude matter and elaborate it into prolific semen, which becomes whitish in the process. Prolific semen is exclusively produced in the testicles, since they alone are equipped with that *vim spermatizantem* that brings about an alteration and digestion of the semen.[30]

In addition to this principal function of rendering the semen prolific, the testicles have a second equally important function, namely that of providing what Zacchia called the "virilem vigorem". The *spiritus turgens* which comes from the main parts of the body (brain, kidney and liver) is communicated to the semen by the testicles, thereby causing a natural and normal sexual stimulus.[31] As such, the testicles are a sure sign and proof of virility, that is "ipsiusque nativi caloris", which gives "in coitu sufficientem vigorem genitali".[32] If both testicles are removed, a man loses not only his capacity to generate but also his virility, and "foeminae similis quoad praedictum animi vigorem evadat".[33] In this case,

---

[28] Cfr. FRANCESCHINI, P., *Il secolo di Galileo e il problema della generazione*, in *Physis*, 4 (1964) 150.

[29] ZACCHIA, P., *QML*, 5.3.1.13.

[30] Ibid., 3.1.5.25-39; 9.3.4.1; 9.3.6.7-8; 9.10.1.10-11; 9.10.2.12-14.

[31] Ibid., 5.3.1.13; 3.1.3.5; 9.3.2.19; 9.3.6.7.

[32] Ibid., 7.1.8.19; 9.3.6.7.

[33] *QML*, 5.3.1.13: "Satis autem nobis sit, testes habere distinctam operationem, atque illam quidem insignem, ac perfectissimam, seminis scilicet conficiendi,

although he would still retain some sexual urge ("aliquam volup-
tatem"), yet only a "viscidum quemdam humorem" or "acquosam
quandam materiam" is produced. On the contrary, the removal of
only one testicle does not normally affect man's virility nor his
ability to generate.[34]

2. The female's role

Zacchia clearly asserted that something similar to the male's
testicles also exists in the female and in this, once again, he was
closely following Galen.[35]

He departed from the premise that, just like men, women have
all the necessary organs to produce, preserve and ejaculate the
perfect semen apt for generation. He argued that once the female is
equipped by nature itself with the same corporal parts as in man,
which parts have in both the same functions, then one cannot but
conclude that women too produce what doctors call the *foemineum
semen*. This perfect white liquid contained in the female's testicles
(which Zacchia admitted are in some way different from those of
the male) is ejaculated by the copulative organs during coitus.[36]

Zacchia was also conscious that there was another current of
thought that, following Aristotle, held that women do not produce
such semen, but only the menstrual blood, which is either expelled
from the body or goes to nourish the foetus during pregnancy. But
he criticised those who held this view, saying that it contradicted
the manifest findings of anatomical dissections which went to prove
that women too, just like men, possess the testicles, which have the

---

...; praeter iam commemoratam operationem, virilem quoque vigorem in maribus
tuentur, cum illis abscissis, mas foeminae similis quoad praedictum animi vigorem
evadat"; cfr. 5.3.7.5; 8.1.14.5.

[34] *Ibid.*, 2.3.7.13; 8.1.14.7; cfr. 3.2.8.13-17. As to the pathology of these
glands, be it congenital or acquired, Zacchia noted that this can be of different
kinds. But more will be said about this in chapter IV, infra, pp. 81 ff.

[35] Besides occasional references to the woman's testicles throughout his
work, Zacchia dedicated to this subject a particular study in two different places:
QML, 7.3.1.17 ff: "Digressio de semine foemineo"; and 9.11. qu. unic: "De
semine foemineo". Cfr. ANTONELLI, J., *De mulieris excisae impotentia ad matrimonium*, Rome 1903; Idem, *Pro conceptu impotentiae et sterilitatis relate ad matrimonium*, Rome 1901; ESCHBACH, A., *Disputationes physiologico-theologicae*,
Rome 1901; Idem, *De novo quodam sterilitatis conceptu*, Rome 1902, in which a
prominent position was accorded to Zacchia's views on this subject and which in
turn served as the launching ground for many an argument.

[36] *QML*, 9.11.1.1-10; 7.3.1.20-24; cfr. 4.2.4.2.; 3.1.7.11; 1.1.6.38f.

same function of elaborating the "materia sanguinea" into perfect and fertile semen. Moreover, even in this case, if these glands are removed, the female is neither sexually aroused nor can she generate.[37]

Zacchia clearly distinguished this perfect semen from menstrual blood which, he claimed, is only the product of the veins and as such just crude matter. Yet he also noted the strict relation between menstruation and the semen. Not only do they generally appear at the same time, but also never, or very rarely, does a woman conceive before she begins to menstruate.[38] This led him to conclude that both the semen and menstruation are in their own way needed for generation, since it is for this purpose that nature itself destined them. If either of them is missing, then generation cannot take place. Still, according to Zacchia, the difference between the two is a great one; for the semen is both the matter and the origin of the foetus, whereas the menstrual blood goes to nourish the foetus.[39]

In accordance with this belief, Zacchia drew the logical conclusion that both the male and the female semen are required for generation,

> "cum conceptus non ex unico semine maris fiat, sed ex eo semini muliebri unito".[40]

The female therefore has an important role to play in the process of generation. If conception is to take place, the woman too must ejaculate her own semen which must also be fertile, that is produced by her in the required quality and quantity. Just like the male's semen, the female's is not matter alone but also an efficient, concurring principle of conception.[41]

----

[37] In refuting the opinion of Aristotle and his followers who denied that the female produced any semen, Zacchia noted among other things that "eadem materia eosdem omnino effectus producat in foeminis, ac in maribus". And he briefly rounded up his whole argument in these words: "Quod si obijcias ex eorum (testium) abscissione foeminam ad venerem non stimulari, non amplius generare, quemadmodum neque mas iisdem abscissis, ad venerem agitur, neque generationi est aptus, promptam habent responsionem, id foeminis evenire ex laesione vicinarum partium, et retractatione caeterorum vasorum ad generationem facientium": 7.3.1.12,23; cfr. 9.10.1.12; 9.11.1.3-4.

[38] Ibid., 7.3.1.23; 9.3.7.1-5; 3.2.8.24; 4.2.4.8-9.

[39] Ibid., 4.2.4.6.

[40] Ibid., 9.1.3.69-70; cfr. 9.1. qu. ult. 127.

[41] Ibid., 3.1.7.11; 9.11.1.1-10; 7.3.1.21-25; 1.1.6.38 f.

3. *The process of generation*

Having established all this, Zacchia went on to explain the dynamics of the generative process. He started by claiming that:

"mulierem non posse absque eo quod a viro cum effectu et realiter cognoscatur per omnimodam applicationem membrorum generationis ullo modo concipere. Unde neque si vir non erigat, neque si membrum illi penitus aut magna ex parte sit abscissum, neque si prope vas aliquo modo polluatur, potest mulier ex eo concipere".

And the two main reasons which he gave for this were that he did not believe that:

"uterus trahat sperma propter suam propriam virtutem"

and that

"cum coniunctio tam arcta maris et foeminae per genitalium membrorum applicationem ad id sit a natura intenta, ut semen quam minimum, immo nullo modo ab aere externo alteratur, eo quod illico et absque mora spiritus illi tenuissimi, ac purissimi seminis evanescant, ut testis est Aristoteles, *De generatione animalium*, l. 2, c. 4, patet quod ubi absque ea coniunctione semen prodeat, infoecundum eam ob causam omnino sit oporteat. Antequam enim ab utero attrahatur, ab aere alterabitur, alteratum non amplius foecundum esse potest".[42]

When man ejaculates his semen inside the vagina, the woman too ejaculates her own "in proprium uterum", so that a mixture of both semina occurs.[43] The male sperm acts as the principal agent which on its own, however, is unable to generate. The female too has an active role. Still this does not mean that there are two agents, two different matters and two effects in the process of generation, since both semina are by themselves only incomplete and partial agents, incomplete and defective matter. From the mixture and union of both semina there results one complete and perfect agent capable of setting the process of generation in motion. Hereditary traits are passed on through the semina to the newly conceived. Zacchia also noted that when both semina mix and unite, the male sperm, which

---

[42] *QML*, 3.1.8.2,10,16; 9.10.1.7,9; 10 cons. 42 per totum.

[43] *Ibid.*, 7.3.1.21. Except for one instance (9.10.1.6), Zacchia never used the term *vagina*, but constantly used the term *uterus* to refer both to the sexual passage in the female from the womb to the external orifice and to the womb itself. According to him, the vagina or "uterus dividatur in os externum, collum et os internum", 7.3.6.10; cfr. 3.1.8.20. Zacchia explained the start of the process of generation in 7.3.1.34.

PARTICULAR ASPECTS RELATED TO THE PROBLEM OF GENERATION

has greater force, moves the female into action; but the latter too has an equal potential and as such could also set in motion the process of generation.[44]

Art. 3. NEW DISCOVERIES AFTER ZACCHIA

1. *Important discoveries*

It is quite evident that Zacchia's theory of generation remained within the traditional framework of thought.

But this was also a time of great progress. In fact, in 1651 William Harvey published his *Exercitationes de generatione animalium,* in which he claimed that while the male's sperm remains in the female's vagina after ejaculation, only an "aura spermatica" reaches the womb to fertilize the matter that is produced by the female. Well known is Harvey's conclusion "omne vivum ex ovo".[45]

The ink was still fresh on the pages of Zacchia's first publications of his complete treatise, when yet another, much more important discovery was made. In a short anatomical treatise published in 1667, Niels Stenson advanced the hypothesis that the female's testicles are in reality ovaries analogous to those found in oviparous animals.[46] In 1672, De Graaf explicitly confirmed that "ova in mulierum testibus generantur ... sed praeter ova nihil aliud testes mulierum ad generationem conferre". For De Graaf, the follicules and the ova were one and the same thing.[47] In this, he

---

[44] According to Zacchia, the semen in itself does not possess the power to produce a living being. What gives the semen this dynamism is the *anima*. In all animals except man, the *anima formatrix* is communicated from parent to offspring through and with the semen. In the case of man, when both the male and the female semen unite during sexual intercourse, at the same moment of conception, God infuses the rational soul, which vivifies, nourishes and develops the newly-conceived human being. In this way, claimed Zacchia, man can really be called the generator of his offspring, since he provides the matter which is so disposed as to receive the form. Cfr. *QML*, 7.3.1.30-34; 9.1.1.5; 9.1.2.22-35; 9.1.3.44-67; 9.1.4.77-85; 9.1. qu. ult. per totam; 9.12.1.13; 10. cons. 42.13.

[45] HARVEY, W., *Exercitationes de generatione animalium. Quibus accedunt quaedam de partu, de membranis ac humoribus uteri, et de conceptione*, London 1651. An Italian edition was published in Padua, in 1666.

[46] STENSON, N., *Historia dissecti piscis ex Canum genere*, in *Nicolai Stenonis elementorum myologiae specimen, seu musculi descriptio geometrica, cui accedunt Canis carchariae dissectum caput et Dissectus piscis ex Canum genere*, Florence 1667.

[47] DE GRAAF, R., *De mulierum organis generationi inservientibus tractatus novus*, Lyon 1672.

obviously erred, but it was only in 1827 that Van Baer would correct this mistake by stating that follicule and ovum are two distinct things and that the latter is contained in the former.[48]

The discovery of the spermatozoon goes back to 1677. Although it was Jan Ham of Arnhem who first made this discovery[49], yet it was Anthony van Leeuwenhoek who, on being informed by Ham of this discovery, not only confirmed it but also realised its true import. In a letter to the Royal Society, Leeuwenhoek made known Ham's discovery, adding that he too had examined the sperm of a healthy man "et tantam in ea materia viventium animalculorum multitudinem vidi".[50] Leeuwenhoek himself came to the conclusion that the testicle is the organ which produces these "animalcula", which in turn are the agents responsible for setting the generative process in motion.[51]

Around 1839, great progress was made with the provision of the cell theory[52] but it was only towards the end of the last century that Oscar Hertwig could observe the successive and reciprocal approaching of the male and the female nuclei until they were completely fused.[53]

2. *The generative system in the light of modern science*

1. *A basic outline*

Modern science has greatly clarified what had been hitherto considered so mysterious in this basic sex system of the human being.[54] The genital system is composed of three functional ele-

  [48] VON BAER, K.E., *De ovi mammalium et hominis genesi Epistola ad Accademiam Imperialem Scientiarum Petropolitanam*, Leipzig 1827.
  [49] Cfr. FRANCESCHINI, P., op. cit. in note 28, pp. 151-152.
  [50] VAN LEEUWENHOEK, A., *De natis e semine genitali animalculis*, in *Philosophical Transactions*, 142 (1677) 1040-1045; quoted by FRANCESCHINI, P., op. cit., pp. 152-153; cfr. p. 154, n. 14.
  [51] VAN LEEUWENHOEK, A., *De visis animalculis ex semine deferentibus vasibus spermaticis expresso* (Letter sent to Robert Hooke in 1684); quoted by FRANCESCHINI, P., ibid., p. 155.
  [52] The names behind the cell theory were: RENÉ JOACHIM HENRI DUTROCHET (1776-1847), JAN EVANGELISTA PURKYNĚ (1787-1869), MATHIAS JACOB SCHLEIDEN (1804-1881), THEODORE SCHWANN (1810-1882) and MAX SIGISMUND SCHULTZE (1825-1874).
  [53] HERTWIG, O., *Beiträge zur Kenntnis der Bildung. Befruchtung und Theilung des thierischen Eis*, in *Gegenbaur's Morphologisches Jahrbuch*, I (1875) 347-434; quoted by FRANCESCHINI, P., *Il secolo di Galileo e il problema della generazione*, in *Physis*, 4 (1964) 175, note 15.
  [54] Cfr. SANTORI, G., *Compendio di sessuologia*, Saluzzo 1972, pp. 1-139.

ments. These are: (a) the *glands* which in the male are called *testes* or testicles, and in the female *ovaries*; (b) the *ducts*. These tubes carry the germinating cells from the testes and ovaries and render fertilization possible. In the male, they are the epididymus, the vas deferens, the ejaculatory duct and the urethra. In the female, they are the fallopian tubes, or oviducts through which the ovum is carried from the ovary to the uterus; (c) the *organs of copulation.* Through these, the male germinal cells, called spermatozoa (zoon = animal; sperma = seed), reach the ovum for fertilization. These organs are the penis in the male, and the vagina in the female. The fertilized ovum remains in the female's uterus or womb, where it is nourished and sufficiently developed to be born.

2.   *The testicle, the spermatozoon and its iter*

The testicles are a pair of oval-shaped glands, enclosed in a cutaneous sack (scrotum). These testicles perform a dual activity. They produce (a) the germinal or reproductive cells, called spermatozoa, and (b) the sex hormones in the male. Male hormones are produced by microscopic cells among the seminiferous tubules, to pass directly into the bloodstream. Spermatozoa are continuously produced in large quantities by the seminiferous tubes. These tubes unite near the top to form a set of larger ones, and these in turn join to form the epididymus which besides other functions serves as a store for the spermatozoa. The tubes forming the epididymus converge into one seminal duct or tube, called the *vas deferens*, which in turn extends into the body carrying spermatozoa to the seminal vesicle by repeated contractions. Just under the bladder, and surrounding the urethra, is the prostate gland, which secretes prostatic fluid, a milky-white and alkaline substance. This secretion helps both to preserve the spermatozoa and to stimulate their motility. The seminal vesicles, situated at the point where the vas deferens enters the prostate gland, produce a gelatinous fluid which, together with the other secretions of the epididymus, the glands of Cowper, the glands of Littré and the prostate, forms the seminal fluid in which the spermatozoa are carried and which is ejaculated during intercourse.

The ultimate external product of the male genital organs is a fluid, consisting partly of the liquid formed from the various secretions of the spermatic ducts and partly of the reproductive cells elaborated by the testicles.

One immediately notes how near to the modern findings was Zacchia in explaining the double role of the testicles. On the other hand, he could not as yet speak of spermatozoa and much less of cells and hormones. He also obviously erred in the way he explained the formation and the nature of the seminal liquid that is ejaculated during intercourse. Basically, however, he was right to affirm that the male generative factor is elaborated in the testicles, which also produce the necessary factor which gives man his virile characteristics.

3.   The ovary, the ovum and its iter

In the female, the ovaries are the most important organs in her generative system. They are located within the pelvis, in the lower abdominal region, one on each side of the upper wider portion of the uterus. Near each ovary the uterine tubes, which extend to the right and to the left of the upper part of the uterus, widen like funnels and form numerous movable fimbriae. By their movement these fimbriae produce a light stream of fluid which conveys the ovum, expelled from the ovary into the abdominal cavity, to the uterine tube, whence the ovum is transported into the uterus.

The ovaries produce egg cells, called ova. These are already contained in the ovary at birth. Between the age of puberty and menopause, many egg cells are in various stages of development within each ovary, but usually only one ovum matures to the point of being released about once every four weeks. Each ovum is surrounded by, and enclosed in, what is called a Graafian follicle. As each ovum matures it is developed in the outer layer of the ovary, which causes the outer ovarian wall to bulge until the Graafian follicle bursts. This takes place in only one ovary. The discharged ovum (ovulation) is caught by the tentacle-like opening at the outer end of the fallopian tube.

Unlike the spermatoza, the ova do no possess in themselves power of motility and so travel very slowly. Protected by an albuminous substance in the fallopian tube, the ovum is slowly propelled towards the womb. It is within this tube that fertilization of the ovum by the male spermatozoon takes place. Once the fertilized ovum (now an embryo) reaches the womb, it adheres to its lining (called the endometrium) and becomes implanted to proceed to further development. If the ovum is not fertilized, it dies and is passed out through the vagina with the menstrual flow.

Besides serving as the maturation habitat of the egg cells, these ovaries are also a hormone factory producing female sex hormones which are passed into the bloodstream.

All this shows that Zacchia was also right on a very fundamental point, namely that the female too has to provide a necessary factor for generation. For pregnancy to occur, union of the male and female elements must take place. Hence his insistence on the presence of the "foemineum semen", which he claimed is produced by the female testicles. The latter, he rightly insisted, also give the woman her feminine characteristics. But Zacchia erred about the real nature of this "semen", saying that it is produced by testicles almost similar to those of the male in nature. He must have been misled by the lubricant fluid secreted by the glands around the entrance to the vagina during sexual arousal and intercourse, not least by that thick, sticky and transparent secretion produced by the glands of Bartholin.[55] Furthermore, although he was not aware of the exact nature of the relation between the ovum and the menstrual flow, yet he was not completely off the mark when he said that the latter served for the nourishment of the fertilized "semen foemineum".[56]

And we know today that both the spermatozoon and the ovum are two corresponding cells similar to each other in some aspects but differing greatly in others. Thus, each of them contains the genetic information of the respective male and female who produce them and which is passed on to the new being that develops from the fusion of these cells. They are likewise similar in the fact that neither can germinate without the other.

Among the most important differences, we have already mentioned that the spermatozoon has a great motility which the female ovum lacks. Besides, while spermatozoa are produced continuously and in large numbers, only one ovum matures in the span of one month; not to mention the difference in size which also exists between the two. Worthy of mention, is also the difference in gender: in fact, it is the spermatozoon (which contains an X and a Y sex chromosome) and not the ovum (which contains two X sex chromosomes) which determines the sex of the individual.

The new being takes its point of origin not from the action of the former on the latter, but from the fusion of these two cells, thereby becoming one, the fertilized ovum.[57]

---

[55] ZACCHIA, P., *QML*, 7.3.1.24: "Itaque materia illa alba, quae in foeminarum testibus reperitur, et quam per eiaculantia vasa illae in coitu effundunt, non solum non erit materia cruda, ut voluit Aristoteles, et cum eo plures eius sequaces, sed erit materia quovis venoso ac arterioso sanguine magis ac exquisitius concocta et elaborata". Cfr. SANTORI, G., cit., pp. 152, 160-161.
[56] Cfr. supra, chapter II, Art. 2, # 2, pp. 52 f.
[57] Cfr. SANTORI, G., ibid., pp. 3-8.

Here also Zacchia was basically right in attributing to both the male and female agents equal potentiality in starting the process of generation. Of course, he could not as yet know the real nature of the process. He likewise erred when he claimed that, for the purpose of generation, penetration is essentially required, since without it the male's semen will neither retain its fertilizing force, nor can it be absorbed inside the vagina.

Although some skepticism still remains even today, yet both authoritative studies and case histories have proved that penetration of the vagina is not necessary for reproduction, although it renders the likelihood of pregnancy far greater. It is not very rare that a woman who possesses an integral and flexible hymen, becomes pregnant. This happens when the sperm, which in a warm and liquid habitat has a longer life, is absorbed by the female's genitals to pass through the opening of the still intact hymen and reaches the fallopian tube where it meets and impregnates the ovum.[58]

---

[58] Cfr. KREMER, J., *La sterilità nell'uomo e nella donna*, in *Sessuologia*, a cura di MONEY, J.-MUSAPH, H., it. tr., vol. 2, Rome 1978, p. 878; SANTORI, G., cit., p. 191; DA GANGI, B., *Dispensatio super rato post conceptionem*, in *Palestra del Clero*, 35 (1956) 657-659; ANTONELLI, G., *Medicina pastoralis*, vol. I, Rome 1932, n. 213; KAHN, F., *La vita sessuale*, Rome 1973, pp. 93-94; ORLANDI, G., *I "Casi Difficili" nel processo super rato*, Padova 1984, pp. 145-149.

CHAPTER THREE

MARRIAGE AND IMPOTENCE

INTRODUCTION.

It is against this wider background that the closely-related question which constitutes the main object of this study, namely Zacchia's contribution to the understanding of sexual impotence, has to be seen.

Since the early Middle Ages, the two main theories about marriage and its ends that were commonly followed had their common roots in Genesis 2:24: "Et erunt duo in carne una". Yet each current of thought followed a different course in the interpretation of this phrase: the one emphasising the institutional character of marriage in relation to the procreation of children, the other stressing its instrumental aspect, in so far as it serves the "sedatio concupiscentiae". The influence of Augustine who considered the conjugal act and the accompanying sexual pleasure as inherently wrong, had a long-lasting effect. In his view, such an act is only legitimate when used for the scope of procreation, or at least, as long as procreation is not purposely avoided. Although not all theologians, moralists and canonists shared this opinion, it still prevailed for many centuries.[1]

---

[1] The bibliography on this subject is practically unlimited. Suffice it here to quote the following: DOMS, H., *Vom Sinn und Zweck der Ehe*, Breslau 1935;

These two approaches have played a determining role in establishing the evaluative criteria of the nature of impotence, nonconsummation and "verum semen".[2]

Art. 1. MARRIAGE AND THE SEXUAL ACT

Zacchia made use of the most varied terminology when he referred to the conjugal act. "Usus veneris", "coitus", "copula", "coniunctio", "commixtio" and "debitum" are all terms which he frequently used, sometimes just on their own, at other times coupled with the qualifying adjective "coniugalis" or "carnalis". Although the choice of the word often depends on the shade of meaning which the author wanted to stress in a particular context yet, basically, all these terms refer to that

> "applicatio maris et foeminae in membris generationis, qua super- fluum expellitur quantum ad finem speciei, vel individui ordinata".[3]

There is no doubt that Zacchia found himself between the two currents of thought and doctrine mentioned earlier. Such tension is reflected in what he wrote about the various ends of marriage. On the one hand he often repeated that "coitus a natura ipsa in generationem speciei propagationem inventus est" and that "certum est matrimonium causa procreandi liberos praecipue contrahi".[4] Yet on the other hand, he surely did not try to conceal his view that the sexual act has a wider scope than mere procrea-

---

ABELLÁN, M., *El fin del matrimonio, según Tomás Sánchez*, pt. I, in *Archivio Teologico Granadino*, II (1939) 35-69; GERLAUD, P., *Note sur les fins du mariage d'après saint Thomas*, in *Revue Thomiste*, XLV (1939) 764-773; SCHAHL, C., *La doctrine des fins du mariage dans la théologie scolastique*, Paris, 1948; BOISSARD, E., *Questions théologique sur le mariage*, Paris, 1948; Idem, *Les fins du mariage dans la theologie scolastique*, in *Revue Thomiste*, 49 (1949) 289-309; LOCHET, L., *Les fins du mariage*, in *Nouvelle Revue Théologique*, 73 (1951) 449-465; 561-586; TROSCH, F., *Das "bonum prolis" als Eheziel bei Thomas Sánchez S.J. und Basilius Ponce de Leon O.E.S.A.*, in *Zeitschrift für Katholische Theologie*, 77 (1955) 1-38; 169-211; SCHILLEBEECKX, E., *Evoluzione e cambiamenti nelle concezioni cristiane del matrimonio*, in AA.VV., *Diritti del sesso e matrimonio*, Mondadori 1968, pp. 29-55; VEREECKE, L., *Mariage et plaisir sexuel chez les théologiens de l'époque moderne (1300-1789)*, in *Studia Moralia*, XVIII (1980) 245-267.
   [2] Cfr. SILVESTRINI, A., *Circa l'impotenza e l'inconsumazione nella giuris- prudenza canonica anche del S. Ufficio*, in *Monitor Ecclesiasticus*, 98 (1973) 118-120.
   [3] ZACCHIA, P., *QML*, 3.1.1.7. He also defined coitus as a "commixtio per membra generationis" (3.1.8.1), and as a "coniunctio maris et foeminae per genitalium membrorum applicationem" (3.1.8.16).
   [4] *Ibid.*, 3.1.3.23; cfr. 3.1.7.1; 9.10.3.15,21; 7.3.5.11.

tion. Accordingly he stated that even where there is no hope of generation, such an act is not only licit, but even praiseworthy, since in marriage "aliud esse debitum reddere, aliud uti matrimonio ad hunc finem, ut sequatur generatio".[5] Although he noted that married couples are bound to leave their conjugal relations open to procreation, as far as this depends on them, Zacchia added that marriage has other ends; so that even where the principal end of procreation ceases, a marriage is not dissolved, since one of the other ends suffices for its validity.[6] Among these other ends, Zacchia mentioned the "individua vitae consuetudo", the "remedium concupiscentiae" and the "mutuum coniugum amorem".[7]

Zacchia's opinion in this regard can perhaps be best summarised in the following words:

"Iamvero ... ex receptissima canonistarum sententia, immo ex divinae sapientiae decreto monuimus, coniuges teneri ad mutuam coniugalis debiti redditionem: quam quidem vel quod filiorum procreationem, vel quod justitiae satisfactionem, vel quod stimulorum venereorum refrenationem, vel quod reciprocam coniugum dilectionem in matrimonio spectemus, ad eorum singula comperiemus esse apprime necessariam. Nam constat ex ea, et non aliter, coniuges prolem sperare posse; nec aliter aut alio modo iustitiae debito satisfieri, neque ullo aptiori medio veneris aculeos retundi posse, neque per aliud quodvis medium, quam per hoc, mutuum coniugum amorem foveri; nam idcirco dictum est a Plutarcho, ..., venerem esse optimum dissidii coniugalis medicum. Debiti itaque matrimonialis redditionem his omnibus matrimonii finibus plenissime satisfacere certum est".[8]

Thus, in a few lines, Zacchia described the multiple scope of marriage; and to achieve these ends, the married couple has no better means than the conjugal sexual act. In his view, the various ends of marriage can be harmoniously reconciled. The sexual act is

---

[5] *Ibid.*, 7.3.1.15; cfr. 3.1.7.1.

[6] *Ibid.*, 3.1.7.1-2: "Cessante ea principali quidem causa procreationis liberorum ... matrimonium non dissolvatur, quia habet nimirum alias causas, quarum una satis est ad eius validitatem"; cfr. 6.1.5.7-9; c. QUATTROCOLO, 21.3.1927, in *SRRD*, vol. 19, p. 84, nn. 2-3: "Unde iam saeculo XVII celebris medicus Zacchias in Q.M. Leg. 9.3.4.2. disserte ad rem tradit: Leges quando iubent matrimonia separari ob impotentiam, non intelligent de impotentia generandi, sed coeundi".

[7] ZACCHIA, P., *QML*, 3.1.5.61; 7.3.1.14. Zacchia perhaps thought that he was stating more than what was commonly admitted, since he added: "salvo semper saniori iudicio", 7.3.1.15.

[8] *Ibid.*, 7.3.1.4-5; cfr. SAPONARO, A., *Vita sessuale matrimoniale*, Milan 1972, pp. 18-20.

not restricted to the biological procreative function. Accordingly Zacchia gave a wider, more personalistic view of these relations between husband and wife.

Without intending to attribute to him more than in reality he himself wanted to admit, yet our conclusion seems founded enough from the way he spoke about the role of sexual relations in marriage. It is not necessary, he went on to say, that conception follows every marital intercourse, so long as the couple does not positively try to obstruct it. His own advice as a doctor was that the husband should not merely seek his own satisfaction in the sexual act, but he should see that his wife too achieves her own, even though in this case, this would serve only "ut mulier etiam delectetur ex coitu".[9] Clearly, for our doctor, the pleasure accompanying sexual relations between husband and wife is not only not to be shunned but is on the contrary a positive factor in the husband-wife relationship.

According to Zacchia the ends of the marital copula are therefore distinct and can exist separately, as in the case of the marriage of old people. On his part he criticised Tomás Sánchez and those canonists who held that the only important thing was for the husband to ejaculate his semen without him being bound to wait for his wife to emit her own. Obviously, argued Zacchia, this was because such canonists held that this was the only essential requisite for the copula that consummates marriage. But on his part, he noted that when the wife asks for her marital rights, she means primarily her right to the sexual act to satisfy her sexual desire. The husband must be attentive enough to these requests of his wife, given that she might not express herself in so many clear words. Moreover, if the husband does not wait for her to reach such a moment when she too feels satisfied, then he does not fulfil such an obligation; and this neither in view of generation, since for this to follow the female must provide her own semen, nor in view of satisfying the libido of his wife, who just like him achieves satisfaction at the moment of orgasm.[10]

Here one must remember what we have said further up regarding Zacchia's erroneously thinking that the white secretions which the female "ejaculates" during sexual arousal and intercourse are necessary for generation.[11] In spite of these errors, however, Zacchia's opinion about sexual satisfaction in the female

---

[9] ZACCHIA, P., *QML*, 7.3.6.4.

[10] *Ibid.*, 7.3.6.3; cfr. 7.3.1.11-12. Cfr. SÁNCHEZ, T., *De sancto matrimonii sacramento disputationum*, 9.17.9, Lyon 1654.

[11] Cfr. supra, chapter Two, Art. 2 # 2, pp. 52 f; Art. 3, # 2.3, p. 58 f.

appears to be more reasonable than that of Sánchez, when one considers that such secretions not only accompany, but are also a sign of sexual arousal and of the "sedatio concupiscentiae".

Far from exhausting its significance in its procreative aspect, the conjugal act has a very important role to fulfil in marital relationship. The "remedium concupiscentiae" is not a negative secondary end, in the sense of providing the partner with a means of avoiding adultery, but contributes to the growth of communion between the married couple.[12] This insight of Zacchia fits well in the description of conjugal love given by Vatican Council II some three centuries later: "Haec dilectio proprio matrimonii opere singulariter exprimitur et perficitur. Actus proinde, quibus coniuges intime et caste inter se uniuntur, honesti ac digni sunt et, modo vere humano exerciti, donationem mutuam significant et fovent, qua sese invicem laeto gratoque animo locupletant".[13]

Art. 2. IMPOTENCE: "STATUS QUAESTIONIS" AT THE TIME OF ZACCHIA

It has always been the teaching of the Church that the very validity of a marriage depends on, among other things, one's ability to exercise the conjugal act. Since "matrimonia in dies et horas, frequentissime contrahantur", Zacchia felt it necessary to dedicate special attention to this question of impotence which is very often brought before ecclesiastical tribunals. He admitted that the problem of impotence creates many doubts and for that reason the advice of the medical expert is necessary. Indeed, even Rotal jurisprudence insists on the intervention of this expert in such matters.[14]

---

[12] Cfr. *QML*, 7.3. per totum. This personal opinion of Zacchia must have met with opposition. A case in point is provided by a Report of Dott. FRANCESCO TOPAI, who maintained that the all-important element of the sexual act is its fecundative aspect: "Quindi si vede che (l'accoppiamento) non ha ragion di esistere se non come funzione che deve essere integrata da funzioni ulteriori, se non come atto iniziale che non può essere sistematicamente scisso dai successivi e complementari. L'accoppiamento è soltanto comprensibile ... come mezzo al raggiungimento del fine che è la generazione". And to prove his point, this Expert pointed out that even Zacchia was of the same opinion. But this is completely false, since it is very clear that our author held a completely different opinion. Cfr. Dott. FRANCESCO TOPAI, *Parere medico-legale*, in S.C. CONCILII, Monasterien. Matrimonii, 16 decembris 1899, in *Thesaurus*, vol. 158, p. 943.

[13] CONCILIUM VATICANUM II, Constitutio Pastoralis, *De Ecclesia in mundo huius temporis, Gaudium et Spes*, 7 decembris 1965 n. 49 b.

[14] ZACCHIA, P., *QML*, 3.1.1.5: "Hinc patet multoties de sufficientia aut

Since Zacchia's approach to the problem of impotence was to be in conformity with the canonical teaching and doctrine, it is essential to have a clear notion of the state of affairs in the different periods, starting from the times that preceded our author. Only against this background can Zacchia's contribution be objectively evaluated.

It is enough to note that our author was writing his medicolegal treatise in the period immediately following on the publication of the Brief "Cum frequenter" by Pope Sixtus V.[15] It was a period not without importance in the canonical tradition. What was the "common" canonical doctrine before the papal document and that which was introduced with it?

1.   *"Status quaestionis" before the "Cum frequenter"*

The whole problem was rather a complex one, since prior to the publication of the "Cum frequenter" there were three different opinions regarding the validity of the marriage of persons lacking the use of both testicles.

The *first* opinion was that persons who had no testicles but could have an erection and effect penetration, could still validly marry even if they did not ejaculate any semen whatsoever. One of the defenders of this view was Martinus de Azpilcueta (Doctor Navarro).

> "Concedo — he said — non solum spadonem, qui unum testiculum habet posse contrahere matrimonium, sed etiam qui nullum habet, etiam si sint thlasiae, quibus testes fracti sunt, sive thlibiae, qui eas habent attritos, modo arrigere collum, et virgam, et coire possint ..."[16].

The *second* opinion was that such persons could validly marry, so long as they were capable of erection, penetration and ejaculation inside the vagina, even if the semen they ejaculated was not apt for

---

insufficientia coeundi dubitare posse, quo in casu, ut in aliis multis, qui circa hanc materiam Iurisconsultos exercent, medici in iudices, tanquam periti adhibentur". Cfr. c. COCCINO, Toletana Nullitatis Matrimonii, 18 februarii 1639, n. 4, in *QML*, 10 dec. LXXX; c. SERAPHINO, Faventina Matrimonii, 1 februarii 1585, n. 5, *ibid.*, 10 dec. VIII.

[15] SIXTUS V, Epist., *Cum frequenter*, 27th June 1587, in *Fontes Codicis Iuris Canonici*, vol. I, n. 169, pp. 298 ff.

[16] AZPILCUETA, M.de, (alias Dr. NAVARRO), *Consiliorum sive Responsorum libri iuxta ordinem Decretalium dispositi*, lib. 4, tit. de frigidis et malef., cons. 3, nn. 11-12, Rome 1590, vol. II, p. 154.

generation. Among the authors who held this view was Petrus de la Palu (Paludanus), who expressed his opinion in these words:

> "Si in eis virga erigitur et semen emittitur, sed invalidum ad generandum, possunt contrahere; sed si semen non emittunt, contrahere non possunt".[17]

Finally, the *third* opinion was that persons lacking both testicles were simply considered not capable of contracting a valid marriage, irrespective of whether they ejaculated any seminal liquid or otherwise. D. Soto thus expressed this opinion:

> "Igitur eunuchi utroque vacui, quamvis virili polleant, illudque erigant et in vas inducant, revera nullum contrahunt matrimonium quia vel non seminant, vel eorum semen non est eiusdem rationis cum prolifico".[18]

Writing after the Brief, Tomás Sánchez pointed out that this third opinion was not only "indubitata" and "communis", but also constituted a "regula infallibilis et certissima". And he listed 37 authors to demostrate this.[19]

But this assertion of Sánchez has been challenged and proved wrong. From a study of twelve of the authors listed by Sánchez, I. Gordon comes to the following conclusion:

> "Attentis expositis fateri debemus auctores ita apparere divisos, ut de opinione vere communi sermo esse non possit; videtur tamen opinio asserens viros sine testiculos esse habiles ad matrimonium, dummodo erigere et seminare possint, fuisse tunc temporis communior, atque, ... haberi posse tanquam 'regula infallibilis et certissima'".[20]

A more recent and fuller study by A. McGrath comes to the same conclusion. After analysing and examining the authors listed by Sánchez in favour of his theory, McGrath concludes:

> "Of all the authors examined, not a single one can be said to support the third opinion unequivocally ... It is manifestly clear that

---

[17] PALUDANUS, P., *Lucubrationum opus in quartum sententiarum*, dist. 34, q. 2, a. 1; quoted by CASTAÑEDA DELGADO, E., *Una sentencia española en el siglo XVI. La validez del matrimonio de los eunuchos y espadones*, in *Revista Española de Derecho Canónico*, 12 (1957) 267.

[18] SOTO, D., *Commentarium in quartum sententiarum*, dist. 34, q. 1, Art. 2, # Atque hinc; Venice 1575, vol. 2, p. 247, col. A.

[19] SÁNCHEZ, T., *op. cit.*, 7.92.17.

[20] GORDON, I., *Adnotationes quaedam de valore matrimonii virorum qui ex toto secti sunt a tempore Gratiani usque ad Breve "Cum frequenter"*, in *Periodica*, 66 (1977) 243, 244.

Sánchez's claim is hopelessly inaccurate. There is not one independent verification of the existence of his theory prior to "Cum
frequenter" ... On the other hand, at least 31 authors, in one way or
another, favoured the second opinion, upholding the ability of
eunuchs and spadones to marry, provided they can have an erection
and emit semen ... Sánchez's opinion cannot truly be called common. Indeed, it would seem that, where the specific question was
considered, it was the second opinion that was common (though the
supporters of the first opinion would widen the bounds of potency
even further). Nor can Sánchez's other claim be upheld when he
says that the third opinion was "indubitata", since he himself bears
witness to the controversy in the matter of the marriage of eunuchs
and spadones".[21]

2. "Status quaestionis" after the "Cum frequenter"

1. The contents of the Brief

On the 27th June 1587, Pope Sixtus V published his Brief
"Cum frequenter". The socio-cultural situation in sixteenth-century
Spain was permitting an increasing number of marriages by men
who had no testicles or only atrophised ones. This situation drove
the Apostolic Nuncio in Spain, Cesare Spacciani, to seek direction
from Rome. From the introduction of the Brief, it is evident that
the Nuncio had asked direction as to "quid statuendum" about the
marriage of persons

> "qui utroque teste carent, et ideo certum ac manifestum est, eos
> verum semen emittere non posse, ... et humorem forsan quemdam
> similem semini, licet ad generationem, et ad matrimonii causam
> minime aptum effundunt".[22]

Those persons could not be considered frigid, since they were
capable of having an erection and penetration. Furthermore they
could even ejaculate a certain seminal liquid. Yet they lacked the
use of both testicles, either because they were missing or because
they were atrophised. The case of the man having one testicle did
not present any problem at all; his marriage was considered valid.

In his reply the Pope gave a double answer. The first was that

> "Nos igitur attendentes, quod secundum canonicas sanctiones, et
> naturae rationem, qui frigidae naturae sunt, et impotentes, iidem

---

[21] McGRATH A., A controversy concerning male impotence. Analecta Gregoriana, vol. 247, Rome 1988, pp. 107, 109-110.
[22] SIXTUS V, Epist. Cum frequenter, cit., in note 15.

minime apti ad contrahenda matrimonia reputantur, quod praedicti eunuchi et spadones, quas tamquam uxores habere non possunt, easdem habere ut sorores nolunt, quia experientia docet, tam ipsos dum se potentes ad coeundum iactitant, quam mulieres, quae eis nubunt, non ut caste vivant, sed ut carnaliter invicem coniungantur prava, et libidinosa intentione, sub praetextu, et in forma matrimonii turpes huiusmodi commixtiones affectare, quae cum peccati, et scandali occasionem praebeant, et in animarum damnationem tendant, sunt ab Ecclesia Dei prorsus exterminandae".[23]

Men who are frigid by nature, said the Pope, are impotent, and cannot therefore contract a valid marriage. The reason he adduced is not that mentioned by the Nuncio in his petition, that is the absence of both testicles and of the "verum semen ad generationem aptum", but the fact that such men are frigid.

The second argument adduced by the Pope to prohibit the future marriages of eunuchs and spadones is that

"ex spadonum huiusmodi, et eunuchorum coniugiis nulla utilitas provenit, sed potius tentationum illecebrae, et incentiva libidinis oriuntur, eidem Fraternitati tuae per praesentes committimus, et mandamus, ut coniugia per dictos, et alios quoscumque eunuchos et spadones, utroque teste carentes cum quibusvis mulieribus, defectum praedictum sive ignorantibus, sive etiam scientibus contrahi prohibeas, eosque ad matrimonia quomodocumque contrahenda inhabiles auctoritate nostra declares ...".[24]

With a view to the ends of marriage, such a union would serve no purpose at all: "nulla utilitas". It is, however, interesting to note that while the Pope pointed out the fact that these men lacked both testicles, yet he made no mention at all as to their ability or otherwise to produce "verum semen", or any semen whatsoever. He just prescinded from this problem. In view of all this, McGrath comes to the evident conclusion:

"in keeping with the common opinion of theologians and canonists, the Brief declared eunuchs and spadones unable to marry, not because of some defect in the composition of what they ejaculated but because they were not able to achieve the secondary end of marriage, the so-called 'sedatio concupiscentiae'".[25]

In reality therefore, the Pope's disposition did not affect those eunuchs and spadones who, though lacking both testicles, were

---

[23] *Ibid.*
[24] *Ibid.*
[25] McGRATH, A., *op. cit.*, p. 110.

capable of both erection and semination. And therefore the Brief was only echoing the earlier common opinion (the second) that if these men could achieve the secondary end of marriage, they were to be considered potent, since they were neither frigid nor unable to achieve at least one of the ends of marriage. This was the true message of the Brief.

2.   The opinion after the Brief

The interpretation that the Brief was given was completely different. Mainly thanks to Sánchez, as we shall see in the next paragraph, moralists and canonists were completely misled in following the earlier third opinion and in holding that those eunuchs and spadones who had no testicles, and were therefore not capable of ejaculating "verum semen in testiculis elaboratum", could not contract a valid marriage. Thus Johannes Gutiérrez, writing again after the publication of the Brief, when referring to whether or not such persons could marry, noted that:

> "hodie tamen, attento motu proprio Sixti V in hoc dato procul dubio matrimonium contahere prohibentur et inhabiles ad hoc sunt declarati".[26]

This interpretation continued unassailed for almost three centuries. The 1917 Code of Canon Law once again spoke of the object of consent as being constituted by those acts "per se aptos ad prolis generationem"[27], a phrase which was almost universally interpreted to mean those acts in which "vir verum semen modo naturali effundit intra vaginam mulieris".[28]

Problems arose when surgical sterilization, for one reason or another, started to be practised with more frequency. Ecclesiastical jurisprudence was faced with the decision of whether those men who had their seminal ducts severed, were capable of contracting a valid marriage or not, given that they too, not unlike eunuchs and spadones, could not emit the "semen in testiculis elaboratum". A

---

[26] GUTIÉRREZ, J., *Quaestiones tam ad sponsalia de futuro quam matrimonia eorumque impedimenta pertinentes*, cap. 112, n. 11, Venice 1618. Cfr. LEFEBVRE, C., *De Joanne Gutiérrez deque constitutione "Cum frequenter" quoad verum semen*, in *Études de Droit et d'Histoire*, Mélanges Mgr. H. Wagnon, Louvain 1976, pp. 591-601.

[27] *Codex Iuris Canonici*, 1917, can. 1081 # 2.

[28] WERNZ, F.X.-VIDAL, P., *Ius canonicum*, tom. V, *Ius matrimoniale*, Rome 1946, p. 258, n. 218; cfr. GASPARRI, P., *Tractatus canonicus de matrimonio*, Paris 1904, nn. 568, 602.

twofold praxis was followed. On the one hand, the Roman Rota in accordance with the mistaken, but common, interpretation of the sistine Brief, required that for the perfect canonical copula, the male must have the possibility to ejaculate the "verum semen", identified with the semen produced in the testicles, inside the vagina, and this through the normal process of erection and penetration.

On the other hand, the Holy Office (the present Sacred Congregation for the Doctrine of the Faith) followed a distinct praxis. Referring to the sterilization being performed in Germany, it stated that "in casu sic dictae sterilizationis iniqua lege impositae, matrimonium ad mentem paragraphi 2 can. 1068 non esse impediendum".[29] Sterilized men who had their spermatic ducts severed or obstructed were openly permitted to marry even though they could not ejaculate the "verum semen in testiculis elaboratum". Similar replies were given in 1957, 1964 and 1965.[30] The result of such a different praxis can well be imagined.

The whole question was raised and discussed during the process for the revision of the Code. It is very interesting to note that "omnes consultores negant necessitatem seminis prout a iurisprudentia rotali requiritur". The "seminatio ordinaria uti in traditione antiqua intellegebatur, id est sine formali respectu ad naturam ipsius liquidi seminalis" is required and suffices.[31]

Finally, in agreement with the new orientation of Vatican Council II and the new canonical codification, the Sacred Congregation for the Doctrine of the Faith, on the 13th May 1977, emanated a Decree in which to the question

> "utrum ad copulam coniugalem requiratur necessario eiaculatio seminis in testiculis elaborati"

replied in the negative.[32]

The centuries-long discussion was finally brought to an end. And the new 1983 Code points out that the marriage covenant is

---

[29] S.C.S. Officii, Resp. to the Ordinary of Aachen, 16*2*1935; in Ochoa, X., *Leges Ecclesiae post Codicem Iuris Canonici editae*, vol. I, Rome 1966, n. 1262.

[30] Cfr. Idem, Responsa, 28*9*1957, in Ochoa, *ibid.*, vol. II, Rome 1969, n. 2692; 28*1*1964, *ibid.*, vol. III, Rome 1972, n. 3161; 11*6*1965, *ibid.*, n. 3289.

[31] Pontificia Commissio C.I.C. Recognoscendo, *Communicationes*, VI (1974) 186-188.

[32] S.C. pro Doctrina Fidei, *Decretum circa impotentiam quae matrimonium dirimit*, 13 maii 1977, in *AAS*, 69 (1977) 426.

"indole sua naturali ad bonum coniugum atque ad prolis generationem et educationem *ordinatum* ."[33] The phrase "actus per se
aptos ad prolis generationem" has been purposely left out, thereby
avoiding all connotations to the "verum semen" which it had
mistakenly carried for so long.

3.   *Sánchez ad Zacchia*

Because of the great influence Sánchez had on the doctrine
that followed the "Cum frequenter", it is imperative to examine in
some detail his opinion in this regard.

For Sánchez, semination by the husband inside the wife's
vagina is an essential element of the perfect copula. It is only when
this "seminatio intra vas" takes place that the spouses become truly
"una caro",

> " quia de ratione matrimonii est traditio potestatis corporis ad
> copulam coniugalis. At non reputatur copula coniugalis deficienti
> semine. Secundo, quia, ad matrimonii valorem desideratur copula
> per quam coniuges efficiantur una caro ... At non efficiuntur
> coniuges una caro absque seminatio intra vas".[34]

Sánchez insisted that the carnal union, i.e. penetration inside the
vagina, is not enough. Penetration is the normal way of achieving
ejaculation inside the vagina, but it is not in itself sufficient for a
perfect copula in the canonical sense. What Sánchez required is a
"commixtio seminum" and not merely a "commixtio carnium":

> "Ergo tota consummationis ratio est seminis receptio, et carnium
> commixtio est omnino impertinens ... Sed dum semen non recipitur
> intra claustrum foeminae, non efficiuntur una caro ... quia copula
> requiritur ad consummationem apta ad generandum".[35]

With this principle firmly established, Sánchez went on to ask
whether the marriage of eunuchs who lack both testicles is a valid
one. As we have seen, the question was very much discussed before
the Brief and there is proof that the vast majority of canonists and
moralists had opted for a positive reply. Yet writing soon after the
Brief, Sánchez alleged:

> "sed indubitata sententia est, eunuchos utroque testiculo carentes
> esse matrimonii incapaces, ac proinde irritum esse matrimonium,

---

[33] *Codex Iuris Canonici*, 1983, can. 1055 # 1.
[34] SÁNCHEZ, T., *op. cit.*, 7.92.7; cfr. 7.64.8.
[35] *Ibid.*, 2.21.5.

quod inierint, quia ad matrimonii veritatem desideratur potentia verum semen intra vas femineum emittendi ... At eunuchi quamvis membrum erigant, atque quamdam aquosam materiam emittant, ea tamen non est verum semen, nec eiusdem rationis cum vero semine".

And to prove his point, Sánchez quoted the text of "Cum frequenter" and added that:

> "haec sententia etiam ante motum proprium Sixti V communis erat Theologorum et Iurisperitorum",[36]

an assertion that has been proved false.

Yet Sánchez left no doubt that all persons who lack both testicles, or whose testicles are atrophised, cannot contract a valid marriage. The reason for this is their inability to produce and emit "verum semen", which he mistakenly considered as essentially required by the sistine Brief for the canonical conjugal copula:

> "Nam cor, jecur, et cerebrum, quae sunt tres nostri corporis praecipuae partes, transmittunt suos spiritus ad testes qui virtutem habent hos spiritus retinendi, ex quibus totum corpus calefit. At si testes deficiant spiritus non retinentur, sed evanescunt illuc transmissi: nec calor per totum corpus reflectitur, unde frigidiores fiunt, et inepti ad verum semen emittendi".[37]

And by insisting that Pope Sixtus V had settled the matter and therefore "hodie dubitari nequit", Sánchez succeeded in drawing behind himself and misleading the other theologians and canonists. Sánchez did not dedicate any special attention to the nature and contents of this "verum semen". He was content to insist on its existence, its passing through the testicles and its ejaculation in the vagina. "Verum semen" is the male semen, ejaculated by a man who possesses at least one testicle. When the copulatory organs exist, the ejaculation of the man always consists of "verum semen", which is in itself naturally ordained to generation, even though this might not in fact result.

What was Zacchia's opinion in this regard? Here we must make an important distinction between what Zacchia said as a doctor and what he was merely adopting from the current doctrinal opinion.

In line with the interpretation of Sánchez, he noted that the most common and unchallenged opinion among canonists was that

---

[36] *Ibid.*, 9.72.17.
[37] *Ibid.*

those men who have no testicles cannot contract a valid marriage. But the way he explained the reasoning behind such an opinion is very indicative, since in reality Zacchia was here pointing out to the confusion made between the two kinds of impotence, namely *coeundi* and *generandi*; a confusion which inevitably leads to the wrong conclusion. This is how Zacchia explained the real reason why men lacking both testicles were considered barred from marriage: only the testicles have the power to transform the seminal liquid "ut generationis materia fiat", so that men who do not have them cannot perform a "copula apta ad generationem", that is a copula "cum spe generationis". In this way, the procreative end of marriage is frustrated, "et sic non poterunt forte tales valide matrimonium contrahere"[38], since

> "ad generationem sint omnino inhabiles unde prohibentur matrimonium contrahere".[39]

But this is only one side of the coin, for Zacchia did not personally share this opinion. In reality he was in favour of the earlier opinion which held that men lacking both testicles can validly marry, so long as they are capable of ejaculating inside the vagina. Zacchia agreed that the absence of testicles deprives the person only of his ability to generate, but leaves him capable of an otherwise normal sexual act from which the other ends of marriage can be achieved. Clearly this is neither a case of frigidity nor a "useless" marriage:

> "Aliqui, ut eunuchi, apti sunt ad coeundum, non tamen apti sunt ad generandum, ob seminis absentiam aut imperfectionem".[40]

And while he prudently left the matter of the validity of such marriages to the canonists' decision, yet he did not refrain from criticising them for their inconsistency and illogical deductions.[41]

---

[38] ZACCHIA, P., *QML*, 3.1.5.9.

[39] *Ibid.*, 3.1.9.13. Cfr. 3.1.5.28: "Potest ... dubium insurgere huiusmodi: nam cum aliqui sint ex frigidis, ... qui coeunt quidem non tamen semen emittunt, aut emittunt quidem, sed in quantitate nullius considerationis, et qualitate tenue, et aquosum et in summa minime prolificum, dubitari potest, an hi, valide matrimonium contrahant, quod videantur posse carnaliter commisceri, et sic matrimonium consummare. Ad hoc dubium, salva semper veriori sententia, negative responderem: et ratio est, quia cum actus coitus tendat ad ulteriorem finem, nempe ad seminis emissionem, cum spe quoque futurae generationis, iam patet in his actum illum suo fine frustrari, et sic non poterunt forte tales valide matrimonium contrahere...; sed hoc canonistae decidant, quibus in omnibus me remitto".

[40] *Ibid.*, 9.3.7.1.

[41] Cfr. *ibid.*, 3.1.9.13; 3.1.5.29; 7.3.4.12-13.

Art. 3. DEFINITIONS AND DISTINCTIONS OF IMPOTENCE

Zacchia started his systematic treatment of impotence by noting, in line with the traditional canonical doctrine, that

> "cum ergo matrimonia in dies, et horas frequentissime contrahantur, palam est ad eorum validitatem requiri de necessitate coeundi potentiam ...; unde regulariter coniugio ineptus est, qui debitum reddere nequit ... Nec solum coeundi potentia sufficere videtur, sed potentia seminis quoque emittendi requiritur ... Idcirco ergo ubi horum utrumque non adsit, separatur matrimonium".[42]

Moreover, as an impediment, impotence has to present certain qualities in order to render a marriage null, for not every anomalous condition in this regard carries with it such an adverse effect. Aware of the firmly established canonical principle that only that impotence which is antecedent, perpetual and certain renders a marriage null, Zacchia pronounced himself accordingly:

> "ad diremptionem matrimonii requiritur ut impotentia sit naturalis, perpetua et insanabilis ... Alias enim ubi sit temporalis vel dubia, matrimonium non dissolvitur".[43]

Furthermore, when speaking of the dynamics of a normal sexual act i.e. of a "naturalis coitus" from which generation can follow, he also noted that all doctors unanimously agreed on the necessity of three elements:

> "Sunt vero tres illae conditiones ad coitum requisitae, membri genitalis erectio usque ad operis consummationem, nempe ad seminis emissionem perdurans, ipsius membri intromissio debita in vas foemineum, et seminis eiaculatio in ipsum uterum".[44]

With these three premises firmly established, Zacchia then passed on to give the various definitions and distinctions of impotence.

---

[42] *Ibid.*, 3.1.1.4.
[43] *Ibid.*, 9.3.1.1. Here Zacchia referred to three Rotal decisions: c. DUNOZETTO, Romana Quarti Dotalis, 15 iunii 1635, nn. 2-4: *QML*, 10 dec. LXXI; c. COCCINO, Pampilonensis Matrimonii, 11 decembris 1615, per totam: *ibid.*, dec. XL; and c. PLATTO, Taurinensis Dissolutionis Matrimonii, 16 martii 1590, n. 7: *ibid.*, dec. XIV: "et tamen ad hoc ut dirimatur matrimonium, debet constare, quod (impotentia) perpetua sit, et insanabilis humano remedio".
[44] ZACCHIA, P., *QML*, 9.3.2.5. It is useful to repeat that Zacchia used the term *uterus* to refer both to the vagina and to the womb; cfr. supra, chapter 2, note 43, p. 54.

1. *"Impotentia coeundi" and "Impotentia generandi"*

Zacchia started by distinguishing between the two main classical types of impotence, namely, the inability to perform the sexual act or *impotentia coeundi*, and the inability to generate, *impotentia generandi*. Following Hostiensis and Brunellus, he defined the former in these words:

> "Impotentia coeundi ... vitium est vel naturale vel accidentale, quo quis impeditur alteri carnaliter commisceri".[45]

Impotent and consequently

> "coniugio ineptus est, qui debitum reddere nequit".[46]

In strict relation with this type of impotence, but clearly distinct from it, Zacchia also mentioned another form of impotence: *impotentia seminandi*. It was held that, if present, even this impotence would render a marriage null.

> "Causae ergo impedientes matrimonii consummationem (de iis tantum loquor, de quibus ad medicum considerare spectat) ad impotentiam coeundi, vel seminandi, vel utriusque simul reducuntur, cum impotentia coeundi per se, etiam si vir seminare possit, et impotentia seminandi per se, etiamsi vir possit coire, et utriusque rei simul impotentia sit ipsissima causa dissolvendi matrimonium".[47]

It is therefore evident that for Zacchia, *potentia coeundi* includes not only the ability to have an erection and effect penetration, but also to effect ejaculation — hence *potentia seminandi*. In this way Zacchia brought about a reconciliation between the first two opinions held before the Brief, *Cum Frequenter*. *Potentia coeundi* would therefore essentially include both moments of the copula — penetration and ejaculation — required for marriage.[48]

Furthermore, when speaking of *impotentia seminandi* Zacchia did not make any reference at all to the nature of the seminal liquid required. Apparently, he purposely left out of his definition any qualification of the semen. Zacchia's silence is very indicative, for he seems to have had a very different opinion on this point from Sánchez and the other canonists.

The other type of impotence, i.e. *impotentia generandi*, only renders a person unable to beget any offspring.

---

[45] *Ibid.*, 3.1.1.6.
[46] *Ibid.*, 3.1.1.1.
[47] *Ibid.*, 9.10.2.1.
[48] Cfr. *ibid.*, 9.3.2.2.

"Impotentia autem generandi vitium item est naturale, vel accidentale, quo quis legitimo vel naturali coitu utens inhabilis est ad sui similis generationem".[49]

According to Zacchia, the inability to perform a normal sexual act always causes in the patient an inability to generate. Persons who cannot generate are called sterile. This sterility is an anomaly due to which

"animal compari iunctum in aetate habili generare sibi simile non potest, vel foetus unquam ad perfectionem deducere".

The term *sterile* was therefore also somewhat loosely applied by him to those women who had only given birth once or due to some defect on their part were not able to carry out a pregnancy to its end.[50] Inability to generate or sterility does not affect any of these essential elements of the copulative act and therefore it does not constitute an impediment to marriage.[51] Finally, Zacchia also noted that either type of impotence can affect both the male and the female individually, or it can be present simultaneously on both sides.[52]

2. Divisions of "impotentia coeundi"

As the abundant references to both doctors and canonists clearly show, Zacchia accepted and followed the already current distinctions made with regards to the concept of sexual impotence, as understood by Sánchez and others after the Brief, *Cum Frequenter*. His main original contribution here consisted in his ability to gather in a single treatise the dispersed medical and canonical doctrine on the subject and present it in a systematical and rather complete way, and this especially from a medico-legal point of view. Very often, by way of clarification and completion he also added a personal critical evaluation of what other authors said.

1. Congenital and acquired

In Zacchia's terminology, "impotentia coeundi" can be either *natural* or *accidental*, depending on whether it is caused by some anomaly present from birth (congenital) or by some illness or other accidental factor (acquired). Both types of anomalies can cause

---

[49] *Ibid.*, 3.1.1.8.
[50] *Ibid.*, 9.10.3.14. Cfr. SANTORI, G., *Compendio di sessuologia*, Saluzzo 1972, p. 436, note.
[51] Cfr. *QML*, 9.10.3.16; 9.3.6.1.
[52] *Ibid.*, 3.1.1.9; cfr. 9.10.3.22-23.

either a *total* or *partial* impotence, again depending on whether it is an illness which strikes the whole person and therefore affects also the genital organs or it is an anomaly, congenital or acquired, which affects only the genital parts. In addition, acquired impotence can be either *intrinsic* or *extrinsic*:

> "... impotentiam coeundi vel ex causa esse connaturali, vel ex accidentali. Naturalis causa vel ex parte totius est, vel ex partium vitio ... Accidentalis porro causa, vel intrinseca est, vel extrinseca ...".[53]

2. *Perpetual and temporary*

This depends on whether impotence can be cured or not. In this case, Zacchia distinguished not only between those causes that can be completely or only partially removed, (or better only apparently removed, as he noted), but also between those that can be cured only after a long time. In the latter cases, he noted, treatment was accompanied by difficulties, suffering as well as possible risking of one's life.[54]

Leaving apart for the time being Zacchia's particular treatment of each case, which we shall deal with in the following chapters, we can mention here the general conclusions which he drew in this regard and which were always in accordance with the current canonical doctrine. He held that a marriage is not to be dissolved where impotence is either temporary or even doubtful. In this latter case, a three-year trial period was to be assigned to find out the nature of such impotence. If the cause of impotence can be removed, then the validity of the marriage is to be upheld. On the contrary, where the impediment proves perpetual, the marriage is to be declared null.[55] Where the impediment can be removed but only with great difficulty and even not without risk to one's life, then the patient would not be bound to seek such a cure. Zacchia considered such an impotence as irremediable. He also noted that all congenital impediments causing impotence, save for some lesser ones, are incurable.[56]

---

[53] *Ibid.*, 3.1.1.10-11; cfr. 9.3.2.5; 9.10.2.2.

[54] *Ibid.*, 7.3.6.1.

[55] Cfr. *ibid.*, 9.3.1.1; 9.10.2.1. This three-year trial period first passed into the official legislation of the Church towards the end of the twelfth century with the decretal *Laudabilem* of Pope CELESTINUS III: "si frigiditas prius probari non possit, secundum authenticum legale cohabitent triennium", c. 5, X, IV, 15. Cfr. also D'AVACK, P.A., *Cause di nullità e di divorzio, cit.*, pp. 526-531.

[56] ZACCHIA, P., *QML*, 9.3.1.3; cfr. 10 cons. 72.16.

3. *Absolute and relative*

Zacchia also distinguished between "impotentia absoluta" and "impotentia relativa". He applied the former to those who are considered unable to have the sexual act with all other persons of the opposite sex; and the latter to those who are unable to have intercourse only with some but not all persons of the other sex. He said that this distinction applies to both "impotentia coeundi" and "impotentia generandi". According to Zacchia, the causes of relative impotence are multiple:

> "Est quaedam impotentiae species tam coeundi quam generandi, quae non simpliciter et absolute impotentia est, sed respective, et ob id respectiva dicta, quatenus alter coniugum respectu alterius potens ad coitum aut generationem non est, cum respectu aliarum personarum ad utrumque aptissimus existat".[57]

4. *Organic and functional*

Modern canonical doctrine and jurisprudence speak also of *organic* and *functional* impotence.[58] Although Zacchia did not use such terms, it is clear that he referred to these forms of impotence throughout his study of the subject. He spoke of organic impotence

---

[57] *Ibid.*, 3.1.6.1.

[58] This twofold division of impotence has prevailed in the traditional praxis followed by ecclesiastical jurisprudence, although in recent years some attempts were evident at specifying even further functional impotence, and a third type defined as "psychic" has also been proposed. In a recent study on the subject, G. VERSALDI points out that this twofold division of impotence into organic and functional is very inadequate and proposes a new one. He distinguishes between *organic* and *psychic* impotence, subdiving the latter into *primary* and *secondary*:

impotence { organic / psychic } { primary / secondary }

"L'impotenza organica viene definita come l'impotenza avente come causa un'alterazione organica di qualsiasi tipo a carico di qualunque struttura o processo fisiologico interessante l'attività copulatoria.

"L'impotenza psichica è definita come l'impotenza causata dai processi psicologici che intercorrono tra l'individuo e l'ambiente in cui vive. È chiamata impotenza psichica primaria quella in cui le cause psichiche agiscono direttamente sui processi sessuali, provocando la disfunzione. È chiamata impotenza psichica secondaria quella che deriva in modo indiretto e accidentale da patologie psichiatriche già in sé definite", *L'oggettività delle prove in campo psichico*. Una ricerca interdisciplinare sulle sentenze della S. Romana Rota dal 1967 al 1976 in tema di "impotentia coeundi" per cause psichiche, Brescia 1981, pp. 205-206; cfr. pp. 1-92.

whenever he mentioned the physical defects of the sexual organs
that rendered a person incapable of performing the sexual act. As
to functional impotence, he referred to this anomaly when he used
the then common terms "frigiditas" and "maleficium", to which he
dedicated detailed attention on different occasions; not to mention
the psychological factors to which he also attributed a share in the
dynamics of the sexual act.[59]

5. *Certain and doubtful*

The last distinction which Zacchia mentioned in connection
with sexual impotence regards its certainty: *certain* and *doubtful*
impotence. Sometimes such an impediment is quite clear, but on
other occasions it is doubtful. He noted that such a distinction is of
special importance to judges, since they must determine the nature
of the alleged impotence in every particular case. Only that
impotence which is certain and perpetual renders a marriage null,

> "alias enim ubi sit temporalis, vel dubia, matrimonium non dissolvi-
> tur, sed expectatur triennium ad experiendum de qualitate
> impotentiae".[60]

We can conclude this chapter by referring to what Zacchia pointed
out, namely that one who is impotent either to perform the sexual
act or to generate, cannot be called healthy. However, in every
case, everyone is to be presumed capable of both acts, since the
presumption is that every individual is healthy rather than unheal-
thy. It is only where there is proof to the contrary that this
presumption is no longer valid.[61]

---

[59] Cfr. ZACCHIA, P., *QML*, 3.1.1.6; 3.1.5; 3.1.6; 9.3.5.

[60] *Ibid.*, 9.3.1.1.

[61] *Ibid.*, 3.1.9.9-11. Cfr. c. ZARATE, Bononien. Fideicommissi de Buccaferris,
24 maii 1655, n. 2, *ibid.*, 10 dec. XCVIII: "Ad generationem habilis unusquisque
praesumitur, nisi inhabilitas probetur: ... nostri aevi alter Hippocrates Paulus
Zacchias, *QML*, 3.1.9.10".

CHAPTER FOUR

ORGANIC IMPOTENCE IN MAN

In this chapter, we shall turn our attention to those factors of an organic nature which Paolo Zacchia considered among the causes that in his opinion prevent the exercise of a "copula apta ad generationem" in man.

Art. 1. ESSENTIAL REQUIREMENTS FOR THE CONSUMMATION OF MARRIAGE.

1. *An important premise*

There is no doubt that our author knew of the different opinions that were current both before and after the publication of the sistine Brief. Nor is there any doubt as to what the prevalent interpretation of this Brief in his time was. As we have already seen, Zacchia did not share this view completely[1]; but it was not in

---

[1] Cfr. supra, chapter 3, Art. 2, # 3, pp. 72 ff.

his competence to decide what the essential elements needed for
the canonical consummation of marriage are. He therefore merely
adopted as his starting point the definition of the copula that
according to canonists is required for the consummation of
marriage:[2]

> "Assumpta canonistarum determinatione quoad matrimonii con-
> summationem, nempe quod tunc dici debeat matrimonium consum-
> matum cum inter coniuges secuta est copula apta ad generationem,
> absque ulla haesitantia firmandum est, matrimonium consummari
> ubi per membra generationis coniuges commixti fuerint prout
> natura exposcit, nempe per insertionem membri virilis in uterum
> muliebrem, et veri seminis intra uterum eiaculatum; haec namque
> tantum copula apta est ad generationem".[3]

According to canonical doctrine, marriage is consummated "cum
inter coniuges secuta est copula apta ad generationem". Only *then*
did Zacchia draw his conclusions in the light of his medical
knowledge; that is, given *this* definition, he enunciated when such a
copula is really "apta ad generationem", saying that for this
purpose two things are required: effective *penetration* inside the
vagina and *ejaculation* of the "verum semen" therein.[4] He concluded that where penetration is not to the necessary degree, or
where the male does not ejaculate "verum semen", or merely
ejaculates outside the vagina, then such a copula can never be
called "apta ad generationem", nor can it be considered sufficient
to consummate that particular marriage.[5]

2. Whether penetration is always required for consummation

1. The problem and its solutions

At the time of Zacchia, it was currently held that conception
could result even without any penetration inside the vagina. Such a
claim, often corroborated by facts, was even made by persons who
enjoyed a certain authority and amounted to different forms of
what today is known as "absorption of the semen"; whether this

---

[2] Cfr. Zacchia, P., *QML*, 7.3.4.10.
[3] *Ibid.*, 9.10.1.8.
[4] *Ibid.*, 9.3.2.5.
[5] *Ibid.*, 9.10.1.9: "Unde si debita coniunctio, et insertio membrorum non
sequatur, si verum semen vir non eiecerit, aut eiecerit prope externum osculum,
vel non debite penetraverit, nunquam haec copula erit apta ad generationem, nec
per eam dici poterit matrimonium fuisse consummatum". Cfr. 3.1.8.13; 9.3.2.5.

followed after an ejaculation "ante portas" or after the semen had in some way come into contact with the external organs of the female, for example "in balneis"[6] or, as some then used to hold, even through the intervention of the devil.

Given the authority of the persons behind such claims, Sánchez accepted this position as "longe verior" and drew two conclusions. He held that since without any penetration, conception can follow, then, it is not necessary for the consummation of marriage.

> "Etiam absque corporum coniunctione, virili semen recepto intra vas, consummatur matrimonium. Ergo tota consummationis ratio est, seminis receptio, et carnium commixtio est omnino impertinens".[7]

Although penetration is the usual way of depositing the semen in the vagina, yet this can also take place by some other means or in some other way, so long as both parties are indeed potent: "quacumque arte", said Sánchez, be it natural or otherwise.[8] And like Sánchez, many other theologians and authors of esteemable authority followed this opinion, claiming that such a copula suffices for generation and through it the spouses become one flesh.[9]

On his part, Zacchia criticised this view, saying that Sánchez and all those holding such an opinion erred when they insisted that penetration is not necessary for the consummation of marriage. Although he was aware of the facts yet, he categorically rejected them since, he retained that "fabulam potius sapiunt". Still, given the authority enjoyed by those who favoured and propagated these theories, Zacchia thought it appropriate to dedicate to this problem a whole chapter, in which he discussed

> "an possibile sit, mulierem ex virili semine concipere absque eo,

---

[6] "Quod si vir solus seminet extraordinarie, i.e. extra vel circa vas naturale ... et semen subintret claustra, esset contracta affinitas et matrimonium consummatum, si praecessissent verba de praesenti; quia hic est seminum commixtio, et inde sequi potest generatio, sicut fit in balneis, vel per daemones incubos, qui ex semine virorum infuso matricibus mulierum generant homines, qui utrique hominum et non daemonorum sunt filii; et in Gallia quaedam mulier salvis claustris, imo cum esset arcta, impregnata est", SILVESTER PRIERAS, *Summa*, v. *Matrimonium*, VIII, n. 15, ad 2, Venice 1572; cfr. THOMAS AQUINAS (S.), *Quodlibetales*, VI, q. 10, a. 1; ZACCHIA, P., *QML*, 3.1.8.2-3.

[7] SÁNCHEZ, T., *De sancto matrimonii sacramento disputationum*, Lyon 1654, 2.21.5.

[8] Cfr. D'AVACK, P.A., *Cause di nullità e di divorzio nel diritto matrimoniale canonico*, vol. I, Florence 1952, pp. 278-283; GÓMEZ LÓPEZ, A., *El impedimento de impotencia en Tomás Sánchez*, Pamplona 1980, pp. 49-54.

[9] Cfr. SÁNCHEZ, T., *op. cit.*, 2.21.2; 9.16.3. ZACCHIA, P., *QML*, 3.1.8.5.

quod cum eo commixta fuerit per membra generationis, sed simplici genitalium approximatione, aut utcunque semine prope muliebre vas eiecto".[10]

Zacchia's conclusion was that such a claim lacks any sound scientific basis and is founded only on a false presupposition which obviously leads to the wrong conclusion.[11]

As for the part which the devil might play, Zacchia retained that it is "absurdissimum" to say that generation can follow from a sexual union between the devil and a woman, or that the devil can intervene to insert inside the vagina the semen which the husband ejaculates outside:

> "Ego quidem ... nisi Sancta Mater Ecclesia aliter doceat, de facto non dari talem conceptionem, et partum existimaverim, immo dixerim in via naturae esse impossibilem, cum daemon non possit excedere naturae creatae vires ... Neque crediderim unquam celer-itatem daemonis in semine adsportando, et iniiciendo in uterum mulieris adaequare posse brevitatem temporis, quo seminis calor evanescit; neque enim in hoc exuperat daemonis potentia potentiam naturae, quia ob sui inenarrabilem tenuitatem, seminis spiritus contineri extra conveniens receptaculum, ne per momentum quidem potest".[12]

Zacchia therefore concluded that one must not be too quick to form a general rule from a rare and sporadic event.[13] And once he had

---

[10] *QML*, 3.1.8.1.

[11] *Ibid.*, 9.3.6.1: "Omnia impedimenta, quae remorantur copulam carnalem ex parti viri, remorantur etiam omni procul dubio generationem, cum impossibile sit, foeminam posse ex viro concipere absque eo quod cum viro per membra generationis secundum naturae institutum copuletur, ac fabulae, somnia, ac mera mendacia sunt quaecunque iactantur de conceptione facta ex semine virili in balneo relicto, vel ex eius effusione extra, licet prope vasa muliebria, aliaeque nugae his non absimilis...". Cfr. supra, chapter 2, Art. 2, # 3. pp. 54 f; *QML*, 3.1.8; 5.3.7.2; 7.3.1.5; 7.3.6.10; 9.3.6.1; 9.10.1.6; 9.10.2.10; 10 cons. 42.

[12] *Ibid.*, 7.1.7.5-6; cfr. 3.1.8.19.

[13] *Ibid.*, 7.1.7.7; cfr. 3.1.8.20. Many theologians and canonists took up this line of argumentation and insisted on the need of penetration for the consumma-tion of marriage, sometimes also committing the same mistake of Zacchia. Cfr. for example; Pragen. Disp. Matrimonii, 29 maii 1869, in *Thesaurus*, vol. 128, p. 409; Cameracen. Matrimonii, 31 iulii 1897, ibid., vol. 156, p. 751: "... plures quoque moderni physiologi Zacchia doctissimum sequi penetrationem vaginae per suffi-cientem virgae introductionem necessariam esse sine dubio asserunt, ut vir sic copulans semen suum in uteri interiora per vaginam eiaculat".

c. CATTANI AMADORI, 8 ianuarii 1913, in *SRRD*, vol. 5, p. 35, n. 10; c. SOLERI, 10 augusti 1922, *ibid.*, vol. 14, p. 282, n. 11; c. QUATTROCOLO, 25 februarii 1930, *ibid.*, vol. 22 p. 109, n. 8.

refuted this view, he rounded up his argument by noting that it was the opinion of doctors in general that for generation to follow "necesse est ut (mas membrum) quam penitissime intrudat".[14]

2. *A critique*

With B. Marchetta, we can say today, that:

"la copula consumativa del matrimonio nel concetto canonico può definirsi come l'unione corporea di due individui di sesso diverso realizzata mediante l'introduzione dell'organo copulatore dell'uomo nella cavità vaginale della donna e la conseguente immissione di seme nella stessa. Tutte le volte che i coniugi sono in grado di effettuare l'amplesso sessuale secondo natura, diventando 'una caro', essi hanno consumato il matrimonio".[15]

It is therefore quite evident that Sánchez's opinion, which admitted the consummation of marriage even without any penetration, is no longer tenable. Both doctrine and jurisprudence have clearly established that "erectio et penetratio membri virilis in vaginam mulieris" is a necessary element of the copula which consummates marriage. In this sense, on the 1st March 1941, the Holy Office gave a reply in which it declared that for the purpose of consummation the semen must be deposited inside the vagina, and this "naturali modo".[16] Rotal jurisprudence too has followed the criterion that without effective penetration a marriage cannot be considered consummated:

"non est consummatum validum matrimonium baptizatorum in quo defuit illa penetratio vel illa interna seminis effusio"[17].

---

[14] ZACCHIA, P., *QML*, 10 cons. 43.9: "Si in coitu celebrando non sufficit, ut conceptio sequatur, ut mas intromittat membrum in matricem, sed necesse est, ut illud quam penitissime intrudat, ut semen prope et quam proxime ad internum uteri osculum effundat, alias non secutura conceptione, ex Hippocratis praecipue, aliorumque medicorum auctoritate, quanto magis non sequatur conceptio si semen prope externum uterum eiiciatur?"; cfr. 7.3.6.10; 9.3.6.1; 10 cons. 82.8.

[15] MARCHETTA, B., *Scioglimento del matrimonio canonico per inconsumazione*, Padova 1981, pp. 20-21.

[16] This response was not published in the *AAS*. However, it can be found in: CASORIA, J., *De matrimonio rato et non consummato*, Rome 1959, p. 237.

[17] Coram MORANO, 18 aprilis 1931, in *SRRD*, 23 (1931) 134; n. 6; cfr. c. GRAZIOLI, 17 augusti 1920, *ibid.*, 12 (1920) 240, n. 7; c. ROSSETTI, 3 augusti 1921, *ibid.*, 13 (1921) 189-191, n. 4; c. FILIPIAK, 11 ianuarii 1952, *ibid.*, 44 (1952) 15, n. 14; c. FELICI, 1 februarii 1952, *ibid.*, 44 (1952) 65, n. 4; c. MATTIOLI, 29 februarii 1960, *ibid.*, 52 (1960) 145, n. 5.

The doctrine of the Sacred Congregation of the Sacraments is also the same: where penetration is not effected, the marriage is considered as not having been consummated.[18]

On the other hand, it is today commonly admitted that conception can follow "per absorptionem seminis", and therefore without there having been any previous and real penetration. On this point Sánchez was, therefore, right.

But unlike Sánchez, Zacchia was right on one very fundamental point, namely that penetration is required for the consummation of marriage. He erred, however, when following Hippocrates, Aristotle and others, he claimed that

> "ob sui inenarrabilem tenuitatem, seminis spiritus contineri extra conveniens receptaculum, ne per momentum quidem potest",[19]

for this led him to reject the possibility of conception taking place without any penetration. Nevertheless, in the case of a husband and wife whose marriage is still "ratum tantum", such a conception would not consummate it, since one of the essential elements, i.e. penetration, is missing. Zacchia's error, therefore, did not affect his fundamental premise on the necessity of penetration for consummation, which in any case was a very relevant intuition and a decisive step forward towards the true definition of the "consummation" of marriage.

Furthermore, it seems that Zacchia was in favour of a penetration "usque ad internum uteri (= vaginae) osculum"[20], precisely in view of the fragility of this "seminis spiritus". It must also be said, however, that behind such reasoning there was the then current opinion which stressed that the copula which consummates marriage has to be "apta ad generationem", which is today no longer the case.[21]

---

[18] Cfr. MARCHETTA, B., *op. cit.*, pp. 21-22; ORLANDI, G., *I "Casi Difficili" nel processo super rato*, Padova 1984, pp. 165 f.

[19] Cfr. supra, chapter 2, Art. 1, pp.44 ff; Art. 2, # 3, pp. 54 f.

[20] Cfr. ZACCHIA, P., *QML*, 3.1.8.14: "Secundo, cum etiam brevitas nimia ipsius penis, ex eo quod ad uteri internum osculum ob id pervenire eiaculatum semen non possit, causa notissima sit sterilitatis: ..., cum tamen aliqua approximatio fiat; et intromissio in uterum: quanto magis si nullo modo approximetur, neque intromittatur, nullaque vi semen ad intima eiaculetur, generationem impediret?"; 9.3.8.1.

[21] Cfr. supra, Art. 1, # 1, pp. 81 f; Response of the Holy Office, 1*3*1941, note 16, p. 85.

3. *Ejaculation*

According to the "assumpta canonistarum determinatione", ejaculation of the "verum semen" was also required if the copula was to be apt for generation.[22]

As we have seen[23], Zacchia retained that the seminal liquid is not produced by the testicles, but only carried in them in a rudimentary form and "ibique concoctam et dealbatam ut generationis materia fiat", so that "perfectum ac verum semen in testibus tantum conficitur, itaque ubi desint testes, verum semen quod generationi sit aptum, reperiri non potest", even though the individual can still produce the seminal liquid as such.[24] By this definition, therefore, the liquid ejaculated by those who lack the testicles or those whose testicles are atrophised can still be called "seminal". Besides, the strict relation which Zacchia made between the testicles, "verum semen" and generation is very evident.

Zacchia further noted that for canonical purposes this mere seminal liquid was not considered appropriate to consummate marriage.[25] He also spoke of those cases in which the seminal liquid, even though it has presumably passed through the testicles, is not rendered prolific, and therefore is not apt for generation. But for canonical purposes, sterile as it is, it is still called "verum semen", so that in such cases

"si coitu utantur et semen qualecunque sed a testibus alteratum in uterum proiiciant, tamen matrimonium consummasse dicendi"[26],

since "semen posse esse verum semen, etiam si non sit prolificum" precisely because, at least so it seems, it has passed through the testicles.[27]

In this regard, there is no doubt that in conformity with his medical knowledge, Zacchia called "verum semen" that seminal liquid which is made apt for generation. And as a private doctor, he surely held this opinion. Still, given the canonical doctrine of the

---

[22] Cfr. ZACCHIA, P., *QML*, 9.10.1.10: "Additum porro est, quod haec copula sequi debeat cum effusione veri seminis intra uterum, quantumvis enim vir mulierem cognoverit, et ad uteri usque intima penetraverit, non consummat matrimonium, nisi intra uterum semen effundat: et dico intra uterum, non enim, ut inculcavi, satis est effundere semen prope uterum".

[23] Cfr. supra, chapter 2, Art. 2, # 1, pp. 51-52.

[24] ZACCHIA, P., *QML*, 9.3.2.16.

[25] *Ibid.*, 9.10.1.11; cfr. 3.1.5.28-29.

[26] *Ibid.*, 9.10.3.18-19.

[27] Cfr. *ibid.*, 9.10.3.15-19; 9.10.1.11.

time and the premise from which he set out, whenever he addressed himself to judges and canon lawyers, Zacchia referred to Sánchez and canonical doctrine, and called "verum semen" also the seminal liquid which though it had been in some way altered by the testicles was, however, not rendered apt for generation. But we shall soon see, it was Zacchia himself who pointed out and stressed the contradictions inherent in this position held by canonists.[28]

Taking as his starting point the "verum semen" which canonists required on the part of man for a "copula apta ad generationem", Zacchia ably pointed out one such contradiction. We must, however, remember what we have already said above[29], namely that although he was wrong in asserting that the woman too ejaculates her own semen, Zacchia did not err in affirming that without her physiological contribution, generation is not possible. Hence his query:

> "Cur foemina semen non potente emittere, vir tamen coitu uti possit, et matrimonium teneat; contra vero viro non potente emittere, coitus sit illicitus, et matrimonium non teneat, cum in nostra sententia etiam foemineum semen, ut masculeum, requiratur ad conceptionem? In utroque certe casu, licet succedere non possit conceptio, possunt intendi, et haberi duo alii matrimonii fines, nempe et debiti solutio et fornicationis remedium".[30]

Zacchia's true personal opinion expressed in this question needs no clarification. Once again, the strict relation between the "verum semen" and generation is very evident.

Once the essential elements for the canonical copula that consummates marriage have been pointed out and clarified, we shall now pass on to see what Zacchia considered more properly as his domain and competence, i.e. his treatment of the causes that prevent the normal exercise of such a sexual act.[31]

Art. 2.   SEXUAL ANOMALIES AND ORGANIC IMPOTENCE.

Zacchia's merit in this regard lies in his extensive and detailed presentation of these anomalies as well as in the rather accurate study which he offers from the point of view of canonical impo-

---

[28] Cfr. infra, Art. 3, # 2, pp. 104 f.
[29] Cfr. supra, chapter 2, Art. 3, # 2.3, pp. 58 ff.
[30] ZACCHIA, P., *QML*, 7.3.4.12-13.
[31] Cfr. *ibid.*, 7.3.4.12-13; 9.3.5.2.

tence, considering whether the person suffering from such anomalies can consummate the marriage or not, whether the defect can be cured or otherwise, etc. As it has already been pointed out above, there existed as yet no such complete and systematic treatment from the medico-legal point of view. For this reason, Zacchia's work soon became the constant point of reference and a very useful tool for judges and advocates in ecclesiastical tribunals.

This notwithstanding, Zacchia still remained a man of his times, with his share of errors and limitations, which we shall try to point out and clarify in the course of this exposition.

1. *Testicular anomalies*

Zacchia considered the various anomalies affecting the testicles in conformity with his main thesis that

> "et coeundi et multo magis generandi impotentiam manifesto arguunt".[32]

In line with the then current opinion, he noted that although the primary role of the testicles is in view of the elaboration of the seminal liquid into perfect and prolific semen, yet their anomalous condition can even, sometimes, deprive the individual of the ability to perform the sexual act:

> "Testium carentia omnimoda, aut eorum parvitas, aut etiam incongrua magnitudo, aut non naturalis situs, haec enim caloris naturalis pauperiem, et consequenter imbecillitatem virtutis testantur. Nam testes in seminis generatione, sive perfectione principatum obtinent ut medici omnes existimant".[33]

1. *Lack of testicles*

Zacchia noted that the overall effects produced by the testicles' absence or removal, depend on whether this defect is congenital or acquired, and this either before or after puberty:

> "haec naturae mutatio ... magis praedominatur in his, qui ante pubertatem eunuchantur, quam in illis qui eunuchantur post puber-

---

[32] *Ibid.*, 3.1.3.2; cfr. 3.1.9.6.

[33] *Ibid.*, 3.1.5.24-25; cfr. 3.2.10.3; 9.3.6.7. Ecclesiastical jurisprudence made frequent references to Zacchia on this point, as can be seen in, for example: Salernitana Matrimonii, 24 ianuarii 1871, in *Thesaurus*, vol. 130, pp. 15-16; Leopolien. Matrimonii, 15 decembris 1877, *ibid.*, vol. 136, p. 605; Curien. Matrimonii, 26 ianuarii 1878, *ibid.*, vol. 137, p. 28; coram CHIMENTI, 16 augusti 1918, in *SRRD*, 10 (1918) 116, n. 9.

tatem, iam enim transacta pubertate calor partibus communicatus est, qui ad virilitatem hominem disponit, quod non potuit succedere ante pubertatem".[34]

The absence of the testicles does not therefore necessarily deprive the individual of the exercise of the sexual act. Indeed, where this is possible, the individual who is capable of some emission is still also capable of having the "remedium concupiscentiae".[35] On the other hand, said Zacchia, the absence of testicles, be it congenital or acquired, completely deprives the individual of all possibility to generate:

> "Maritus cum testibus careret, semen generare non poterat, neque absque semine filios".[36]

This would therefore corroborate Zacchia's position and criticism of his contemporary canonists, who claimed that lack of testicles "dirimere matrimonium iam contractum"; and this all the more so, since such persons can, normally, achieve the other ends of marriage.[37]

2. A single testicle

The lack of one testicle, be it congenital or acquired,

> "nec naturam in muliebrem immutare, nec mores deteriores effi-cere, nec quicquam de virilitate demere"[38],

so long as the remaining testicle presents no deficiency. Persons suffering from monorchidia are considered capable of performing the sexual act and of generating:

> "quia et in erectione et in seminis productione et concoctione et emissione non magis deficiunt, quam caeteri, qui ambobus donan-tur, virtus enim unitur in his".[39]

As to the consummation of marriage, this case presents no impediment at all.[40]

---

[34] ZACCHIA, P., QML, 8.1.14.5-7; cfr. c. CATTANI AMADORI, 8 ianuarii 1913, in SRRD, 5 (1913) 31, n. 6.
[35] ZACCHIA, P., QML, 3.1.9.13-14.
[36] Ibid., 9.3.6.10.
[37] And hence, Zacchia concluded: "An vero hoc satis sit ad matrimonii validitatem canonistis decidendum relinquam": ibid., 3.1.9.14; cfr. 9.10.2.14.
[38] Ibid., 8.1.14.7.
[39] Ibid., 3.1.9.5.
[40] Cfr. ibid., 9.10.2.14.

3. Testicles' change of place

This anomaly, known as criptorchidia, is caused by the lack of descent of the testicles in the scrotal sac. Zacchia attributed this lack of descent to the "caloris imbecillitate", so that those who suffer from such an anomaly are not capable of producing prolific semen nor do they seem to possess sufficient genital vigour to enable them to exercise the sexual act.[41]

Although Zacchia showed himself rather doubtful in this regard, yet it seems that he was more inclined to believe that such an anomaly affects primarily one's ability to procreate. It is interesting to note Zacchia's position in view of the canonical "copula apta ad generationem":

> "Dicendum tamen ex mea sententia esset, quod si constare possit huiusmodi viros semen generare, non obstante ea mutatione situs testiculorum, esse aptos ad generationem et consequenter non ob id ineptitudinem generandi, esse a matrimonio repellendos, si modo generandi impedimentum est causa sufficiens ad impediendum, ne contrahant".[42]

The problem is only one of "impotentia generandi" for such persons are really capable of performing the sexual act.

4. Atrophised testicles

Zacchia noted that the same can be said in the case where the testicles, though retaining their natural position, "magnitudine tamen duritie, ac vigore sint nullius considerationis". If on the one hand, such testicles are to be considered as non-existent "quia proprio fine, qui est seminis prolifici generatio et conservatio frustrantur"[43], yet on the other, it is only when they are accompa-

---

[41] *Ibid.*, 9.3.6.7: "Circa testes dubitationem facit eorum situs mutatus, nam in aliquibus conspiciuntur in inguinibus sitos, cumque hoc ex caloris imbecillitate omnino procedat, ex consequenti videretur dicendum, non esse ipsos ad prolificum semen generandum aptos, neque etiam in coitu sufficientem vigorem genitali tribuere, ut ad instar caeterorum hominum ad coitum vir sufficiat". Cfr. 9.10.2.14.

[42] *Ibid.*, 9.3.6.7. This was Zacchia's reply to the question which he proposed to the canonists: "an tales valide matrimonium contrahant, nam si ad matrimonium requiritur copula apta ad generandum, Sánchez, *De matrimonio*, 2.21.5, si huiusmodi testium non naturalis situs potest seminis confectionem et generationem, ut dictum est impedire, certe hi non poterunt matrimonium valide contrahere", *ibid.*

[43] *Ibid.*, 9.3.6.8.

nied by an inability to perform the sexual act, that such an anomaly
marks the presence of frigidity[44], which is not normally the case.
    Contrary to what some other doctors held, Zacchia excluded
the possibility of a cure, and this definitely after puberty.[45]

5. *Large testicles*

    Zacchia directly linked the "crassities et magnitudo testium" to
the ability or otherwise to procreate. In line with other doctors he
said that when this particular state is congenital, it does not affect
the generative faculty. Whereas if it is caused by some disease, then
it may affect this faculty, at least until the cure becomes effective,
"nisi quid maius obstat".[46]
    Medical science has proved that Zacchia was fundamentally
right in attributing to the testicles the two vital tasks of producing
spermatozoa for the propagation of the species and of elaborating
the hormones which give man his virile characteristics; although he
obviously erred when he also thought that the testes also serve as a
store for the spermatozoa. On the other hand, medicine could not
as yet offer him the necessary means to diagnose certain anomalous
conditions such as hypogonadism, eunuchoidism or Klinefelter's
syndrome, nor the existence of such diseases as orchitis, epididymi-
tis and varicocele; so that Zacchia was necessarily very limited in
diagnosing the real causes and in proposing the possible cure of
such anomalies. Furthermore, hormonal treatment can now easily
control the endocrinal activity of these sexual glands as well as the
development and functioning of the genital apparatus; so that a
person suffering from certain testicular anomalies, which were
considered so difficult to cure in the past, can now enjoy a normal
sexual life, including the ability to perform the sexual act with a
normal ejaculation and "sedatio concupiscentiae".[47]

---

[44] *Ibid.*, 3.1.9.18: "Neque etiam proprie eunuchos esse dixerim eos, qui testes
adeo exiguos habent ut ciceris, seu fabae magnitudinem non aequent ...; nam et
hos, si veneri non sufficiant, potius frigidos quam eunuchos dixerim"; cfr.
9.10.2.14.
[45] *Ibid.*, 9.3.6.8.
[46] *Ibid.*, 9.3.6.9; cfr. 9.10.2.14.
[47] Cfr. supra, chapter 2, Art. 3, pp. 55 ff; SANTORI, G., *Compendio di
sessuologia*, Saluzzo 1972, pp. 96-104, 257-271; NANGERONI, A.-SAPONARO, A., *La
vita sessuale dell'uomo*, Milan 1971, pp. 99-102; BERSINI, F., *Matrimonio e
anomalie sessuali e psicosessuali*, Rome 1980, pp. 137-144; CAMPBELL, M.F.-
HARRISON, J.H., *Urology*, Philadelphia, London, Toronto 1970, vol. I, pp.
161-186; vol. II, pp. 1625-1654.

2. *Epididymus and seminal ducts*

1. *The epididymus*

When speaking about the removal of the testicles, Zacchia noted that sometimes, during this process "relicta est superior pars alterius vel amborum testium". Yet it is evident that he had no exact knowledge as to the difference that exists between the didymus and the epididymus. Science had not as yet reached the stage of distinguishing between the two; and the term testicle was an all-inclusive one, comprising both.

Zacchia said that according to Holler when the upper part of the testicles is left intact, the ability to generate is not lost. On his part, however, he was not very much inclined to share this opinion. Nevertheless, while stressing that these persons are not able to produce "verum semen" and consequently cannot consummate their marriage in the canonical sense, he also added that in such cases doctors have to check[48]

> "an illa superior testiculorum pars, nempe venae parastatae, seu glandulae, ubi se dilatare incipiunt, et ad testes seruntur, in excisione testium illis relictae sint, et tamen hoc etiam probato, vix probatum crediderim, illos coire et generare posse, nisi simul probaretur, eos semen ferre, atque illud qualitate et quantitate laudabile et prolificum".[49]

In short Zacchia was very doubtful and rightly so. In fact, modern science distinguishes between the didymus or testicle and the epididymus. Only the former produces the semen and therefore he who possesses only the latter cannot generate.[50]

2. *The seminal ducts*

The importance of such ducts is well known. Along these channels the sperm that had started its voyage in the didymi, having passed through the epididymus, proceeds to be ejaculated into the vagina. On its way it is joined by other secretions. Just as with the epididymi, so also these ducts can be obstructed because of some anomaly. However, so long as this does not indirectly cause the

---

[48] ZACCHIA, P., *QML*, 3.1.5.25; cfr. 3.1.9.7; 9.10.1.10.
[49] *Ibid.*, 3.1.9.11.
[50] Cfr. SANTORI, G., *La questione del "verum semen"*, in *Il Diritto Ecclesiastico*, 82 (1971) 67-70; Idem, *Compendio di sessuologia, cit.*, pp. 300-308; BERSINI, F., *op. cit.*, pp. 144-146.

irremediable incapacity for the sexual union, the closure of these
ducts is today considered as causing only sterility and not impotence in the strict sense.

Speaking in general terms about the causes that lead to
"impotentia coeundi", Zacchia noted that this can also be due

> "ex parte aliorum vasorum ... si illa sint male conformata, si
> naturalem situm non habeant, si sint obstructa",

or even to the fact that one has desisted for a long time from having
sexual intercourse, in which case "testes ac vasa spermatica
contabescant".[51]

But it was explicitly in relation to "impotentia generandi" that
he spoke of the importance of these seminal ducts. Referring to the
possible anomalies he said:

> "Aliae denique respective ad vias, per quas semen eiaculatur, ut
> exampli gratia carunculae sunt in ipso virgae meatu quas dubium
> non est aut in totum, aut ex parte remorari, et impedire seminis
> eiaculationem, et consequenter generationem"[52].

And in agreement with Gabriele Falloppia and other doctors, he
retained that due to such a defect not only the force of ejaculation is
lost, but the semen itself loses its vigour. Yet, despite the fact that
such obstructions are both difficult and dangerous to remove,
Zacchia concluded,

> "generaliter firmandum, carunculas neque coitu unquam, neque
> generationem semper impedire"[53].

3. *Malformations and impairments of the penis*

Zacchia attributed three main functions of this genital organ:
erection, insertion into the female's vagina and ejaculation, all of
which are essentially required for a natural sexual act.

The malformations and impairments which can affect this
organ often render sexual intercourse very difficult and in certain
cases even impossible. On various occasions Zacchia referred to
these anomalous conditions and in line with the anatomical and
medical knowledge of his time, he noted that by far the majority of
them are congenital and in some cases they can even be an
indication of frigidity.[54]

---

[51] ZACCHIA, P., *QML*, 3.1.1.12,16.
[52] *Ibid.*, n. 25.
[53] *Ibid.*, 9.3.6.14; cfr. 10 cons. 65.
[54] Cfr. *ibid.*, 3.1.1.12; 3.1.3.1; 3.1.5.22; 3.1.8.4; 8.1.14.10.

1. *Long penis*

Zacchia followed all doctors who held that generally speaking in this case the sexual act is not rendered impossible. Occasionally, however, it can give rise to relative sexual impotence[55], although sterility is much more common. In fact, Zacchia pointed out that a very long penis, which presses against the back of the vagina, can easily cause pain to the woman during intercourse and make her lose all gratification, thereby not allowing her to emit any semen. However, he also noted that the husband can be cautious enough and act in such a way as to avoid his wife all unnecessary pain.

Although some doctors held that in the case of persons who have a long genital organ, the semen loses its vigour and force before it reaches the female's interior parts, Zacchia argued that this is not always the case.[56]

Finally, while noting that in this case the inability to perform the sexual act

> "neque evidens, neque certum est, neque haec erit fortasse censenda iusta causa separationis"[57],

nevertheless, given the "incommoda quae mulier pati potest et sanitatis quae ex ea causa potest incurrere"[58], Zacchia compassionately suggests that she might turn to the Church and see

> "an haec causa sufficiens esse possit ad illam excusandam a debiti redditione, vel ad thori separationem illi concedendam".[59]

2. *"Penis crassus"*

This impairment deserved greater attention for

> "si magna et excedens sit, ita ut communem crassitiem caeterorum membrorum exuperet",

it can easily become a cause of relative sexual impotence.[60] Generally, however, such an impairment is not very grave and it will gradually disappear with time and treatment.[61]

But there might be other cases where such "crassities sit

---

[55] *Ibid.*, 3.1.6.5.
[56] *Ibid.*, 9.3.6.2; cfr. 10 cons. 68.6.
[57] *Ibid.*, 3.1.6.6.
[58] *Ibid.*, 9.3.3.1.
[59] *Ibid.*, 7.3.5.10.
[60] *Ibid.*, 9.3.3.1.
[61] *Ibid.*; cfr. 7.3.5.9.

exorbitans", so that penetration results impossible or even dangerous for the wife. In these cases, stated Zacchia, given the impossi-
bility to exercise the conjugal act, the marriage can be dissolved.
But since it is very often only a case of relative impotence, the
person can remarry.[62]

In strict relation with this anomaly, he also referred to a case
mentioned by Hostiensis, where the husband had a "membrum
nimis carnosum". But he noted that there, the thickness was not
congenital, but caused by a disease known as elephantiasis. Given
that such a disease was a very grave one, nor did it admit of any
remedy, the copula resulted impossible, so that the marriage could
be dissolved.[63]

3. Short and slender penis

There was no doubt for Zacchia that such a "brevis et exilis"
organ is among the most known cases of sterility.[64] He therefore
dedicated considerable attention to these two characteristics which
can be found together or separately. He noted that such a short
penis can in some instances not only diminish the possibility of
coitus, but can even wholly prevent it. As an example of the latter
case, Zacchia referred to a patient "qui penem adeo brevem
habebat, ut praeter glandem cum praeputio, nihil praeterea a
corpore promineret". Following other doctors, among whom Falloppia and Platter, Zacchia attributed the cause of this irremediable
anomaly to the frigid nature of the individual in question, adding
that this is especially the case where such a shortness is also
accompanied by slenderness. But not all cases are so grave, and
very often this underdevelopment of the penis leads only to some
inconvenience, and at most to sterility, but not to impotence in the
strict sense.[65]

What happens, asked Zacchia, where a man has a short penis
and he is capable of erection and ejaculation, yet "non posset ad
interiora pervenire et hymenis membranam disrumpere", especially if the wife has a rather long vagina?[66] Here, he seemed rather
hesitant, just as he always was wherever it was a question of what
really constitutes "impotentia coeundi" and "impotentia generan-

---

[62] *Ibid.*, 3.1.6.2.; cfr. 9.3.3.1; 9.10.2.8.
[63] *Ibid.*, 9.3.3.2; cfr. 2.3.6.17; 3.3.5.8; 3.3.6.16.
[64] Cfr. *ibid.*, 3.1.8.14; 9.3.6.1.
[65] *Ibid.*, 9.3.3.3-5; cfr. 9.10.2.9.
[66] *Ibid.*

di" for canonists. Once again, Zacchia seemed to be at a loss, giving the impression of being very doubtful of the canonical position. In fact, in his reply he noted that there would be those who claim that since there has been an ejaculation and the semen has somehow reached the vagina (clearly the allusion is to Sánchez), then the marriage in case is considered to be consummated, for they would say that such a copula is "apta ad generationem". They would say that even without penetration, from such a marriage

> "coniuges consequi finem praecipuum, qui est procreandi liberos, neque aliis matrimonii bonis defraudari, licet quoad concupiscentiae remedium non sit adeo efficax, ut in aliis quoad mulierem".[67]

But according to Zacchia, this marriage should be dissolved and this because persons having such an organ

> "non possunt scilicet eorum instrumento usque ad internum uteri osculum pervenire",

and also because

> "censendum enim est, huiusmodi membrum nullius valoris, et utilitatis esse posse, cum tantopere natura in eius formatione defecerit".[68]

4. *Torsion of the penis*

Among the various sexual anomalies, Zacchia also referred to the "penis tortuositate, obliquitate et distorsione", which can be either congenital or acquired. In the first two cases, the defect is not considered without cure, at least if it is not caused by some paralysis; and the copula, which can still prove somewhat difficult to perform, is however not impossible. But in the last case, not only is erection accompanied by great pain, but penetration inside the vagina also results impossible.[69]

---

[67] *Ibid.*, 9.10.2.9.

[68] *Ibid.*, 9.3.3.3-5; cfr. 10 cons. 43.9-10: "Dico ergo quod si ad hunc matrimonii finem assequendum, qui praecipuus est, filiorum procreatio, sufficeret approximatio tanto membrorum generationis utriusque coniugis, et effusio seminis virilis prope, et extra vas foemineum, incassum ad matrimonii validitatem requireretur talis coniunctio, ut vir possit penetrare ad interna uteri, et ibi seminare, quod tamen requiri ad matrimonii validitatem firmant unanimiter canonistae omnes".

[69] *Ibid.*, 9.3.3.7-9; cfr. 9.3.6.3; 9.10.2.10.

5. *Epispadias and hypospadias. Phimosis*

In a question which he dedicated to the impediments that prevent generation in the male, Zacchia noted that worthy of attention is also the case of those who

> "nascuntur cum pene nullo foramine pervio; hi si quam aliam viam natura sibi non comparent ad urinam expellendam in ipso vitae primordio pereunt sed in aliquibus natura aliam sibi viam parat, aperiendo orificium aliquod vel in ipso medio, vel ad veretri radices, vel sub testibus in perinaeo, vel in inguinibus, vel alibi".[70]

It was common belief that whenever such an outlet is not in its natural position, generation is wholly obstructed, since the semen cannot be ejaculated directly "ad uteri internum osculum" but is only emitted along its external sides. When this happens, the semen loses all its vigour and generative force. But Zacchia pointed out that one cannot be so generic since one case can differ from the other, depending on the position of such an outlet.[71]

Is the marriage of a person having such a defect a valid one, given that it is very doubtful whether he can ejaculate inside the vagina?

Zacchia said that canonists held that it is consummated, at least in those cases where, given that the outlet is quite near to the gland, the semen is somehow drawn into the vagina. This was because these canonists were convinced that

> "quocunque modo semen virile intra uterum (= vaginam) effunda-tur (accipiunt autem pro utero etiam ipsius collum) sequi posse generationem".

On his part, Zacchia was skeptical,

> "licet in hoc casu non impossibile videatur, generaliter tamen non admiserim".[72]

---

[70] *Ibid.*, 8.1.14.12.

[71] *Ibid.*, 9.3.6.4.

[72] *Ibid.*, 9.10.2.10; 9.3.6.5: "Verumenimvero quanto orificium hoc distat a glande, tanto maius impedimentum generationi affert, quod si in radice sit, non remanet dubio locus, quod generatio in toto impediatur, nam impossibile est semen intra uterum recipi posse, in quo casu dubium insurgeret, an talis vir posset matrimonium consummare, quia cum non possit intra uterum seminare, sed semen necessario extra uteri labia excidat, deficit haec matrimonii consummatio a praecipua conditione, cum non satis sit ad consummandum matrimonium vas foemineum penetrare, sed requiretur de necessitate, ut virile semen vas sponsae subintret, ut dicit Sánchez, *De matrimonio*, 2.21.5. Dicendum ergo an matrimo-nium cum huiusmodi viro contractum sit nullum, et irritari illico debeat, cum

In connection with this, Zacchia also spoke of phimosis. Where this abnormality occurs, the preputial orifice is so tightly constricted that the foreskin cannot be retracted back over the glans. In agreement with other doctors, he said that such a defect «non habet tantam sanationis repugnantiam". He also noted however, that where a true adhesion of the prepuce to the glans occurs, it renders a marriage null, unless of course it responds favourably to cure.[73]

What we have already said with regards to Zacchia's treatment of testicular anomalies can also be applied here. Although he spoke at some length about penile anomalies and diseases, understandably enough, he was more to the point in their medico-legal implications than in explaining their true cause or in suggesting an effective treatment. Modern medicine has come a long way in diagnosing the anomalies and diseases of the penis and the urethra and in suggesting the required treatment, although in some cases this is still lacking.[74]

4. Hermaphrodism

The question of the hermaphrodite's ability to contract a valid marriage has always been the subject of much discussion in the theological and canonical doctrine and praxis of the Church. As such, it could not escape Zacchia's attention.

> "Dicuntur hermaphroditi, qui sexu sunt indistincti, nempe qui vel neutrum, vel utrumque habere videntur, et hoc nomine hic comprehendi volo quoscunque, qui aliquomodo in sexus qualitate dubium excitare possunt".[75]

In line with this general definition, his contemporary authors usually distinguished four types of hermaphrodism: three in man and one in woman. Zacchia, however, preferred a different distinction which he thought he could reduce to four classes:

> "Primo, a conformatione genitalium; secundo, a situ eorundem; tertio, a potentia coeundi; quarto, a potentia generandi".[76]

---

constet, vitium hoc sine remedio esse...". Cfr. BERSINI, F., *Matrimonio e anomalie sessuali e psicosessuali, cit.*, pp. 149-151.

[73] ZACCHIA, P., *QML*, 9.3.6.4-6.

[74] Cfr. CAMPBELL and HARRISON, *cit.* in note 47, vol. II, pp. 1573-1625, 1834-1854; BERSINI, F., *Matrimonio e anomalie sessuali e psicosessuali*, cit., pp. 149-152.

[75] ZACCHIA, P., *QML*, 7.1.8.1.; cfr. 3.1.9.1.

[76] *Ibid.*, 7.1.8.4.

What interests us here is whether, in Zacchia's opinion, the hermaphrodite is really capable of performing the sexual copula or not. He immediately noted that this is not an easy question, precisely because of the great variety of hermaphrodites:

> "nam quidam neque agere, neque pati commode possunt, quidam ad utrumque apti, quidam ad agendum tantum, quidam tantum ad patiendum, prout hic aut ille sexus praevalet, cui sexui etiam adscribendi".[77]

But how can one know which sex prevails in a given case of hermaprodism? Zacchia agreed with Doctor Navarro that one's ability or inability for the sexual act provides the real answer. Yet, on the other hand, he completely refused to accept that the final word is to be left to the patient, or even to the doctor's advice resting solely on such a word. In this, Zacchia claimed, both Navarro and Sánchez erred, thereby showing that they were wanting in knowledge. He pointed out that there are other means by which a doctor can judge as to one's potency or impotency, as well as to the prevalent sex.[78] He also warned that, although there can be some exception, it is excessively rare to find a hermaphrodite who possesses the perfectly constituted male and female genital organs. Zacchia's conclusion was that that sex prevails "qui magis conspicuus est"[79], and in which these individuals

> "potentiores sunt ... et cuius usum natura magis insinuat, stimulis-que urget acutioribus"[80]

In his opinion, therefore, hermaphrodism as such does not impede the individual from performing the sexual act. As long as one sex prevails the ability to marry is not lost. If however, "uterque (sexus) tam exilis (est), ut neque ad agendum, neque ad patiendum, satisfaciat"[81], so that "nulla sexus distinctio apparet", then these hermaphrodites "in censu eunuchorum esse habendos".[82] And, concluded Zacchia, since such an impediment can in no way be removed without grave risk to one's life, it is useless to wait for the usual three years before declaring such a marriage null.[83]

---

[77] *Ibid.*, 3.1.9.3; cfr. 7.1.8.4.
[78] *Ibid.*, 7.1.8.15-18.
[79] *Ibid.*, 3.1.9.3; cfr. 7.1.8.4,24-31.
[80] *Ibid.*, 7.1.8.32.
[81] *Ibid.*, 3.1.9.3.
[82] *Ibid.*, 7.1.8.3.
[83] *Ibid.*, 3.1.9.3: "Caeterum impotentia agendi, seu patiendi in his, ex sexus exilitate facile internoscitur; praevalet enim, qui magis conspicuus est, sed potest,

Art. 3.   Eunuchi, Spadones, Castrati and "Impotentia coeundi".

1. *Terminology*

1. *General definition of eunuch*

In view of the widespread confusion created by the vast amount of writings on this subject, Zacchia started by giving an all-inclusive and general definition, comprising these three fundamental types of persons. Their common characteristic is that because of some congenital or acquired cause, they have lost the use of their testicles and consequently the ability to generate. All these three Zacchia called *eunuchi*. Eunuch, therefore, is

> "hominem ex virilium laesione (sive ea laesio per privationem, et exectionem, contingat, sive aliter) non generantem, etiamsi unius tantummodo testis, vel particulae, et instrumenti vitio id contingeret".[84]

Such a definition is obviously too wide and, precisely due to this fact, it did not prove practical enough to be concretely applied.[85]

2. *Causes of eunuchism*

Such causes can be either congenital ("a natura") or acquired ("ex accidenti"). To the former, Zacchia reduced all the testicles' pathological states present from birth, such as their absence, their atrophisation or change of place. He noted, however, that "neque hos, neque immediate praecedentes omnino inter eunuchos adnumeremus".[86]

---

ut dixi, uterque tam exilis esse, ut neque ad agendum, neque ad patiendum, satisfaciat... Hoc autem impedimentum vel nullo modo omnino, vel nonnisi cum manifesto vitae discrimine auferri potest; itaque eo apparente, triennio opus non est ad discernendum, an sit illud impedimentum amovibile". Cfr. Bersini, F., *op. cit.*, pp. 291-292; Santori, G., *Compendio di sessuologia, cit.*, pp. 238-256.

   [84] Zacchia, P., *QML*, 2.3.7.1; cfr. 2.3.7.36.

   [85] Zacchia himself said that "plures spadonum, eunuchorum et castratorum differentias afferemus" (2.3.7.1). Besides, this definition also includes other anomalies which he himself listed under other categories. Thus for example, the "virilium laesio" seems to include also the lesion of the penis; yet Zacchia expressly excluded this anomaly from this heading (2.3.7.5). And he also included the lack of one testicle, which is in contrast with what he elsewhere stated (cfr. supra, Art. 2, # 1.2, pp. 90 f).

   [86] Zacchia, P., *QML*, 2.3.7.4.

Acquired ("ex accidenti") causes can be either due to a medical intervention ("ex arte") or to some disease. In some detail, Zacchia described the three methods which were usually used to remove the testicles, namely
— "per excisionem"
— "per contusionem vel attritionem", and
— "per frigida quaedam pharmaca".
In all cases the person was deprived of his ability to generate.[87]

Disease too can deprive a person from the normal use of his testicles, so that he will surely lose his ability to procreate.[88] Sometimes, such a disease can even affect one's ability to perform the sexual act, and this due to the testicles'

> "extincto prorsus ipsarum partium vigore ac calore ... Praeterea ex eunuchis seu spadonibus alii sunt qui non solum generationi inhabiles existunt, sed ad venerem etiam ignavi, et impotentes, ut quibus neque tantum flatuosi spiritus a corde subministretur, ut penem arrigere possint, aut veneris stimulos persentiscere; alii autem et ad venerem stimulantur, et eam valide exercent ... Sed alii neque coeunt, neque quicquam emittunt ... Licet autem ex iis, qui concumbunt, semen non emittant, tamen voluptatem aliquam coeuntes experiuntur: ut qui seminis vice viscidum quendam humorem non sine voluptate in coitu, excernat ... vel aquosam quandam materiam ...".[89]

3. *Proper meaning of terms*

While noting that "tam spadonis, quam eunuchi, ac castrati nomen, vel in sua propria significatione sumitur et stricto modo, vel latius"[90], Zacchia passed on to explain what, in his opinion, was the proper meaning of each of these three terms.

Spado.   He said that in its wider sense, this term can be taken to include all those who lack either or both testicles and who due to this defect are unable to exercise the sexual act. But he noted that such a definition is both improper and abusive. According to him, the true and proper meaning of *spado* is more restricted and refers to

> "is cui arte ambo testiculi, vel alteruter, excisi sunt".[91]

---

[87] Cfr. *ibid.*, 2.3.7.7-10.
[88] Cfr. *ibid.*, 3.1.4.18; 2.3.7.12.
[89] *Ibid.*, 2.3.7.12-13.
[90] *Ibid.*, 2.3.7.14.
[91] *Ibid.*, 2.3.7.15: "Spado proprie dici videtur debere is, cui arte ambo testiculi, vel alteruter excisi sunt; spado enim a verbo graeco, quod avellere, vel

Eunuchi. Zacchia went through a whole list of authors briefly reproducing their different ideas as to the proper meaning and application of the word. In his opinion, the term should be restricted to those whose testicles are absent from birth, though he would not mind if those who were deprived of their testicles before puberty are also included in this definition.[92]

Castrati. Choosing from among the different opinions, Zacchia restricted this term to include all those "quibus testes, unus aut ambo, arte excisi sunt", i.e. "per excisionem", saying that this was the meaning which the term was generally given.[93]

As one can see, for Zacchia there is no difference between spadones and castrati as such. The difference exists only between those two on the one hand, and eunuchi on the other.

4. *The castration of women*

Zacchia also felt the need of dedicating some of his attention to this problem since both doctors and jurists were saying that such an operation was possible. He warned, however, that the removal of the female's "testicles" is much more difficult than in the case of the man.

> "Idcirco videndum nobis est, utrum eadem in foemina castrata, quae in castrato masculo procedere debeant; nam foemina excisis testibus mari castrato similis efficitur".

He concluded that while in man the removal of only one testicle still leaves him the possibility to generate, in the case of woman, it deprives her even of this,

> "quia necesse est foeminam castratam, ob multorum vasorum ac variarum partium incisionem, sterilem evadere, etiamsi unus tantum testis avellatur".[94]

---

abscindere significat, derivatur ... Improprie autem, et abusive spadonum appellatio late patere videtur ... Omnes enim quicunque testiculis, uno vel ambobus carent, aut ex eorundem vitio ad venerem impotentes facti sunt spadones appellantur; atque hoc modo sumptum spadonis nomen, generis potius videtur, quam speciei peculiaris".

[92] *Ibid.*, n. 31: "Ego inter tot sententias, meam etiam proferam, ...: Eunuchum proprie dici crediderim sine testibus natum; quod si etiam ad eos id nominis extendi velis, qui ante pubertatem sunt execti, ego nil moror: ratio est, quia tam spadonis, quam castrati, et caeterarum huiusmodi nomina, habent certam et indubitatam significationem; relinquitur ergo (nam caetera nomina convenire non possunt iis, qui nati sunt absque testibus), ut solus eunuchi nomen iis aptetur"; cfr. 2.3.7.24-30.

[93] *Ibid.*, nn. 32-35.

[94] *Ibid.*, nn. 48-50.

There is therefore no question of "impotentia coeundi" in the case where either one or both ovaries are removed, at least as long as the woman's vagina remains capable of receiving the male's organ and ejaculation inside it. But to this we shall return further on.[95] Besides, very evident even in this case is the relation between cause and effect, the removal of testicles and sterility, in which "foemina mari similis efficitur"!

2. Zacchia's opinion about the marriage of Eunuchi, Spadones and Castrati

So far for the problem of terminology. But there is still a very important question to clarify, which is whether, in Zacchia's opinion, these persons are capable of marrying or not. This was where Zacchia and Sánchez greatly differed. For on the one hand, to all intents and purposes, Sánchez required the ability to generate, while on the other, Zacchia said that it is enough to be able to perform the sexual act. And he left no chance pass by without making this point clear.

1. Their ability to perform the sexual act

It is by now very clear that the only reason why these persons whose testicles are absent were canonically barred from marriage, was their inability to produce testicular semen, and not their inability to perform an otherwise normal sexual act, which serves the other ends of marriage.

Zacchia clearly considered such persons, namely those who could perform an erection and ejaculation inside the vagina, as capable of marrying[96]

2. The comparison with Impuberes and Senes

This conclusion finds further confirmation in what Zacchia had to say about the ability of certain categories of persons to marry validly.

In the case of *impuberes*, Zacchia noted that their main characteristic is their "ineptitudinem ad generandum"[97], since at most, they can produce only

---

[95] Cfr. infra, chapter 6, pp. 129 ff.
[96] Cfr. supra, chapter 3, Art. 2, # 3, pp. 72 ff; supra, Art. 2, # 1.1, pp. 89 f.
[97] ZACCHIA, P., QML, 1.1.4.39-43.

"rudimentum quoddam seminis, vel, ut dilucidius loquar, semen quoddam crudum, et imperfectum intra se".[98]

Nevertheless, if they are capable of performing the sexual act, they can still contract a valid marriage, as all canonists admit.

But if these children are considered quite capable of contracting a valid marriage, despite their inability to generate, why are these eunuchi and spadones barred from it? In other words, if such a copula suffices in the former case, why does it not also suffice in the second?

"Nota ergo quod si in particularibus ante determinatum annorum terminum adveniat coeundi potentia, matrimonium contrahi potest ... etiamsi semen non effundant, quia sufficit ad contrahendum matrimonium ut succedere possit copula carnalis, etiamsi generatio nulla expectetur. Quamquam Rota in Hipp. praeter. matrimonii, coram Comitulo, n. 14, dixerit ad validitatem matrimonii requiri, quod corpus sit aptum generationi, licet alii contrarium senserint. Hoc tamen, ut ingenue fatear, durum mihi prima fronte videbatur: nam si frigidi illi qui arrigunt quidem, et venerem exercent, sed semen non emittunt, non possunt matrimonium contrahere, ... profecto neque isti posse deberent; quod si possint, idipsum liceret spadonibus quibusdam et eunuchis, qui cum valide venerem exerceant, tamen generare ob seminis defectum non possunt; sed et huiusmodi eunuchi prohibentur matrimonium contrahere, prohiberi ergo debent et isti".[99]

This same argument can be applied also in the case of the marriage of old men. If, despite the fact that for a valid marriage the ability for a "copula apta ad generationem" is canonically required, old men who are not sufficiently capable of generating are permitted to marry, why is marriage not permitted also in the case of persons who lack both testicles?[100].

---

[98] *Ibid.*, 9.3.1.4.

[99] *Ibid.*, 3.1.2.12; cfr. 9.3.7.2.

[100] Cfr. *ibid.*, 3.1.5.30: "Dices autem, cum matrimonium inter decrepitos, qui ad generationem sufficientes non praesumuntur, sit validum, cur et horum matrimonium non erit pariter validum? Respondeo, quod quantumcunque in decrepita aetate vir constituatur, dummodo coire possit, ac matrimonium consummare, nunquam est omnino extra spem generandi; sed huiusmodi viros, non aliter quam eunuchos, nullam generandi spem habere posse et sic si impotentia generandi sufficiens est ad invalidandum matrimonium, illudque impediendum, certe hi nunquam valide matrimonium contrahere poterunt".

Zacchia also presented a similar argument by making a third comparison, this time between eunuchi and frigidi: cfr. *ibid.*, 3.1.5.30; 9.3.2.7.

Chapter five

FUNCTIONAL IMPOTENCE IN MAN

I. The classical doctrine. II. Functional impotence according to Zacchia. — Art. 1. Frigidity. # 1. Its definition. # 2. Different types of frigidity. 1° Anerection. 2° Some erection but no penetration. 3° "Eiaculatio praecox". 4° Erection without ejaculation. 5° Erection, penetration and ejaculation of a seminal liquid "ad generationem omnino ineptam". 6° Emission during sleep and masturbation, but not in sexual act. — Art. 2. "Maleficium". # 1. Definition and distinction. # 2. "Maleficium ex opera daemonis". 1. Limits. 2. Practical norm and application. 3. Mistaken proofs of "maleficium". 4. The true proofs of "maleficium". # 3. "Veneficium". — Art. 3. Other causes of functional impotence. # 1. Psychological anomalies and perversions. III. A critique.

I. The classical doctrine.

Faced with the problem of the man who, despite the absence of any genital defect, was unable to perform the sexual act, classical authors held that this was a case of *frigidity* or *maleficium*,

> "et nota — wrote Tancredus — quod hic est differentia inter frigidos et maleficiatos, quoniam frigidus nullam potest cognoscere mulierem, nec movetur ad voluntatem coeundi, sed maleficiatus potest alias mulieres cognoscere, praeter illam cum qua maleficiatus est".[1]

---

[1] Tancredi, V., *Summa de matrimonio*, ed. Wunderlich, Gottingen 1841, p. 65; quoted by D'Avack, P.A., *Cause di nullità e di divorzio*, Florence 1952, p. 463; cfr. Thomas Aquinas (S.), *Commentaria in quattuor libros sententiarum*, New York 1948, IV, d. 34, q. unic., a. 2; Hostiensis, *Summa*, IV, *de sponsalibus et matrimonio*, tit. 15, nn. 8,9, Venice 1574.

As we shall soon see, the causes of frigidity or "defectus naturalis caloris", were very often of an organic nature; whereas in the case of "maleficium", the resulting impotence was attributed to the devil.[2]

II. FUNCTIONAL IMPOTENCE ACCORDING TO ZACCHIA.

Our author retained this basic classical distinction between "frigiditas" and "maleficium"; but as we shall gradually point out, he rejected many of the explanations and reasons brought forward by other authors to corroborate their claims, and this especially with regards to "maleficium".

Art. 1. FRIGIDITY

1. *Its definition*

Here also, Zacchia started by giving a general definition:

"frigidi dicuntur qui in aetate habili ad venerem exercendam omnino ad eam sunt inepti".[3]

However, he preferred a much stricter concept, saying that,

"Frigidi in sua propria acceptatione dicuntur qui ob partium genitalium ignaviam, ab imbecillitate nativi caloris prodeuntem, ad coitum in aetate habili sunt impotentes: nativus enim calor nusquam magis quam in semine laedi solet".[4]

---

[2] GONZALEZ TELLEZ, "Saepe maleficiatus quandoque ad unam solam impotens est, atque ablato ligamine, manet potens; quae diversitas ex causa naturali nequit provenire. Cum ergo non proveniat a causa naturali erit effectus daemonis. Accedit nam cum daemon voluntarie et non ex necessitate operatur, potest impedire facultatem coeundi respectu unius, et non respectu alterius, praecipue cum saepe impedimentum maleficii proveniat ex impressione daemonis in hominis imagine ex qua omnino tollit concupiscentiam ad illam", *Commentaria perpetua in singulos textus quinque librorum Decretalium*, IV, *De sponsalibus et matrimonio*, tit. 15, n. 6, Lyon 1715; cfr. HOSTIENSIS, *ibid.*; BERNARDUS PAPIENSIS, *Summa decretalium*, IV, tit. 16, # 3; SOTO, D., *Commentarium in IV sententiarum*, IV, d. 34, q. 1, a. 3; DE LEDESMA, *Tractatus de magno matrimonii sacramento super doctrinam Angelici Doctoris*, q. 58, a. 2, Venice 1595; SÁNCHEZ, T., *De sancto matrimonii sacramento disputationum*, *cit.*, 7.94.1.
[3] ZACCHIA, P., *QML*, 3.1.5.1.
[4] *Ibid.*, 9.3.2.1. Here Zacchia noted that this definition is in line with the decretal *de frigidis et maleficiatis*, of Gregory IX; cfr. GREGORY IX, *Decretales*, 1.4, tit. 15 (FRIEDBERG, II, 704-707).

From this class, he also excluded both *impuberes* and old men.[5]

Although Zacchia mentioned two types of frigidity, i.e., congenital and acquired through some illness or disease[6], yet by definition he seemed to understand that true frigidity consists only in the congenital inability to perform the sexual act:

> "Qui autem nequeunt coire, in communi modo loquendi, dicuntur impotentes, et siquidem vitium a natura sit, frigidi".[7]

He also said that true frigidity is absolute, that is, it renders a person completely incapable of performing the sexual act with all the persons of the opposite sex. Yet he noted that a type of relative frigidity, which he called *semifrigidity* does exist; but this does not amount to impotence. *Semifrigidi* do not achieve an erection strong enough to permit them to effect penetration, if not without great difficulty. This would happen, for example, when such men try to have intercourse with a woman who has a narrow vagina, or who has not yet been deflowered; with other women, however, these *semifrigidi* can achieve a normal sexual act.[8]

2. *Different types of frigidity*

Zacchia pointed out that not all men suffering from frigidity are affected in the same way and to the same degree, saying that

> "frigidos inter se multum differre, et alium altero minus autem magis ab hac vel illa actione, in venere exercenda requisita, prohiberi; quia cum eam ineptitudinem ex frigidiori intemperantia vel totius, vel partium nonnullarum patiantur, necesse est, eam intemperantiam plures, aut pauciores gradus sortiri, cum multam habeat latitudinem ...".[9]

Elsewhere, he looked at frigidity from the point of view of its effects. Referring to the three essential elements that constitute the natural copula namely erection, penetration and ejaculation, he added that frigidity can affect one of these three stages:

---

[5] ZACCHIA, P., *QML*, 3.1.5.1; 1.1.4.29-31; 1.1.5.77-80; 1.1.9.11.

[6] *Ibid.*, 3.1.5.2: "Neque enim pueri antequam ad pubertatem accedant, eo quod inepti ad coitum sint, frigidi dicuntur; neque item frigidi proprie dicendi ex mea sententia, essent decrepiti, etiamsi vere ob frigiditatem, vel potius ob nativi caloris depauperationem coitum exercere non possint, sed lato tantum modo potest et ipsis frigidi nomen aptari".

[7] *Ibid.*, 9.3.2.2; cfr. 3.1.5.2.

[8] *Ibid.*, 9.3.2.21; cfr. 3.1.5.14.

[9] *Ibid.*, 3.1.5.14; cfr. 3.1.5.7-11.

"Nonnulli igitur ab una aut altera, aut ab omnibus simul ex iis conditionibus deficiunt, unde plures frigidorum classes constitui, debent".[10]

1°   *Anerection*

This class includes all those men

"qui nullam erectionem habent, ac nullo modo possunt mulieribus commisceri".

Zacchia divided these in two sub-groups. The first consists of those "quibus coles resolutus est" or who can even have an initial erection which, however, they soon lose. Both types of persons are capable of emitting some seminal liquid outside the external labia of the vagina. The second group includes those who do not ejaculate any seminal liquid at all. These latter are, according to Zacchia, the true frigid in the proper sense of the word, since they do not even have any sexual desire and their genital organs are as if they were dead.[11]

2°   *Some erection but no penetration*

This class is constituted by those persons who though they achieve some erection, yet it is very weak and certainly not sufficient to permit any penetration inside the vagina. Ejaculation

---

[10] *Ibid.*, 9.3.2.5: "Caeterum quia ad coitum naturalem tria requiruntur, ad quem nempe sequi possit generatio, ut unanimiter omnes medici docent; evenit, ut ubi ad una, vel pluribus earum conditionum vir deficiat, frigidus dicatur. Sunt vero tres illae conditiones ad coitum requisitae, membri genitalis erectio usque ad operis consummationem, nempe ad seminis emissionem perdurans, ipsius membri intromissio debita in vas foemineum, et seminis eiaculatio in ipsum uterum. Nonnulli igitur ab una, aut altera, aut ab omnibus simul ex iis conditionibus deficiunt, unde plures frigidorum classes constitui debent".

[11] *Ibid.*, 9.3.2.5: "Aliqui ne membri quidem erectionem habent, ac nullo modo possunt mulieribus commisceri, et hi in duplici sunt differentia, nam vel semen etiam flaccido existente membro prope uteri externum ostium emittunt, vel nullo modo seminant, ..., atque hi neque ullo desiderio, aut stimulo venereorum per tempus ullum irritantur, sed omni huiusmodi sensu orbati, genitales partes veluti emortuas habent ... Hi ergo inter omnes summo iure frigidorum nomen merentur". Cfr. 9.3.2.18. On this point, Zacchia was often quoted by ecclesiastical jurisprudence. Cfr. for example: Theatina Dispensationis, 20 novembris 1894, in *Thesaurus*, vol. 84, p. 301; Neapolit. Matrimonii, 24 aprilis 1858, *ibid.*, vol. 117; pp. 120-121; Neapolit. Nullitatis seu Dispensat., 14 iunii 1862, *ibid.*, vol. 121, p. 213; Viennen. Dispensat. Matrimonii, 30 aprilis 1904, *ibid.*, vol. 163, p. 492.

itself is very little and of a poor quality; and it is accompanied by a very little sense of gratification.[12]

3° "Eiaculatio praecox"

The third class listed by Zacchia includes those persons who suffer from premature ejaculation. In such cases, he noted that these men experience a sexual urge and have an erection,

> "sed cum coire tentant, in ipso ostio, et vestibulum ante ipsum, primoque in limine semen effundunt absque ulla penis intromissione".[13]

This can happen, said Zacchia, for two reasons. It can be caused by a person's "intemperies nimis calida", in which case, an excessive "calor" in the body causes a too great sexual stimulus which does not permit the individual to retain the semen till the right moment of ejaculation inside the vagina.[14] Or it can also be caused "ex fervore amoris et acutioribus veneris stimulis".[15]

This anomalous condition was not a new discovery and for all intents and purposes it was considered to have the same juridical effects as frigidity. As an example, Zacchia once again mentioned Sánchez.[16]

---

[12] The second type of frigidity is that "in qua nulla erectio fit, aut modica, et quae ad opus non sufficiat, et cum qua semen et quidem paucum ex se effluit cum nulla, aut modica voluptate, et qui talia patiuntur habent quoddam copulae carnalis desiderium, non magnum, et quando semen emittunt (quod tamen fluidum et aquosum est, et frigidum persentitur, aut non omnino calidum, neque ullo odore insigne) membrum inter emittendum non modo non servatur durum, ut semen eiaculatur, sed magis flaccescit et emoritur", QML, 9.3.2.10; cfr. 3.1.5.8; Camerinen. Matrimonii, 20 septembris 1794, in Thesaurus, vol. 63, p. 241.

[13] QML, 9.3.2.11; cfr. 3.1.5.10.11; Plocen. Matrimonii, 28 iunii 1887, in Thesaurus, vol. 146, pp. 272-276, nn. 20-25.

[14] QML, 3.1.3.5; cfr. 3.1.5.10; 9.3.2.4; 9.10.2.7.

[15] Ibid., 3.1.5.11.

[16] Ibid., 3.1.5.10. The reference is to SÁNCHEZ T., De sancto matrimonii sacramento disputationum, cit., 7.92.8. HOSTIENSIS had already spoken of the case where the man "quam cito apponit virgam, semen spargit" (Summa, cit., IV, tit. 15, n. 13). Likewise, SALMANTICENSES, Cursus theologiae moralis, II, tract. 9, c. 12, n. 106: "Et non solum impotentia perpetua judicatur quando vir ob debilitatem vel frigiditatem sui, quae in iure nomine frigiditatis comprehenditur ... nequit claustra pudoris per instrumentum virile penetrare, sed etiam quando propter nimium calorem ... nequit in totum, vel in partem semen intra vas naturale immittere, et semper talis effusio antevertit coitum, si tale impedimentum sit perpetuum ita ut nullo medicamine aut arte tolli possit: quia de ratione matrimonii est traditio corporum in ordine ad copulam aptam ex se prolis generationi, ad quod utrumque requiritur et penetratio et effusio seminis intra vas".

On his part, Zacchia set out to clarify this condition better:

> "nam eos qui arrigunt, et semen effundunt, antequam ad opus perveniant, impropriissime frigidos vocari dixerim, immo promptius eos calidos et salaces, quam frigidos vocaverim, cum ex nimia caliditate, et seminis ipsius acrimonia ac pruritu id evenire possit, quanquam etiam ex fervore amoris, et acutioribus veneris stimulis idipsum possit contigere".[17]

His conclusion therefore was that where premature ejaculation is caused by either of these causes, the person suffering from this condition cannot be considered frigid, and consequently impotent. This is even more so, since Zacchia claimed that premature ejaculation

> "remediabilis est quocunque modo, et in quacunque aetate eveniat, ac vera tales iniuria inter frigidos connumerantur, cum potius a calore patiantur, quam a frigiditate".[18]

His reference to psychological factors such as love and sexual attraction, at play in this anomaly certainly constituted a valid contribution!

On the contrary true frigidity, and consequently impotence, is present in those cases where premature ejaculation is caused

> "ex nimia laxitate, et debilitate partium cum frigida et humida earum intemperie".[19]

4° *Erection without ejaculation*

Here Zacchia referred to those

> "qui virgae erectionem sufficientem habent, et penetrare possunt quidem claustra muliebria coitum exercentes, sed quantumvis se exagitent, semen emittere non possunt".[20]

To those who, like Felix Platter, held that it was naturally impossible for a person to achieve erection and penetration without any ejaculation, since it is the semen that causes sexual arousal, Zacchia intuitively answered that

> "erectio non fit ab ipso spermate, sed a flatu spirituoso";

---

[17] ZACCHIA, P., *QML*, 3.1.5.11; cfr. 9.3.2.11.
[18] *Ibid.*, 9.3.2.11.
[19] *Ibid.*, cfr. SANTORI, G., *Compendio di sessuologia*, cit., pp. 391-399.
[20] *QML*, 9.3.2.12; cfr. 3.1.5.9.

so much so that even children, who as yet do not produce any semen, are capable of having an erection[21]. It is indeed possibile that one achieves an erection, while suffering from anejaculation, concluded Zacchia.[22]

5° Erection, penetration and ejaculation of a seminal liquid "ad generationem omnino ineptam"

This other class of frigidity is constituted by those who can achieve both erection and penetration, and even emit some semen

> "non tamen verum, sed crudam quandam materiam, paucam et aquosam ac nullius odoris, et ad generationem omnino ineptam".

In this case, frigidity is not as grave as in the other cases; but the absence of "calor" in the body prevents the semen from being elaborated to perfection.[23]

6° Emission during sleep and masturbation, but not in sexual act

In this last type of frigidity, Zacchia included all those who, although they cannot emit any semen during intercourse, yet they easily ejaculate in sleep or through masturbation.[24] He observed:

> "Denique non absque culpa frigiditatis fit, ut aliqui in venere exercenda semen emittere non possint, quod tamen vel in somnis, vel manusturpatione, hoc est frictione manus emittunt".[25]

---

[21] Ibid., 9.3.2.17; cfr. 3.1.5.28. FELIX PLATTER (1536-1614) was a professor of anatomy and medicine at Basle. His Praxis Medica (1602-1608) gave what amounts to the first attempt at the classification of disease. Cfr. CASTIGLIONI, A., A history of medicine, New York 1947, pp. 429-441.

[22] Such an ejaculatory incompetence is thus described by W.H. MASTERS and V.E. JOHNSON in Human sexual inadequacy, Boston 1970, p. 116: "A man with ejaculatory incompetence rarely has difficulty in achieving or maintaining an erection quality sufficient for successful coital connection. Clinical evidence of sexual dysfunction arises when the afflicted individual cannot ejaculate during intra-vaginal containment. Frequently this inability to ejaculate intra-vaginally occurs with first coital experience and continues unresolved through subsequent coital encounters". Cfr. KAPLAN, H., Nuove terapie sessuali, Milan 1976, p. 357; SANTORI, G., op. cit., pp. 405-409.

[23] ZACCHIA, P., QML, 9.3.2.16.

[24] This condition has been recently designated as "eiaculatio seiuncta" by MAGNUS HIRSCHFELD. It is today considered to be one of the more difficult cases for a dispensation. Cfr. MARCHETTA, G., Scioglimento del matrimonio canonico per inconsumazione, Padova 1981, pp. 131-139.

[25] ZACCHIA, p., QML, 9.3.2.20; cfr. 3.1.5.15. On this point a decision coram TEODORI, 12 maii 1942 referred to Zacchia, describing him as "in rebus medico-legalibus facile princeps": SRRD, 34 (1942) 381-382, n. 3.

Nevertheless, Zacchia believed that such a condition was not

> "extra omnem spem curationis, nisi frigiditas, aetas maior, et alia id
> genus curae impedimento sint, licet quomodocunque verum semen
> effluat, semper de sanatione bene sperari possit, cum id clare
> demonstret, calorem adhuc vigere, stante quod sufficiat ad generan-
> dum verum semen".[26]

By way of general conclusion to this section, we can therefore say
that according to Zacchia, where frigidity is truly congenital it is
very difficult, not to say completely impossible to cure.[27] On the
other hand, where it is caused by some accidental cause, then the
chances of a cure vary, depending not only on the nature and
gravity of such a cause, but also on the constitutional make-up of
the person himself.

As a general rule, therefore, congenital frigidity would render
the individual suffering from it, incapable of contracting a valid
marriage since an essential element of the copula would be missing.
In practice, however, things were somewhat different. Zacchia
claimed, for example, that in the case of those who have sufficient
erection to penetrate inside the vagina, yet do not ejaculate therein
(class 4), the canonical praxis was to allow such persons to marry
"cum impedimentum patens non sit", although he surely insisted
that such a marriage would be null.[28] On the contrary, in the case of
those who perform an apparently normal copula but do not
ejaculate "verum semen" (class 5), Zacchia agreed with those
canonists who permitted such men to marry, the reason being that

> "hoc in propatulo non est et in dubio unusquisque praesumitur
> potens ad generandum".[29]

---

[26] *QML*, 9.3.2.20.

[27] Cfr. *ibid.*, 9.3.2.6-20.

[28] *Ibid.*, 9.3.2.13. Comparing this type of a frigid man with the eunuch,
Zacchia states: "in hoc casu praesupponimus virum testibus non solum dotari, sed
nullo eorum defectu laborare, qui in conspectum se prodat; itaque licet eunuchis
ob absentiam testium, impedimentum nempe patens, matrimonium contrahere
non permittatur, tamen his, de quibus loquimur, cum impedimentum patens non
sit, non denegatur; at in rei veritate non aliter, quam eunuchi, si contrahant,
invalide contrahunt, quia ad matrimonii validitatem non sufficit copula carnalis,
sed requiritur veri seminis emissio"; cfr. 9.3.2.14-16; 3.1.5.28.

[29] *Ibid.*, 9.3.2.17: "Haec tamen, quia non adeo patent ad sensum, a canonistis
non magnifient, cum tamen de his dubitari iure possit, an valide matrimonium
contrahant, et an contractum teneat; ac si secundum canonistas ferri debeat
sententia, non apparente alio impedimento, nec ullo corporis, ac praecipue
genitalium notabili vitio, ex quo manifeste elici possit tales viros non posse
generare verum semen, et contrahere matrimonium poterunt, et contractum
tenebit; licet enim supponetur eos non generare verum semen, hoc in propatulo

Obviously, the true reason behind his position is that he considered an ordinary ejaculation sufficient for the purpose of a true copula.

Finally, as to the marriage of those who are capable of ejaculation but not during the sexual act (class 6), Zacchia realised the difficulty inherent in such cases; that is why he was in favour of a three year trial period. However, he also added that where no cure has been forthcoming after this period, the marriage is to be dispensed from for non-consummation, since no semen is ever ejaculated during intercourse inside the vagina.[30]

Art. 2. "MALEFICIUM"

As already pointed out, classical doctrine generally dealt with relative functional impotence under the heading of "maleficium", often attributing a great role to the devil in causing such an adverse condition.

Even though with some hesitation on the part of some, like Pope Innocent IV[31] and Bazianus[32] yet, generally speaking, canonists accepted that such an impotence could render a marriage null and void once its perpetuity was sufficiently proved.

Sánchez himself followed such authors as Hincmar of Rheims, Tancredus and Hostiensis[33] in holding that

"procul dubio tenendum est, impotentiam ex maleficio consurgentem, si illud sit perpetuum, dirimere subsequens matrimonium",

---

non est, et in dubio unusquisque praesumitur potens ad generandum (unde etiam verum semen generare) nisi probetur contrarium". Cfr. 3.1.5.29: BERSINI, F., *La dibattuta questione del "verum semen"*, in *Monitor Ecclesiasticus*, 101 (1976) 262-263.

[30] ZACCHIA, P., *QML*, 9.3.2.20: "Interim tamen determinandum a canonistis esset, utrum hoc vitium, si nullo ingenio curari possit, expectato etiam triennio, sufficiens esset ad dissolutionem matrimonii, quia si non dicitur matrimonium vir consummare, nisi semen intra muliebre vas effundat, certum est, quod in hoc casu non potest dici matrimonium consummari per seminis emissionem, cum intra conveniens vas non recipiatur; nulliter ergo hi viri contrahent, et matrimonio erunt interdicendi, et tamen videretur quod hi, cum verum semen generent, et venerem exerceant, vasa sufficienter penetrantes, et possint debito matrimoniali satisfacere, non sint ad matrimonium inhabiles".

[31] INNOCENT IV, *In quinque Decretalium libros commentaria*, IV, *De sponsalibus et matrimonio*, tit. 15, c. 7, n. 2, Venice 1610: "melius videtur quod propter maleficium nullum matrimonium separandum sit".

[32] BAZIANUS († 1197) argued in favour of Innocent's IV position: "quia vix potest aliquis certificare, quando praecedat et subsequatur, vel quando sit perpetuum vel temporale, cum ab illis, quae faciunt, dissolvatur quandoque"; quoted by D'AVACK, P.A., *Cause di nullità e di divorzio, cit.*, p. 468.

[33] HINCMAR OF RHEIMS, c. 4, C, XXXIII, q. 1 (FRIEDBERG, I, 1150); TANCREDI, V., *Summa de matrimonio, cit.*, tit. 30; HOSTIENSIS, *cit.*, tit. 15, n. 9.

the reason being that such a person could not give the "ius in corpus".[34]

Therefore, for all intents and purposes regarding the validity of marriage, "maleficium" had the same negative effects as frigidity. Nevertheless, it was very important to establish the real cause behind the impotence in each case, for while frigidity rendered a person absolutely impotent and consequently deprived him of every possibility to marry, "maleficium" rendered the person unable to perform the sexual act only with one particular person, but not with others, so that he could still remarry.[35]

The doctor's advice was therefore very welcome. Zacchia, being a man of his times and faithful to the doctrine of the Church, did not completely deny the possible occurence of a "maleficium" as it was understood by many. However, he surely tried to redimension certain opinions, trying to provide an explanation that was more in conformity with reality and medicine.

1. *Definition and distinction*

Zacchia defined "maleficium" through its effects:

> "Maleficiati porro sunt qui vel ob malorum medicamentorum applicationem per se, vel arte, et daemonis auxilio adiuncto, redduntur ad venerem impotentes, vel alia quavis noxa afficiuntur".[36]

And in view of this definition he went on to distinguish two types of "maleficium":

> "Quoniam autem patet, maleficium esse in duplici differentia, nempe unum ex opera daemonis procuratum, daemoniacum dicendum; alterum per oblationem alicuius medicamenti venenosi, et apti ad eam affectionem convocandam et ad reddendum hominem in re

---

[34] Sánchez, T., *De sancto matrimonii sacramento disputationum, cit.*, 7.94.8.

[35] Bernardus Papiensis, *Summa decretalium*, IV, tit. 16, ## 6,7, ed. Laspeyres, Ratisbonne 1860, p. 179: "Illud in summa notandum quod in aliis impossibilitatibus coeundi non datur licentia nubendi, nisi potenti coire, in maleficiis autem datur utrique... Item illud praecipue notandum, quod ubi divortium pro frigiditate est factum, si postea viro reddatur potestas cognoscendi aliam mulierem, matrimonium est redintegrandum ...; si vero pro maleficio fuerit divortium factum, et vir accipiat aliam et cognoscat, non propter hoc reddetur priori. Ratio diversitatis est, quia frigiditas impedit virum a cuiuslibet foeminae cognitione, maleficium autem solummodo a coitu suae uxoris".

[36] Zacchia, P., *QML*, 3.1.5.3.

venerea impotentem, quod vel maleficium simpliciter nominatur, vel magis proprie veneficium".[37]

2. *"Maleficium ex opera daemonis"*

1. *Limits*

Although Zacchia did not outrightly deny the devil's share of responsibility in this type of impotence, yet he made it clear that he would attribute the cause of impotence in a particular case to this diabolic "maleficium" only with great hesitation and after making sure that no other natural explanation, no matter how uncommon, really existed. And the reason he gave was that.

"daemonem nihil agere posse, quod naturae vires exuperet".[38]

Admittedly, on this point Zacchia was somewhat contradictory, since while on the one hand he refused to believe that lucky charms and enchantments could have any power, yet he seemed to admit the possible presence of collusion with the devil and even speaks about his supernatural power.[39] However, as we shall see, his fundamental thesis remained unchanged.

Furthermore, he also noted that

"daemon eis solummodo causis utens, frequentius viros et plurifariam quam mulieres, maleficio illaqueare solet".[40]

2. *Practical norm and application*

On the practical level, Zacchia's conclusion is very clear: presumption favours the presence of a natural cause:

"Et tamen, crediderim ego, quod ubi in dubium vertatur an vir ex maleficio, vel ex naturali potius impedimento impotens sit ad carnalem copulam, semper praesumptio debeat esse impedimenti naturalis, seu frigiditatis, cum frequentior et magis naturalis causa

---

[37] *Ibid.*, 9.3.2.30. Cfr. 9.3.2.24: "In tantum autem potest in homine alias ex sui natura ad coitum potente, aliqua causa ignota, et non facile animadvertibilis irrepere, quae ipsum in posterum impotentem reddat, ut ex nova victus institutione, ex animi vehementibus, ac diuturnis passionibus, imo ex frequentato etiam quorundam ciborum usu facile id succedere interdum sit animadversum»; 3.1.5.47,56.

[38] *Ibid.*, 3.1.5.45; cfr. 2.1.18.13-17; 4.1.5.41-46; 7.1.7.6; 9.3.2.29.

[39] *Ibid.*, 3.1.5.50-54; 10 cons. 49.2.

[40] *Ibid.*, 3.1.5.45.

existat; praesumptio autem semper esse debeat ex parte causae, quae magis naturalis est et magis prompta ad agendum".[41]

But how is one to distinguish between a natural cause and one induced by the devil? Even here Zacchia was very practical. In Consilium 49, where he deals with an alleged case of impotence, Zacchia started by recommending that all rumors which are often originated by ignorant and easily impressed people, are to be rejected as foundless. Furthermore, the fact that very often such an anomaly is accompanied by many symptoms, which are not so common and even perhaps very curious, should not be allowed to mislead the doctor into an easy but mistaken diagnosis. Zacchia said that while each symptom is to be evaluated individually and traced to its originating cause, yet all the symptoms must be complexively evaluated in the whole perspective presented by that particular sickness. Otherwise confusion would reign. As an example, Zacchia mentioned the successive alternating phases of weakness and vigour, so that at one moment one is very weak, almost on the verge of dying but very healthy and radiating strength in the next. If considered only separately, such seemingly incompatible symptoms can easily lead to the mistaken diagnosis of a "morbus daemoniacus".

Nor does a great resistance to treatment necessarily imply the presence of the devil's action. It is only when this is accompanied by the unsuccessful diagnosis of the real cause behind such a malady that, according to Zacchia, one can conclude that behind this impotence there might be the malice of the devil.[42]

However, Zacchia's real insistence always remained on the same point: a proper diagnosis of the malady itself: its nature, course and the way it strikes and affects the individual.[43]

3.   Mistaken proofs of "maleficium"

In agreement with Codronchi[44], Zacchia noted that while frigid persons usually show some sign of their anomaly, it is generally more difficult to say when a person is suffering from a "maleficium", since he does not usually offer any particular symptoms.[45] Zacchia also claimed that the three differences usually made between frigidity and "maleficium" did not hold.

---

[41] *Ibid.*, nn. 43-44.
[42] *Ibid.*, 10 cons. 49.1-14.
[43] *Ibid.*, n. 16.
[44] CODRONCHI, B., *De morbis veneficis*, 1.3, chapter 13, Venice 1595.
[45] ZACCHIA, P., *QML*, 3.1.5.17.

In the *first* case, it was commonly held that

> "frigidum non posse cum aliqua muliere coitum exercere, malefi-ciatum cum omnibus posse praeterquam cum una".

But as far as impotence due to "maleficium" is concerned, such a difference, said Zacchia, is not always verified nor is it universally applicable. At most it is a practical conjecture. For there are "maleficiati" who are unable to have the sexual act with all women; just as there are others who can succeed to have intercourse with none except only with one.[46]

Functional impotence due to a "maleficium" can therefore take any of three forms:

> "unum, quo homo impotens redditur cum quavis foemina; secun-dum, quo redditur impotens cum una tantum, non cum aliis; tertium, quo redditur impotens cum omnibus, praeterquam cum una, puta cum uxore".[47]

This conclusion of Zacchia, especially in the first case, would certainly have called for a revision of the canonists' norm regarding the second marriage of such "maleficiati", since in this case, the distinction between absolute and relative impotence did not exist.

Some jurists also made a *second* distinction, pointing out that the difference lay in the fact that

> "frigidus virgam non erigit, maleficiatus maxime, sed cum ad opus appropinquat, membrum flacescit, ac desidit, ita ut coire non possit".

Zacchia also discarded this distinction, saying that there are frigid persons who not only have an erection, but can also perform a normal sexual act, though they are unable to ejaculate any semen.[48]

---

[46] *Ibid.*, 3.1.5.4-6: "Sed haec differentia non est semper vera, nec generica, complectens omnes, qui ad coitum non sunt apti ob frigiditatem, aut maleficium, et inter hos, aut illos enumerandi quia ex maleficiatis etiam nonnulli sunt, et esse possunt quoad omnes mulieres maleficiati, ita ut ad nullam omnino arrigant. Quin et alii ex iis sunt, et esse possunt, qui ad nullas arrigant praeterquam ad unam..."; cfr. 9.3.2.28.

[47] *Ibid.*, 9.3.2.22.

[48]*Ibid.*, 3.1.5.7: "Neque etiam vera est altera differentia allata ... quod nimirum frigidus a maleficiato differat, quia frigidus virgam non erigit, maleficia-tus maxime, sed cum ad opus appropinquat, membrum flaccescit, ac desidit, ita ut coire non possit. Non est (inquam) vera, neque universalis haec differentia, quia nonnulli ex frigidis sunt, qui non solum arrigunt, sed etiam venerem utcunque exercent, sed semen non possunt effundere; frigidorum enim ... plures sunt differentiae".

Likewise untrue, said Zacchia, was a *third* difference, namely that while the persons affected with "maleficium" can ejaculate seminal liquid, those affected by frigidity can never do so.[49] That this is not so, clearly results from the different types of frigidity enumerated by Zacchia.

We can therefore conclude that for Zacchia the distinction between frigidity and "maleficium" was to be drawn not from the consequences that each implies, i.e. whether the resulting impotence is absolute or relative, or whether there is an erection or semination or otherwise, but from the cause that gives rise to the respective deficiency.

4. *The true proofs of "maleficium"*

On the practical level, however, a difficult question still remained as to how to distinguish frigidity from "maleficium". According to Zacchia, since "maleficium" presented a very difficult case, due to the lack of characteristic symptoms, many doctors reduced their diagnostic criteria to two: the lack of any symptoms of frigidity and the negative response to the medical remedies applied.[50]

Once again, Zacchia found himself at odds with these doctors and he refused what he called simple conjectures for they do not correspond to reality.[51] According to him, if there is any proof that can be considered reliable,

"illa erit quae desumi potest ex celeritate adventus ipsius impotentiae coeundi";

and this, whether it is caused by the devil, by some kind of food or drink, or is the result of some psychological factor.

It is therefore imperative to diagnose the cause behind such impotence. If the person has enjoyed good health and the ability to perform the sexual act and then all of a sudden he is rendered impotent, then it is surely a case of "maleficium". By way of further proof, Zacchia added that where one is found impotent with only one woman, then this would also serve as a presumption in

---

[49] *Ibid.*, 3.1.5.15: "Apparet etiam ... falsam quoque esse tertiam differentiam inter frigidum et maleficiatum ..., nimirum quod maleficiati semen emittant, frigidi autem nequaquam...".

[50] *Ibid.*, 9.3.2.23.

[51] *Ibid.*, 9.3.2.24-26.

favour of the presence of a "maleficium". However, this is only a conjecture, since it is not universally applicable.[52]

With regards to "maleficium daemonis", Zacchia further noted that by the very fact that one alleges that he has been affected by it, he is implying that before his misfortune happened, he had been capable of exercising the sexual act. And therefore such a person must prove that in fact he was potent before. If he cannot prove this, then there is no need to wait for three years, but the marriage can be dissolved there and then, for in such a case there is no question of "maleficium". The three year period is to be set only in cases of doubt.[53] If the impotence is proved to be perpetual and it was antecedent to the marriage, then the marriage is to be dissolved. If in the end, it is proved that the impotence in case is due to the devil, then "vix crediderim naturalem admittere curationem".[54]

3. "Veneficium"

The other type of functional impotence referred to by Zacchia was thought to result from the drinking of some potion or the eating of some food. Zacchia agreed that certain herbs such as the lettuce, mint, rue, thyme, etc, could extinguish the sexual stimulus in man, thereby causing anerection and even sterility.[55]

In the case of "veneficium", Zacchia considered the cause of impotence as a natural one, and as a general rule it did not resist to treatment. However, a number of factors, such as age, the nature, mode and duration of use, as well as the physical constitution of the patient must also be kept in mind. As a rule Zacchia said that if after an interval of six months or at least a year, no positive outcome results, then it is to be considered as irremediable.[56]

---

[52] *Ibid.*, nn. 27-29.

[53] *Ibid.*, n. 24. Zacchia based this assertion of his on two Rotal sentences, one c. PENIA, Romana Invalid. Matrimonii, 28 februarii 1603, nn. 12-13, in *QML*, 10 dec. XXII; the other c. COCCINO, Toletana Nullitatis Matrimonii, 18 februarii 1639, nn. 13-15, in *QML*, 10 dec. LXXX.

[54] ZACCHIA, P., *QML*, 3.1.5.56-57. Such a proof is to be sought in line with what Zacchia himself had suggested.

[55] Cfr. *Ibid.*, 3.1.5.48-49; 9.3.2.24,30.

[56] Cfr. *Ibid.*, 3.1.5.55; 9.3.2.30; 9.10.2.13.

Art. 3. OTHER CAUSES OF FUNCTIONAL IMPOTENCE

1. *Psychological elements*

A very important contribution which Zacchia made to the question of impotence is undoubtedly his insight with regards to psychological factors at play. He drew the attention of jurists and doctors alike,

> "quod nonnulli ob aliquam animi passionem ... redduntur ad coitum impotentes, et tunc ad eam non advertentes, falso credunt se maleficio tentatos fuisse".[57]

In fact, this element would explain why a person is capable of having a normal sexual act with other women but not with his proper wife. He also added that where the presumption is that the impotence in case is the consequence of some psychological cause, then not only "maleficium" but even frigidity is to be ruled out.[58]

Zacchia's own experience as a doctor had taught him that inability to perform the sexual act

> "provenire possit ex aliqua vehementi passione, ut amoris, timoris, verecundiae, aversione a rebus venereis et aversione etiam a propria sponsa".

The problem would be even more grave where the couple has desisted from having sexual relations for some time.[59]

He was very much aware of the important role which such a psychological factor can play in cases of relative impotence. Shyness, hate, aversion towards one's wife, or even an excessive love are all potential factors that can psychologically condition a man to such an extent as to render him unable to have sexual intercourse with his wife. Zacchia also noted how a man who lacks sexual stimulus can be moved by a woman's physical aspect to have a normal relationship with her, and how such factors as some bodily defect or lack of hygiene can adversely affect him.[60]

He therefore concluded that whenever there is no apparent reason such as premature age, some defect or illness, why a man cannot succeed in having sexual intercourse with his wife, then he

---

[57] *Ibid.*, 3.1.5.58; cfr. 9.3.2.24.

[58] *Ibid.*, 3.1.5.59: "Idcirco eliciendum ex his, quod ubi praesumptio aliqua vel amoris vel odii viri erga uxorem adsit, facile ex ea alia suboritur praesumptio impotentiae coitus, quod vel ex amore, vel ex odio, potius quam ex frigiditate proveniat".

[59] *Ibid.*, 3.1.2.12,16.

[60] Cfr. *Ibid.*, 3.1.1.20; 3.1.5.19; 3.1.6.9.

should be given a month's time during which he is to attempt daily to perform the sexual act. Only if there is no positive outcome is the presence of a graver cause to be considered:[61]

> "An autem haec impotentia sufficiens esse causa possit separationis matrimonii, ego alias pro eo, quod ad medicum spectat, negative respondi. Rationem esse dixi, quod omnis pudor consuetudine et familiaritate aboletur, omnis amor effervescit, omne item odium mitescit, quod etiamsi ex nimia mulieris deformitate dependeret, tamen et tenebris et temporis diuturnitate demulcetur".[62]

2. Diseases and wounds

But apart from all this, illnesses and diseases too can cause functional impotence. To this also Zacchia turned his attention and even dedicated two whole "quaestiones" to this subject.[63]
He noted that

> "cum morbus sit praeter naturam, ipsique naturae de directo contraria, absque ullo dubio eius omnes operationes aut debilitat, aut depravat".[64]

He was of the opinion that such diseases more often than not cause only sterility and not sexual impotence; and this especially while they hold sway. Even in the latter case, once treatment is successful, the ability to perform the sexual act will normally return.[65]
What mostly interested Zacchia with respect to marriage were naturally those conditions that cause an irreversible sexual impotence in man, which often consists in the absence of erection, as he himself stated when he took up the question in more detail in Book nine.[66] In reality these illnesses are of a purely organic nature,

---

[61] *Ibid.*, 3.1.2.12.
[62] *Ibid.*, 3.1.6.9; cfr. 3.1.5.60-61.
[63] *Ibid.*, 3.1.4: "De impotentia ex morbis"; 9.3.4: "De impotentia copulae ex morbis aut praesentibus aut praegressis"; cfr. 7.3.6. and 6.1.5. per tot.
[64] *Ibid.*, 3.1.4.3; cfr. 1.1.9.75; 2.1.3.11-12; 2.3.2.2; 3.1.4.3.
[65] *Ibid.*, 7.3.6.1; cfr. 3.1.4.16.
[66] *Ibid.*, 9.3.4.1: "Non loquar hic de impotentia temporanea sed de perpetua, vel saltem quae longo tempore, ut annorum spatio perdurat, et quae aut impossibilitatem, aut summam difficultatem sanationis minatur, ea enim quae ob praesentiam aliquorum morborum causatur, et post eorum recessum non multum durat, in dubium non venit, an matrimonium dirimere, vel divortio dare causam possit, cum in nullo censu habeatur tanquam si numquam adfuisset".
Zacchia's doctrine in this regard was often quoted by ecclesiastical jurisprudence. Cfr. for example, Uritana Dispensat. 7 iunii 1777, in *Thesaurus*, vol. 46, pp. 86-91; Firmana Separationis Thori, 16 maii 1789, *ibid.*, vol. 58, pp. 98-101; Sedunen. Separationis Thori, 14 decembris 1850, *ibid.*, vol. 109, pp. 434-446.

affecting not only the genitals but also the parts of the body in such a way as to cause impotence. Among these he mentioned:

— "omnes ac singuli morbi qui insigniter ipsum cerebrum debilitant et in frigidam intemperiem illud labi faciunt";
— "paralyses insignes";
— "vulnera insigna capitis eiusque vehementes percussiones";
— "sectiones venenarum nonnullarum in capite";
— "copiosas ac excessivas sanguinis et aliorum humorum eva-cuationes";
— "laesiones nonnullarum partium praecipue autem cervicis, spi-nae medullaris ac lumborum attritus ac vehementes compres-iones";
— "vulnera renum, vulnus in inguine et in perinaeo";
— "morbi qui cor, stomachum, hepar infestant".[67]

In this context, Zacchia also spoke about *syphilis* and *gonorrhoea*, and noted their consequences on the sexual life of the patient and on marriage. More commonly known as "lues venerea" or "morbus gallicus", syphilis was considered as a highly contagious infection, whose gravity could vary. Even though Zacchia did not say that such a disease would cause impotence, yet he was of the opinion that

"si gravis sit ... absque dubio matrimonium dirimi poterit, quia communicabilis ab omnibus in omnes, et quia notabilem affert turpitudinem, et quia morbus permanens est, et si confirmatus nunquam curabilis".[68]

Zacchia's reasoning behind this statement was that in such cases "timeri potest maximum periculum", given that "lues venerea coitu maxime et accubitu, dehinc etiam convictu, et consuetudine communicatur".[69] Such a disease would consequently render sexual intercourse and life in common impossible. However, he also pointed out that "decisio harum rerum ad canonistas pertinet".[70]

On the other hand, according to Zacchia, true gonorrhoea consists in

"involuntarium veri seminis profluvium absque penis erectione et absque praevia venerearum rerum ulla imaginatione"[71];

---

[67] ZACCHIA, P., *QML*, 9.3.4. per totam.
[68] *Ibid.*, 3.3.6.7; cfr. 3.2.10.2,6; 3.3.5.12-14; 3.3.6.22; 9.10.3.10-13; 9.10.4.9; 9.10.5.13-14; 10 cons. 26.10; 10 cons. 82 per totum.
[69] *Ibid.*, 3.3.6.1.
[70] *Ibid.*, 3.3.6.21,29.
[71] *Ibid.*, 8.1.14.2.

and he was of the opinion that

> "ita ut quandocunque constaret, hominem huiusmodi morbo affici, praesumptio insurgere facile debet frigiditatis et impotentiae ad coitum",

at least in the case where this flow is a frequent one, for it would weaken the individual.[72]

The impotence which results from all these cases was considered by Zacchia to be both perpetual and without any cure, so that where their presence is proved, the marriage in case can be declared null.[73]

3. *Psychosexual anomalies and perversions*

A second class of anomalies which Zacchia considered under this heading consists in those illnesses which give rise to hypererotism in man:

> "alii morbi sunt qui hominem proniorem et potentiorem ad venerem faciunt".[74]

Among these he also mentioned *satyriasis* and *priapism*,

> "in quibus homo effraenato, licet involuntario coitus desiderio flagrat".[75]

But although he noted that such anomalies cause an "inordinatam coeundi cupiditatem", yet Zacchia did not say that such psychosexual anomalies were sufficient to invalidate a marriage, at least on

---

[72] *Ibid.*, 9.3.4.5; cfr. 7.3.5.4-5; 8.1.14.4; 10 cons. 55.

[73] *Ibid.*, 9.3.4.1: "Iamvero de morbis facientibus impotentiam coeundi et generandi ... peculiarius nunc quaedam pertractanda, quae copulae carnali impedimento sunt ob id maxime, quod penis erectionem prohibeant; ob hoc enim praecipue vitium matrimonium dirimi permittitur, cum perpetuum est, et remedio caret, vel saltem est magna cum difficultate remediabile. Horum autem morborum quos recensebimus, unusquisque per se non solum quando praesens est, sed quando etiam praecessit, potest facere maximam et si praeesens est, indubitatam praesumptionem ac plenam probationem impotentiae, ita ut allegante muliere impotentiam viri, atque afferente causam ex morbo aliquo praesenti, aut praegresso, qui est horum, quos recensebimus, numero habeant posset facile Iudex in eius favorem pronuntiare".

[74] *Ibid.*, 3.1.4.8-9.

[75] *Ibid.*; cfr. 8.1.14.13-14; Santori, G., *Compendio di sessuologia, cit.*, pp. 469-493; Bersini, F., *Matrimonio e anomalie sessuali e psicosessuali, cit.*, pp. 231-246.

the ground of sexual impotence. He was very aware, however, of the problems they can cause in a marital relationship.[76]

Finally, Zacchia also referred to a case of psychosexual perversion, namely masochism. This was the case of the man

> "qui flagris ac plagis in coitum accendebatur, ita ut usque ad sanguinis effusionem pateretur se caedi, quinimo irasceretur caedenti, nisi fortius atque acrius caederet; hoc modo enim hic sanguinem accendebat, et semen calidius reddendo cum maiori voluptate, ut credere par est, coibat".

Although he did not comment on the ability or otherwise of such a person to contract marriage, Zacchia did state that "forte non extra omne dubium esset, an stante hoc vitio licite ducere (uxorem) posset".[77]

III. A CRITIQUE.

In line with tradition, functional impotence is considered to be present where "the organs themselves are organically perfect but for one reason or another (either physical or psychical) they function imperfectly".[78] It affects either one or both moments of the copulative act, namely erection and/or ejaculation. In both cases, the incapacity to complete the physical act may result from such causes as deficient hormonal functioning, circulatory problems, nervous or psychological conditions. In this latter case, there is a conflict between the sexual instinct and its expression because of fear, anxiety or anger which manifests itself in the inability to perform the sexual copula.[79]

Precisely in view of the fact that these multiple causes can be either of an organic or psychic nature, G. Versaldi, while pointing to the recent tendency in canonical doctrine and jurisprudence, has suggested that where the cause behind such an impotence is of a purely psychological nature, the resulting "functional" impotence should rather be termed psychic. The term organic should be reserved to that impotence resulting from all organic causes.[80]

---

[76] Cfr. ZACCHIA, P., *QML*, 7.3.5.8.

[77] *Ibid.*, 9.3.2.20.

[78] WRENN, L.G., *Annulments*, Washington 1983, p. 10.

[79] Cfr. ORLANDI, G., *I "Casi Difficili" nel processo super rato, cit.*, pp. 148-159; MARCHETTA, B., *Scioglimento del matrimonio canonico per inconsumazione, cit.*, pp. 200-211; BERSINI, F., *Matrimonio e anomalie sessuali e psicosessuali, cit.*, pp. 156-170; SANTORI, G., *Compendio, cit.*, pp. 363-414.

[80] VERSALDI, G., *L'oggettività delle prove in campo psichico*, Brescia 1981; cfr. *supra*, chapter 3, note 58.

In accordance with this new division of impotence, many of the anomalous conditions resulting in functional impotence as described by Zacchia under frigidity, "veneficium", diseases, illnesses and wounds would have to be more properly listed under organic impotence; whereas those others caused by a "maleficium" in the strict sense or from psychological factors would be more properly listed under psychic impotence.

Speaking of incapacity to perform the sexual act due to some psychological factor, it must be said that this was indeed one of the most important insights offered by Zacchia in this regard. We have noted above how much he insisted that it is the first duty of the doctor to ascertain, where functional impotence is alleged, that no such factor exists, before looking for any other organic or extraordinary cause. In this regard, his advice remains, even today, very appropriate.[81]

But apart from this, even Zacchia's description of the various pathologies of erection and ejaculation remains to a very large extent a valid one. True, his explanation of what really lies behind the complicated mechanism of these two moments of the copula or of the anomalous conditions that can affect them can no longer be upheld. It is interesting to note, however, that he seems to have been on the right track when, for example, he said that the dysfunction of the genital organs can be caused "ab imbecillitate nativi caloris", which "nusquam magis quam in semine laedi solet"[82]; in which, looking back, we can see today a vaguely tentative reference to endocrine motives. But obviously, Zacchia could not make such a conclusion. Medicine had still a long time to wait to provide such explanations.

A case in point was Zacchia's explanation of the mechanism of premature ejaculation. He did provide a clear explanation of the pathology itself; but he could not explain the real cause behind this dysfunction, although he was very coherent with the then available medical knowledge.[83]

In the end, however, two very important contributions made by Zacchia with regards to functional impotence must be recognised. The first was his insistence that in every case no effort is to be spared to find a natural explanation behind any type of anomalous condition. And this was a particularly valuable advice given the

---

[81] Cfr. *supra*, note 72.
[82] Cfr. *supra*, note 4.
[83] Cfr. SANTORI, G., *op. cit.*, pp. 391-399.

socio-cultural environment of his times. The second conclusion, which is of a more forensic character, regards the essential elements of the copula which are required and sufficient for the consummation of a marriage. Zacchia once more insisted that only where penetration is effected inside the vagina and is in fact accompanied by ejaculation therein, can the marriage be said consummated. Only when the individual can effect these two conditions, can he be said to be potent. Where either is missing, the copula is deficient and the individual to be considered impotent.

CHAPTER SIX

ORGANIC IMPOTENCE IN WOMAN

Art. 1. The doctrine before Zacchia. — Art. 2. Organic impotence in the
female according to Zacchia. # 1. "Angustia vulvae". # 2. Malformation of the
clitoris. # 3. Malformations of the vagina and of the hymen. A. Vagina "arcta". 1.
Hypoplasias of the vagina. 2. "Coalescentia uteri". B. Vagina "imperforata". 1.
The hymen. (a) Definition of the hymen. (b) Anomalies of the hymen. (i) Rigid
hymen. (ii) Elastic hymen. 2. Septal partitions. C. Possibilities of treatment. # 4.
Prolapse of the Uterus. # 5. Morbid conditions. # 6. Two cases of impotence. 1. Is
the woman who does not seminate to be considered impotent? 2. The case of the
"mulier velata". Is she impotent? # 7. Some canonico-moral questions. — Art. 3.
Zacchia and modern medicine.

This chapter is limited to the malformations of the female
genital organs. Such anomalous conditions obstruct a sufficiently
normal sexual intercourse and create problems in the conjugal
relationship.

Art. 1. THE DOCTRINE BEFORE ZACCHIA.

Impotence on the part of the female was taken into consideration by canonists much later than that on the part of the male.
There are various reasons for this. Man was considered much more
liable to such an anomaly, given that on his part impotence could be
caused by a number of factors. Furthermore, while the man was
always thought to be the active partner in the sexual act, the female
was considered to be rather passive, and all she required was the
ability to receive the male organ inside her vagina. Thus the
conditions that could cause impotence in the female were practically reduced to one, namely the narrowness or closure of the vagina.[1]

---

[1] Cfr. SÁNCHEZ, T., *De sancto matrimonii sacramento disputationum, cit.*,
7.94.3; ESMEIN-GENESTAL, *Le mariage en droit canonique*, vol. I, Paris 1929, p.
276.

The first reference to female impotence appears to be that found in a letter of Pope Gregory II to St. Boniface in 726.[2] A reference to the lack of legislation about this matter is also contained in a Glossa to this text[3] and in a decretal of Pope Alexander III.[4]

However, once the problem was raised, it gradually gained both attention and importance. The pontifical decretals at the end of the XIIth century and still more at the beginning of the thirteenth century, started to dedicate express attention to female impotence. They pointed out that when proved to be antecedent and perpetual, such an impotence can have the same negative consequences on the validity of a marriage, as impotence in man has.

Of fundamental importance in this regard was the decretal *Fraternitatis* of Pope Innocent III. This decretal dealt with the condition of "arctatio mulieris". The woman in case had remarried after having had her first marriage declared null precisely because of such an "arctatio". Asked about the value of this second marriage, the Pope replied that it was null and the woman had to return to her former husband:

> "perspicaciter attendentes, quod impedimentum illud non erat perpetuum, quod praeter divinum miraculum per opus humanum absque corporali periculo potuit removeri ... cum pateat ex postfacto quod ipsa cognoscibilis erat illi, cuius simili commiscetur".[5]

---

[2] c. 18, C. XXXII, q. 7 (FRIEDBERG, I, 1144-1145): "Quod posuisti, si mulier infirmitate correpta non valuerit viro debitum reddere, quid eius faciat iugalis: bonum esset, si sic permaneret, ut abstinentiae vacaret. Sed quia hoc magnorum est, ille, qui non poterit continere, nubat magis; non tamen ei subsidii opem subtrahat, quam infirmitas prepedit, non detestabilis culpa excludit". Cfr. OESTERLE, G., *Impuissance*, in *Dictionnaire du droit canonique*, vol. 5, Paris 1953, coll. 1262-1265; WERNZ-VIDAL, *Ius canonicum*, tom. 5, *Ius matrimoniale*, Rome 1946, n. 222; KELLY, W., *Pope Gregory II on Divorce and Remarriage*, Analecta Gregoriana, 203, Rome 1977, pp. 279-294.

[3] GLOSSA, *Nubat*, ad c. 18, C. XXXII, q. 7: "Ibi dicit quod non invenitur aliquis canon de arcta, sed certe bene invenitur, sed non expresse".

[4] ALEXANDER III, c. 4, X, *de frigidis et maleficiatis, et impotentia coeundi*, l.4, tit. 15 (FRIEDBERG, II, 705): "Consultationi tuae, qua nos consuluisti, utrum feminae clausae, impotentes commisceri maribus, matrimonium possint contrahere, et si contraxerint, an debeat rescindi, taliter respondemus, quod licet incredibile videatur, quod aliquis cum talibus contrahat, matrimonium, et quamvis de huiusmodi expressum canonem non habeamus, sacrosancta Romana tamen ecclesia consuevit in consimilibus iudicare, ut quas tanquam uxores habere non possunt habeant ut sorores. Verumtamen talibus artificio aliquando consuevit succurri, ut valeant apte reddere debitum et accipere". Cfr. OESTERLE, G., *op. cit.*, col. 1256.

[5] c. 6, X, 4, 15 (FRIEDBERG, II, 706-707).

In order to render a marriage null, such "arctatio" had to be perpetual, i.e. it could not be removed "per opus humanum absque corporali periculo". But even this gave rise to different interpretations in the subsequent doctrine, ranging from Hostiensis' "periculum gravis morbi"[6] to the "periculum mortis" required by others.[7] Furthermore, the Pope seemed to imply that if a woman is not considered to be "arcta" with one man, neither is she with another. In other words, here was the question whether an "arctatio relativa" is possible. Although there were those who, like Sinibaldus Fliscus (the future Pope Innocent IV) held that

"Si mulier est arcta uni, omnibus arcta est, et si uni cognoscibilis, non est arcta"[8],

yet there were also others, who although they accepted as a general rule that this "arctatio" is "absoluta respectu omnium", yet they also pointed out that such a rule does admit of an exception in the case where the physiological nature of the other man is different from that of the first, so that sexual intercourse is possible. In such a case, the first marriage would be declared null "ex arctatione respectiva mulieris".[9]

This latter opinion was the one that in the end was admitted by

---

[6] HOSTIENSIS, *Summa*, IV, *De sponsalibus et matrimonio*, tit. 15, n. 3, Venice 1574; cfr. PALUDANUS, P., *Lucubrationum opus in quartum sententiarum*, IV, d. 34, q. 2, a. 2, conclu. 2, n. 13, Salamanca 1552; ANTONINUS (S.), *Summa maior*, P. III, tit. 1, c. 12, # 1, Venice 1503.

[7] Cfr. DE TABIA, *Summa*, v. *Impedimentum*, 12, n. 2, vol. II, Venice 1569; SOTO, D., *Commentarium in IV sententiarum*, d. 34, q. un., a. 2, Venice 1575, vol. II, col. 7; SÁNCHEZ, T., *cit.*, 7.93.18; GUTIÉRREZ, J., *Canonicarum quaestionum*, tom. III, c. 112, n. 28, Frankfurt 1607.

[8] INNOCENT IV, *In quinque Decretalium libros commentaria*, IV, *De sponsalibus et matrimonio*, tit. 15, n. 1, Venice 1610; Cfr. D'ANDREA, J., *In decretalium libros novella commentaria*, IV, *De sponsalibus et matrimonio*, tit. 15, c. 6, n. 13, Venice 1581; DE TABIA, *cit.*, 12, q. 5, n. 6; DE LEDESMA, *Tractatus de magno matrimonii sacramento super doctrinam Angelici Doctoris*, q. 58, a. 1, dub. 5, Venice 1595; SOTO, D., *cit.*, d. 34, q. un., a. 2, col. 6.

[9] Cfr. ABBAS PANORMITANUS, *Commentaria in Decretales*, IV, *De sponsalibus et matrimonio*, tit. 15, cap. 6, n. 19, Venice 1578: "Ego dicerem hoc dictum procedere ex praesumptione, quando non constat differentiam inter utrumque, scil. virum et uxorem, nam si vir est adeo carnosus quod nunquam posset deflorare mulierem sine periculo mortis, secundus vero vir magis gracilis potuit eam cognoscere, tunc puto quod non sit restituenda primo ... et hoc probo per istud textum qui dicit quod ista erat cognobilis a primo ex quo potuit commisceri secundo, quia erat similis primo, secus ergo ubi non erat similis"; DE TRANI, G., *Summa in titulos Decretalium*, IV, *De sponsalibus et matrimonio*, tit. 15, n. 11, Venice 1586; PRAEPOSITUS, *Commentaria in decretales*, IV, *De sponsalibus et matrimonio*, tit. 15, c. 6, n. 6, Venice 1579.

all. "Arctatio absoluta", which was considered to be perpetual, would therefore render a woman absolutely unable to marry; while in the case of an "arctatio relativa" the woman still had the possibility to contract a valid marriage.

The doctrine of Thomas Sánchez moves along this line of thought. He noted that

> "nil refert an ex parti viri, an ex defectu foeminae consurgat impotentia seminandi intra vas, atque ita consummandi matrimonium, ut coniuges efficiantur una caro".[10]

According to Sánchez, a woman is truly impotent "si tam arcta esset ut non posset semen intra vas recipere".[11]

He also agreed that it can be either absolute or relative, and considered the latter to be present only

> "quando est notabilis dissimilitudo inter utrumque virum. Cum enim praesumptio iuris sit, ut foemina, quae uni non est arcta, sed ab eo cognosci potest, nulli sit arcta, sed ab omnibus cognoscibilis, oportet ut haec praesumptio eludatur, notabilem differentiam inter utrumque virum reperiri".[12]

On the contrary, he did not consider impotent the woman who can receive the semen inside her vagina without, however, retaining it. Still less, did he consider impotent the woman who, while she is able to receive the semen inside her vagina, does not however, ejaculate her own semen, since Sánchez did not think this necessary for generation.[13]

---

[10] SÁNCHEZ, T., op. cit., 7.92.11; cfr. GÓMEZ LÓPEZ, A., El impedimento de impotencia en Tomás Sánchez, Pamplona 1980, pp. 59-60.

[11] SÁNCHEZ, T., ibid., 7.92.11. In conjunction with this anomaly, Sánchez mentioned also the case of a woman who is likewise "incapax matrimonii ... si prae latitudine alia latenti aegritudine cognosci minime potest a viro", ibid. Such a woman would therefore only be impotent if she could not permit sexual intercourse. Cfr. 7.93.15: "Si iudicio medicorum impedimentum impotentiae medicabile sit absque corporali periculo, quamvis foemina renuat incisionem, aut medicamenta necessaria, quibus apta reddatur viro, firmum esset matrimonium. Quod eius firmitas ac valor minime ex feminae voluntate pendeant; sed ex ipsa rei natura, iuxta quam impedimentum illud temporale est, utpote quod potest per artem absque corporis periculo tolli".

[12] Ibid., 7.93.13.

[13] Ibid., 7.92.9-11.

Art. 2. Organic impotence in the female according to Zacchia

That the female too, just like the male, can suffer from impotence was, for Zacchia, a conclusion that logically follows from his very definition of coitus:

> "coitus enim est applicatio maris et foeminae in membris generationis".[14]

In line with the then current canonical and medical tradition, he pointed out that whereas there were so many causes that could obstruct the copula in man,

> "una tantum est quae illam in foemina intercipiat, nempe clausura, arctatio, seu angustia oris externi, et cervicis ipsius uteri (= vaginae)".[15]

As a doctor, however, who had read a good number of the latest books on anatomy, he could not just simply accept this limited view presented and discussed by canonists. He knew very well that there did in fact exist other forms of anomalies that could not permit the female to perform a normal sexual act. Precisely because of a limited view accepted by many, Zacchia felt the need to delve deeper into the subject and present a more complete list of the various organic causes of such an impotence. He also sought to suggest the possible treatment.[16]

Admittedly, Zacchia was not always very clear when he treated the various malformations causing sexual impotence. Very often, his ideas are scattered in the various "quaestiones", throughout his work; and it is not always clear when such malformations affect directly the vagina itself or the pre-vaginal vulvar parts. Fortunately, however, towards the end of his work, he did dedicate to this subject a whole chapter entitled "De impedimento coitus ex parte mulieris".[17] It is here that he was more schematic.

1. "Angustia vulvae"

Referring to the anomalous conditions that can at times affect the entrance of the vagina, Zacchia noted that one such defect

> "respicit foramen ipsius vulvae, et est ipsius angustia, quae aliquando tanta est, ut impediat penis etiam mediocris intromissionem".

---

[14] Zacchia, P., QML, 3.1.1.7; cfr. 3.1.1.9.
[15] Ibid., 3.1.1.22. Cfr. supra chapter 2, note 43, p. 54. Zacchia here referred to the Decretals Fraternitatis (c. 6, X, IV, 15) and Laudabilem (c. 5, X, IV, 15).
[16] Ibid., 9.3.5.5.
[17] Ibid., 9.3.5. per totam.

He was here referring to the fusion of the labia, which is frequently accompanied by some form of hermaphrodism, and he mentioned various examples taken from doctors, among whom Realdo Colombo. Such an excessive reduction of the vulvar orifice, Zacchia said, is surely a ground of nullity.[18]

This condition can be either congenital or acquired. Personally, he was more inclined to think that it is not curable, though there were some doctors who thought that congenital fusion can be solved by an incision of the labia and the use of some medicaments and pessaries. Zacchia, however, was not very convinced and said that unless some positive result appears in the first two or three months, when some cure has been attempted, it is useless to wait any longer before declaring the marriage null. He considered the acquired fusion of the labia as incurable and said that no incision is to be attempted since such an operation is dangerous because of inflammation, possible heavy haemorrhage and grave pain, not to mention death itself.[19]

2.   *Malformation of the clitoris*

With the backing of doctors like J. Hucher and D. Sennert, Zacchia noted that a no less serious impediment to the copula in the female is constituted by a clitoris which

"in nonnullis mulieribus ita excrescit, ut coitum undequaque impediat, non potente vulva ob eius obstaculum penem admittere, quod non modo evenit cum ex se, ad venerem muliere irritata, excrescit, sed etiam absque intumescentia, licet multo magis cum erecta induratur".

Any possibility of cure would depend on its constitution, for in certain cases where it is of great proportion, it is completely beyond any remedy, and it constitutes a perpetual impediment to the copula. In other cases, although not without much difficulty and danger, it can be remedied, and the husband can gradually succeed in deflowering his wife and consummate the marriage. However, Zacchia left it to the canonists to decide

"quid sit determinandum, nam ex re ipsa patet, matrimonium cum tali impedimento validum esse non posse, praesertim si amovibile non sit".[20]

---

[18] *Ibid.*, 9.3.5.7; cfr. 9.10.2.17.
[19] *Ibid.*, 9.10.2.17.
[20] *Ibid.*, 9.3.5.9; cfr. 9.10.2.18.

3. *Malformations of the vagina and of the hymen*

Zacchia had much to offer to the canonist and the jurist in this regard. Although the terms "arcta", "atreta", "imperforata", and "velata" were very often indiscriminately used to refer to the same condition, yet one readily understands that they do not amount to the same anomalous condition. Zacchia himself was not always consistent in the use of these terms, and sometimes he did even interchange them.[21] It seems, however, that he did distinguish two types of anomalies in this regard; namely those which render the vagina impenetrable due to its abnormal narrowness, to which he reserved the terms "angustia", "arcta" or "coarctata". This would correspond to a hypoplasias of the vagina. In the second case, the vagina cannot be penetrated because of some other obstacle, which can be a tough and rigid hymen or even a septal partition. In these cases, Zacchia preferred to use the terms "atreta", "imperforata" or "velata".

A. *Vagina "arcta"*

1. *Hypoplasias of the vagina*

Today we know that such a condition results from an improper fusion of the müllerian ducts, the canal being short and narrow. Zacchia considered hypoplasias as a congenital condition due to the

> "angustia, parvitate et exilitate viarum, unde non potest congredientem virum sustinere".

He also added that a corporal inspection of the parties is here necessary, since such a condition can easily give rise to a case of relative impotence. If the husband is proved to possess a genital organ which is disproportionately great, then there would clearly be no hope of a future success in attempting sexual intercourse. Zacchia noticed that where this situation results, then things are clear and there is no need of setting a trial period.[22]

But there can also be a second case, where the girl has a narrow vagina "procedente ex minori, ac teneriori cute". In such

---

[21] Cfr. *Ibid.*, 3.1.3.3.; 3.1.5.45; 3.1.7.24; 9.10.2.16-17: "De uteri clausura verba feci, ac monstravi non semper esse unius eiusdemque rationis, sed variari pro causae occludentis conditione, cuius respectu facilius, aut difficilius remedia admissibilia sunt, quae in uno casu sunt omnino inania; in altero vero possunt aliquid boni operari".

[22] *Ibid.*, 3.1.2.12; cfr. 9.3.5.3.

cases, the advice of Zacchia was to set a trial period, which if need be, is not to be restricted to just one year. The reason he gave is that as the girl grows older and she gradually gets accustomed to her husband, sexual intercourse will become possible; unless of course, there is some other impediment. It often happens, explained our author, that what initially rendered the copula impossible was only the young girl's fear of pain, but this she will eventually overcome.[23]

2.   *"Coalescentia uteri"*

Once again the reference is to the vagina. This "uteri coalitus vel coalescentia, vel symphisis" which Zacchia noted in some women and which, he said, very often escaped the attention of canonists, in practice amounts to an *agenesis* or absence of the vagina. Today we know that such a malformation results from a failure of the lower end of the müllerian duct to develop properly, and its development as a fused solid cord is recognised as vaginal absence. Lesser degrees of malfusion are seen as vaginal hypoplasias. The only treatment possible consists in the constitution of the vagina by plastic surgery.

Zacchia pointed out that the possibility of cure depended on the nature and gravity of every particular case, since such a fusion could vary in degrees. Indeed, not necessarily congenital, it could also result from some disease or be induced by the use of certain ointments. In all cases, however, the genital parts are so joined together that they do not permit any penetration by the male's organ.[24]

B.   *Vagina "imperforata"*

Zacchia pointed out that a number of causes can block the vaginal canal, though not all are of equal gravity nor cause an equally serious impediment. For this reason the possibility of a remedy can vary from case to case:

> "... de uteri clausura verba feci, ac monstravi non semper esse unius eiusdemque rationis, sed variari pro causae occludentis conditione, cuius respectu facilius, aut difficilius remedia admissibilia sunt, quae in uno casu sunt omnino inania: in altero vero possunt aliquid boni operari".[25]

---

[23] *Ibid.*, 3.1.2.12.
[24] *Ibid.*, 3.1.7.30,32; cfr. 9.3.5.5; 9.10.2.16.
[25] *Ibid.*, 9.10.2.16; cfr. 9.3.5.3-4.

1. *The hymen*

The hymen itself can be one such cause. Zacchia noted that there was confusion in this regard. This he attributed to the fact that authors were neither clear nor in agreement about the very existence and nature of the hymenal membrane. Many doctors doubted and even denied that it exists in all not-as-yet deflowered women. These doctors would rather consider the hymen as something preternatural (i.e. outside the ordinary course of nature) and morbid. On the contrary, others insisted that the hymen is naturally found in all virgins.[26] Because of such a situation, canonists did not usually distinguish as to the nature and cause of this blockage of the vagina.

(a). *Definition of the hymen*

Such a confusion gave rise, said Zacchia, to a number of definitions when referring to the hymen:

> "nam pro hymene nonnulli intellexerunt membranam quandam duriusculam uteri collo adnatam, non semper uno eodemque loco sitam, sed modo interius, modo exterius in ipsius matricis collo".

But in reality, he added, this is not the hymen and it was only mistakenly considered to be so by some. As such, it is not naturally found in a virgin.[27]

According to our author, those who had studied the matter more accurately, like Riolan, Pineau, Falloppia and Vesling,

> "pro hymene non aliud intelligi debere docuerunt, quam connexionem nonnullarum membranarum ... Post nymphas (quae duo membranosa corpuscula sunt alarum modo expansa immediate post pudenda, et labia uteri sita), interius versus intimum uteri osculum, quattuor carunculae apparent, quae myrtoides, quod myrti folia referant, appellantur, vel triangulares, quod triangulari figura dotentur, quarum singulae in singulis lateribus, nimirum superno, inferno, dextro, sinistro prominent; invicemque ita per acutiorem partem sese respiciunt ...; coniunguntur autem, invicemque cohaerent omnes per membranulas quasdam, aut per fibras colligantur, et haec pars ita constituta verus hymen est".[28]

Elsewhere, he noted the presence of an orifice in this membrane.[29]

---

[26] *Ibid.*, 4.2.2.1.
[27] *Ibid.*, 4.2.2.4.
[28] *Ibid.*, 4.2.2.5-6.
[29] *Ibid.*, 4.2.1.28-29. This orifice is necessary for the expulsion of the

According to Zacchia, therefore, the integral hymen is struc-
turally made up of four triangular pieces of flesh united together by
membranes. From the context it appears that the anatomists whom
he was following had seen the hymen both in its integral form as
well as after its rapture through penetration. However, it seems
that their description was based on a reconstruction of the lacerated
triangular parts left after it has been broken.[30]

(b). *Anomalies of the hymen*

Zacchia distinguished two conditions in this regard.

(i). *Rigid hymen*

A blockage of the vaginal canal may result from a rigid though
otherwise normal hymen, which does not break during intercourse.
For

> "et haec ipsa pars, licet naturaliter in virginibus reperiatur ... tamen
> aliquando callosa duritie rigida arietantis penis impetum illaesa
> sustinet, ... et tunc fit unum clausurae genus ex duritie praedictae
> membranae".[31]

(ii). *Elastic hymen*

Another blockage could result from the presence of an elastic
or flexible hymen[32], whose texture is such as to allow intromission
of the male organ without its being broken into the process.

---

menstrual flow so that where, by a congenital defect it is missing, surgical
intervention is absolutely required. This is how modern authors describe the
hymen. It is a "membrana mucosa che nella vergine occlude incompletamente
l'ingresso della vagina. Esso è costituito da una lamina connettivale, tappezzata
sulle due faccie da epitelio pavimentoso stratificato. Presenta un'apertura di solito
molto ristretta, che può avere forma diversa (imene anulare, semilunare, setto o
subsetto, cribriforme, labiato duplice, ecc.). Nella deflorazione spesso l'imene si
lacera, in maniera più o meno estesa. Dopo il parto di solito rimangono solo alcuni
resti dell'imene, chiamati 'caruncole imenali'", PESCETTO, G.-DE CECCO, L.-
PECORARI, D., *Manuale di clinica ostetrica e ginecologica*, vol. I, p. 19, n. 10, Rome
1981; cfr. SANTORI, G., *Compendio, cit.*, p. 59.

[30] When speaking about these tags, Zacchia stated: "Quoad colligantiam et
unionem, omni procul dubio apparent in virginibus inter se cohaerentes, et medio
tenuissimarum membranularum colligatae, in corruptis vero disgregatae, ac
invicem dissitae; abscedunt enim invicem illae carunculae, ob illarum membranar-
um violationem ac disruptionem", *ibid.*, 4.2.2.9; cfr. 4.2.1. per totam.

[31] *Ibid.*, 9.3.5.3.

[32] Cfr. SANTORI, G., *Compendio, cit.*, p. 61; MARCHETTA, B., *Scioglimento del
matrimonio canonico, cit.*, pp. 117-118.

Zacchia added that it is also possible that the semen ejaculated inside the vagina is drawn "per orificium quod perpetuo in ea membrana (est)" and the woman conceives. He also attributed this elasticity of the hymen to a number of factors, among which the internal secretions of the vagina.[33]

2. *Septal partitions*

Besides the hymen, Zacchia mentioned a second condition that can block the vagina, i.e. the presence of another membrane inside the canal. This was the case of the "vagina vel mulier velata":

> "... coitus in muliere aliis quoque ex causis impediri potest, quam ab hymene ... Membrana igitur (loquor autem semper hic de membrana praeternaturali, non de hymene) aut erit tenuis, aut crassa, et carnosa, aut erit perforata, aut non, aut erit posita interius versus internum uteri osculum, aut in medio colli uterini, aut prope os externum".[34]

Such segments are therefore situated along the vaginal canal between the hymen and the lower end of the womb. If they appear in the lower part of the vagina, they too can be an impediment to the copula, unless they can be removed.[35]

In view of this, one particular point calls for some further clarification, namely the case of the woman whose vagina is blocked by such an imperforated membrane. From the whole

[33] ZACCHIA, P., *QML*, 4.2.1.28-33. On this point, Zacchia was a frequently quoted authority in matrimonial decisions. Cfr. for example, c. ANSALDO, Neapolitana Matrimonii, 18 iunii 1703, in *Volantes*, vol. 5, p. 230; Corduben. Dispensat., 20 septembris 1760, in *Thesaurus*, vol. 29, pp. 122-123; Romana Matrim., 17 septembris 1808, *ibid.*, vol. 74, pp. 139-140; Neapolit. Matrim., 2 martii 1861, *ibid.*, vol. 120, pp. 48-49; Parisien. Dispensat. Matrim., 28 martii 1908, *ibid.*, vol. 167, p. 245; Varsavien. Dispensat. Matrim., 23 ianuarii 1904, *ibid.*, vol. 163, pp. 70-71; c. ROSSETTI, 16 maii 1914, in *SRRD*, vol. 6, p. 209, n. 3; c. GUGLIELMI, 24 iulii 1931, *ibid.*, vol. 24, p. 32, nn. 22 ff.

[34] *Ibid.*, 9.3.5.4; cfr. 7.3.5.11: "Sunt enim mulieres nonnullae, quibus membrana in medio uteri collo obtenditur, aliquando tam dura, ut nulla irruenti viri violentia disrumpi possit: has atretas, imperforatas ac velatas vocant"; 3.1.7.24; 9.10.2.16. Even in this matter Zacchia proved a useful source to subsequent matrimonial jurisprudence: Forolivien. et Caesentana, Nullitatis Matrimonii, 29 aprilis 1899, in *Thesaurus*, vol. 158, pp. 304-305; Monasterien. Matrimonii, 16 decembris 1899, *ibid.*, pp. 935-936; Mechlinien. Dispensat. Matrimonii, 26 iulii 1879, *ibid.*, vol. 138, p. 340; Ravennaten. Matrimonii, 11 septembris 1880, *ibid.*, vol. 139, pp. 500-503.

[35] Cfr. ZACCHIA, P., *QML*, 9.3.5.4; 9.10.2.16. Cfr. also infra, # 6.2, pp. 145-146.

context it appears that Zacchia was treating this condition in the woman of marriageable age, even though he did not explicitly say so.[36] It is therefore evident that such a woman must have also been suffering from some other anomaly which caused primary amenorrhoea in her.[37] However, perhaps because he was more interested in the impediment to the sexual act which such a segment could cause, Zacchia did not consider this problem.

C. *Possibilities of treatment*

What possibilities of treatment did Zacchia envisage for these different conditions? To the canonist, this was an important question, since only in those cases where no real and possible cure is available can a particular marriage be declared null.

Zacchia repeatedly affirmed that any possibility of cure depends on the type of closure or blockage in each case as well as on the position where such a blockage occurs within the vaginal canal. It is one thing if the vagina is closed merely by the hymen, and quite another if it is blocked by the fusion of the lateral sides, so that no real vagina is present. In each case, the nature and gravity of each impediment has to be evaluated while the general circumstances of the patient are also to be kept in mind. Another element not to be discarded is the risk to the woman's health and life.[38]

Zacchia did not consider blockages caused by the hymen serious enough to constitute an impediment to the sexual act.[39] Not so in the case of segments, especially if they are imperforated. The presence of such partitions can very well prove to be such as not to leave any possibility of treatment or at least not without incurring a grave risk to the patient's life. The thicker such a membrane is, the more rigid and the deeper it is located inside the vagina, the more difficult and risky the operation to remove it would be. On the contrary, the more subtle and the nearer to the vaginal orifice, the easier it is to remove. As to the sexual act, when such a membrane is located further up from the vaginal orifice, penetration can take place, although the membrane itself would not break under the pressure exerted by the male organ.

---

[36] Cfr. *Ibid.*, 3.1.7.24; 7.3.5.11; 9.3.5.4; 9.10.2.16.
[37] Cfr. PESCETTO, G.-DE CECCO, L.-PECORARI, D., *Manuale di clinica ostetrica e ginecologica, cit.*, vol. I, pp. 208, 670.
[38] Cfr. ZACCHIA, P., *QML*, 3.1.7.29-30; 9.10.2.16; 8.2.4.5.
[39] Cfr. *Ibid.*, 9.10.2.16.

In all cases, the advice of the doctor and surgeon is necessary.[40]

As a general conclusion, one can say that it is in cases where such treatment proves non-existent or can only be achieved with grave danger to the person that Zacchia thought that there is no need of assigning a trial period of time. In other cases, such a period is to be set, but it is not to exceed thirty days. If the husband whose genital organs are normally constituted, does not succeed to have intercourse with his wife, after having tried to do so daily during this period, then this would surely be indicative of some grave impediment that cannot be removed.[41]

4. *Prolapse of the Uterus*

Such an anomalous condition of the womb is today found to be comparatively uncommon and usually occurs in women who have had one or more children and especially if the perineum has been torn at the confinements. Such a prolapse can be of different degrees, complete displacement being reached when the vaginal walls are completely everted and the uterus is wholly or partially outside the vagina. Treatment is today provided by a surgical operation, while pessaries (instruments worn in the vagina to prevent uterine displacements) are only exceptionally used.[42].

Zacchia had something to say even in this regard. He noted that sexual impotence can also be caused by the

"exitum et summam declinationem ipsius uteri, qui interdum per collum et externum os foras prolabitur".[43]

In this context, he is using the term "uterus" to refer to its proper meaning, namely the womb. He added that such a prolapse can create an impediment to the sexual act, unless the uterus is returned to its proper place. Saying that such a prolapse can be of varying degrees, he stated that where old age has set in, not only treatment is much more difficult, but there is also the fear of an easy recurrence. In younger women, treatment is easier. He added that certain pessaries are provided to keep the uterus in its place

---

[40] *Ibid.*, 9.3.5.3-4; 9.10.2.16.

[41] *Ibid.*, 3.1.2.12.

[42] Cfr. TAYLOR, S., (ed.), *Harlow's modern surgery for nurses*, London 1979, pp. 713-716; PESCETTO, G.-DE CECCO, L.-PECORARI, D., *op. cit.*, vol. I, pp. 413-418; CAMPBELL and HARRISON, *Urology*, *cit.*, vol. III, pp. 1975-1976.

[43] ZACCHIA, P., *QML*, 3.1.3.3.

once it has been restored therein. Such pessaries do not cause any
impediment neither to the copula nor to the generative act. The
anomaly itself only causes an impediment when there is no
successful treatment, since the sexual act is impeded only when the
uterus cannot be returned in its place.[44]

5. *Morbid conditions*

The copula can also be rendered impossible by the presence of
some "apostemata", which block the vaginal canal. It seems that
under this general heading Zacchia was referring to what is today
more commonly known as tumors and distrophic lesions of the
vulva and the vagina.[45] Zacchia noted that although not all such
"apostemata" are of the same nature or of the same condition, yet
all of them can render the performance of the sexual act impossible.
Although all present a great difficulty to cure, yet any possibility of
treatment is greater when such a condition is in its initial stages.
The sexual act itself is rendered more impossible when the condition affects the lower parts of the vagina and the labia, since in such
cases it makes it very difficult to allow any sort of penetration.
Where the malign tumor has developed to such a degree which does
not allow the exercise of the sexual act nor admit of any treatment,
then surely, said Zacchia, there is a cause of dissolution of
marriage[46], obviously if such an anomaly has been antecedent to
the marriage.

6. *Two cases of impotence*

By now Zacchia's position as a doctor with regards to the then
current interpretation of the essential requirements of the sexual
act that consummates marriage, on the part of both man and
woman, is quite evident. Zacchia could not understand why
canonists required only the man to emit "semen aptum ad gener-

---

[44] *Ibid.*, 9.3.5.10; 9.10.2.19.
[45] Cfr. PESCETTO, G.-DE CECCO, L.-PECORARI, D., *op. cit.*, vol. I, pp. 557-589;
TAYLOR, S., *op. cit.*, pp. 758-761.
[46] ZACCHIA, P., *QML*, 9.3.5.12: "Verum adhuc plerisque aliis morbis uterus
molestetur, qui copulae carnali impedimentum praebent, ut sunt apostemata
omnia ipsius matricis, quae maximae collum ipsius occupant; ... Cum igitur haec
talis naturae apostemata cervicem etiam uteri obsident, mulieres virum admittere
nequaquam possunt, et cum sint extra omnem spem sanationis, videretur secundum canonistarum decreta praebere ea iustam causam dissolvendi matrimonium,
ubi illud consummare non permiserint"; cfr. 9.10.2.20.

ationem", while the woman, whose contribution is as essential for the purposes of generation, was not required to do so. The following two questions further manifest his disagreement on the use of such different criteria.

1. *Is the woman who does not seminate considered impotent?*

Zacchia noted that for the validity of marriage canonists required not only *potentiam coeundi*, but also *potentiam seminis emittendi*, and added that

> "idcirco, ergo ubi horum utrumque non adsit, separatur matrimonium".[47]

Nor is there any doubt that for Zacchia the female's contribution is as much necessary for generation as the male's, so that without it the copula cannot be said to be *apta ad generationem*.[48]

All this naturally begs the question: what role did Zacchia assign to female semination in the consummation of marriage and in female impotence? In other words, did this author consider the female who does not ejaculate her proper semen just as impotent as the male who does not ejaculate? This question is not without importance, at least from a canonical point of view, for we have already seen that as a doctor Zacchia strictly related the presence of the semen, even in man, to the generative faculty and not to one's ability to exercise the sexual act.

Zacchia made a clear parallelism between the male and the female semen, stating at the same time that both have analogous bodily parts to produce the respective semen which serves for identical purposes, namely generation.[49]

Furthermore, he also noted that without the woman's contribution there can be no generation. Consequently he concluded that "foemina excisis testibus mari castrato similis efficitur".[50]

---

[47] *Ibid.*, 3.1.1.1-2.

[48] Cfr. *Ibid.*, 1.3.6.3; 1.3.6.22; 1.4.3.29; 3.1.7.9-23; 4.2.4. passim; 7.3.1.16 ff; 7.3.6.4; 9.11.1. passim.

[49] *Ibid.*, 9.10.1.12: "Ceterum ex tradita veri seminis definitione eliciendum est, foeminas verum semen habere: nam in eis quoque ex vasis spermaticis defertur materia sanguinea ad testes, ubi concocta, ac dealbata in semen perfectum abit generationi aptissimum, ad eamque a natura, ut semen marium destinatum. Praeterea, quod ea ipsa materia ab ipsa foemina in coitu, vel quomodocunque cum eadem delectatione, quam mares seminantes effunditur, et quod excedens eius excretio ipsas mirum in modum, ut mares, debiles efficiat; quicquid ergo deblaterent contrariae sententiae assertores, relinquentes sensum propter imaginarias quasdam ratiunculas, veritas rei ita se habet...", cfr. 3.1.7.10.

[50] *Ibid.*, 2.3.7.49; cfr. 3.2.8.16-17; 7.3.1.23.

On the other hand, Zacchia was well aware that canonical doctrine did not consider the "seminatio" an essential requirement of "potentia coeundi" in the female. Which seems to have been an itchy problem for our author. This is evident from the fact that he referred to it more than once. Although in the end, Zacchia accepted this state of affairs, at least as far as canonical doctrine was concerned, he could not but show how perplexed he was. And moreover, he drew the attention of canonists and asked them to dedicate further study to this question, in order to provide a suitable solution.[51]

Zacchia produced another argument to corroborate his position. He said that where the woman suffers from frigidity, she neither feels any sexual drive nor does she produce any semen, so that she is sterile.[52] Yet canonically speaking, such a condition "non impedit eam ad patiendum", and therefore it does not constitute an impediment to marriage, "nisi obstet impotentia generandi".[53] And this made him turn once again to canonists and ask:

> "Cur foemina semen non potente emittere, vir tamen coitu uti possit, et matrimonium teneat; contra vero viro non potente emittere, coitus sit illicitus, et matrimonium non teneat, cum in nostra sententia etiam foemineum semen, ut masculeum, requiratur ad conceptionem? In utroque certe casu, licet succedere non possit conceptio, possunt intendi et haberi duo alii matrimonii fines, nempe et debiti solutio, et fornicationis remedium. Si ergo ad primum finem, nempe ad procreationem filiorum non facit hic matrimonii usus, potest aliis duobus suppleri, non minus quam possit, ubi alia quacunque ex causa omnis spes habendae prolis sit irrita, ut in matrimonio evenit inter decrepitos contracto".[54]

---

[51] *Ibid.*, 9.3.7.4: "... dixi tam in mare, quam in foemina requiri seminis intra se generationem, si ex eorum copula sequi debeat generatio... Unde cum sponsi per copulam carnalem effici debeant una caro, ut matrimonium dicatur consummatum, idque fiat concursu seminis ex parte utriusque, ... non dicetur matrimonium unquam consummatum, nisi puer seminet, et puella ... seminet simul. Haec ergo Canonistis discutienda propono, nec quicquam, nisi quod ex arte mihi certo innotescit, determinare ambigo, sed ipsis omnia ex canonum decretis resolvenda relinquo"; cfr. 9.3.7.2

[52] *Ibid.*, 9.3.5.2; cfr. 9.10.2.15.

[53] *Ibid.*, 3.1.6.36.

[54] *Ibid.*, 7.3.4.13; cfr. 9.3.5.2: "et tamen si matrimonium irritatur, si vir semen non generet, quid causae esse potest, quin etiam mulier semen non generans irritet matrimonium?".

2. The case of the "mulier velata". Is she impotent?

A related question concerns the condition of those women commonly referred to as "velatae". As we have already seen, at least in some cases, the location of the septal partition inside the vagina is such as to permit some penetration, so that the husband can also ejaculate therein.[55]

Zacchia held that the condition of such a woman does not present any difficulties as far as the consummation of the marriage is concerned. He noted:

> "Non impeditur aliquando sponsus matrimonium consummare, quia membrum intromittendo in vas, et semen eiaculando, licet membrana non disrumpatur, consummatur matrimonium, ... ita ut sponsa etiam non disrupta ea membrana, concipere possit, si aliquo vel plurimis foraminibus sit pervia".[56]

But can such a woman marry validly, since the semen appears to be blocked within the vagina?

In agreement with Hippocrates and Avicenna, Zacchia said that when this segment is "rarae texturae", the semen can pass through it into the inner parts of the vagina, so that conception can follow. Nor is it necessary that the woman dies at childbirth, as Hippocrates had previously claimed since, at least in some cases, the membrane can be removed by surgery or it can also be broken at childbirth, thus permitting a safe delivery.[57]

Zacchia was of the opinion that such a woman is capable of contracting a valid marriage, since she not only achieves the primary end of marriage but also fulfills its other ends. Furthermore, even in the case where the woman cannot conceive, hers is still a valid marriage since in that case she would only be sterile, and the marriage of sterile people is valid:

> "Nullo enim fine videtur destitui hoc matrimonium, ita ut irritari possit, dum ultra caeteros etiam hunc, qui praecipuus est, habere potest, nempe sobolis procreationem ... Immo etiamsi hoc fine destitueretur ... neque ipse vir, neque mulier impediuntur, quin semen emittant, unde uterque eorum potest habere remedium

---

[55] Cfr. *ibid.*, 3.1.7.24; 9.3.5.4.

[56] *Ibid.*, 9.3.5.4; 9.3.3.4. Cfr. BERSINI, F., *Matrimonio e anomalie sessuali e psicosessuali, cit.*, p. 176.

[57] ZACCHIA, P., *QML*, 9.3.5.4; 10 cons. 42.12; cfr. 1.3.3.30; 3.1.7.24-26; 3.1.8.20; 4.2.1.28-32; 8.1.7.25-26. This same opinion is also reflected in some marriage nullity decisions of the S.C. CONCILII, for example: Bonearen. Matrimonii, 16 iunii 1900, in *Thesaurus*, vol. 159, pp. 443-482; Monasterien. Matrimonii, 18 martii 1899, *ibid.*, vol. 158, pp. 131-172.

concupiscentiae et usu matrimonii mutuam dilectionem fovere.
Ergo etiamsi ex hoc capite mulier sterilis esset tamen non esset illi
denegandum debitum, quia et sterilium matrimonium valet, et
sterilibus etiam ex alia magis irreparabili causa debitum esse reddendum, quia etiam abstracta a coniugio omni spe habendae prolis,
tamen coniugium non est irritum".[58]

7. *Some canonico-moral questions*

When treating marital relations (*de debito coniugali*), Zacchia
raised a number of doubts of a canonico-moral nature, some of
which are strictly related to the anomalous conditions just mentioned. In all of them, he treated in some detail certain questions
which "ad medicum cognoscere spectat", leaving the canonists to
decide "an matrimonium cum his foeminis valeat, an debitum reddi
debeat, et huiusmodi alia dubia".[59]

Evidently there would be no place for such doubts where the
anomaly is such as to prevent any penetration and/or ejaculation
inside the vagina, for this would immediately render the marriage
null. In fact, Zacchia's opinion was that where these two essential
elements of the copula can be performed, both husband and wife
are bound to give and accept the right to conjugal acts; unless of
course there is some reason which is serious enough to excuse them
from this. But then, this was in the canonists' competence to
decide.[60]

One very delicate question was

> "an mulier quae concipiendo rationabili periculo exponitur morien-
> di in partu, teneatur reddere debitum".

Noting that canonists replied in the negative, Zacchia said that the
question still presented difficulties. What if the female retains her
semen, thus avoiding conception? In this way she can satisfy her
conjugal obligation towards her husband and at the same time
avoid any danger to her own life. In view of this, Zacchia proposed
this doubt to the canonists, asking them whether in such circumstances

> "mulier possit proprii seminis emissionem impedire, aut concursum
> saltem proprii cum semine viri, ad hoc ut conceptio non succedat".[61]

---

[58] ZACCHIA, P., *QML*, 7.3.5.11; cfr. 9.3.5.4. Zacchia's reference is to
Sánchez, *op. cit.*, 7.92.26.
[59] *Ibid.*, 7.3.5.11.
[60] Cfr. *ibid.*, 7.3.4.9-10.
[61] *Ibid.*, 7.3.3.21-22.

Zacchia was only making a simple question in the shoes of a doctor and not going against his own beliefs as a Christian. This is proved by the fact that earlier he himself had answered this question, saying that the wife does fulfil her own conjugal obligations properly,

> "si cum viro congrediatur absque eo quod semen proprium effundat, satisque esse, si ipsa semen data opera non retineat, ne sequatur generatio, aut alio quocunque actu ipsam generationem impediat. Quod est peccatum mortale".[62]

Another doubt was "an vir teneatur reddere debitum uxori imperforatae, nempe quae uteri clausuram patitur incurabilem". Zacchia's answer was in the affirmative, since the copula in such a case is not destitute of any of its essential elements or ends. "Si ergo inter hos matrimonium valet, recte matrimonio uti poterunt".[63]

Art. 3. Zacchia and modern medicine.

There remains but one thing to see in this chapter, namely how valid was Zacchia's contribution in this field of medicine. It has already been pointed out that traditionally female impotence was reduced to what was commonly known as "arctatio". Zacchia, however, basing himself on the available but as yet still scattered and partial material provided by the latest studies of his time as well as on his own experience as a doctor, produced a treatise on the subject that was valuable not only for the medical knowledge it offered, but also for the forensic applications it contained. The constant references to his work in cases of non-consummation and nullity of marriage on the ground of female impotence is a sure sign of this.

Besides, if one compares what Zacchia had to offer about the various organic anomalies of the female's genital tract with the findings of modern clinical gynaecology, one remains surprised at the amount of rather accurate and extensive information which he supplied. Basically, his description of the vulvar, vaginal and hymenal abnormalities that can be an impediment to the sexual act coincides, though obviously not in the many details, with that provided by the modern textbooks of gynaecology.[64]

---

[62] *Ibid.*, 7.3.1.15. Once again the reference is to Sánchez, *op. cit.*, 9.20.1.
[63] *Ibid.*, 7.3.5.11.
[64] Cfr. Taylor, S., *cit.* in note 42, pp. 750-766; Pescetto, G. - De Cecco, L. - Pecorari, D., *cit.* in note 37, vol. I, pp. 170-200, 357-400, 557-589; Santori, G.,

Obviously, modern science provides a more systematic presentation and a better identification of the nature and causes of
these various malformations, lesions and tumors that can affect the
female's genital organs, with the possibility of causing sexual
impotence. Medical terminology is also very often different, and
the treatment which is available today was still beyond Zacchia's
imagination. But one can easily understand this. Anatomy had not
reached the stage of providing a sufficiently detailed picture of the
female's genital tract, nor medical science provided the required
means to remedy for every anomalous condition without great
difficulties.

Today, many of these anomalies can be remedied through a
surgical intervention with relative ease[65], and therefore, very often
they do not constitute a perpetual impediment for canonical intents
and purposes.

In the end, moreover, modern canonical doctrine and jurisprudence have proved that Zacchia was right on the very fundamental
point that as long as the female's vagina is such as to permit
sufficient penetration all be it a partial one, and semination by the
male inside, the woman in question is considered capable of
performing the sexual act.[66]

Compendio, cit., pp. 281-286; SAPONARO, A., *La vita sessuale della donna*, Milan
1982, pp. 81-84.
    [65] Cfr. *Ibid.*
    [66] This is most evident in the case of the woman with a "vagina occlusa" or
"aequivalenter occlusa" due to some internal blockage in the vaginal or uterine
canal. In such a situation the husband can still perform the conjugal copula, but
the semen cannot pass from the vagina into the uterus. Such an anomaly has
received much attention in the past and for a time the woman affected by this
condition was considered impotent. "En la actualidad, habiendo desaparecido el
diferente trato existente entre el hombre y la mujer en esta materia, se juzga que
no debe ser considerada impotente la mujer que tiene la vagina occlusam vel
aequivalenter occlusam", AZNAR GIL, F.R., *El nuevo derecho matrimonial
canónico*, Salamanca 1985, p. 224; cfr. ORLANDI, G., *I "casi difficili" nel processo
super rato"*, cit., p. 19; BERSINI, F., *Matrimonio e anomalie sessuali e psicosessuali*,
cit., pp. 172-175; *Communicationes*, 6 (1974) 197; BAMBERG, A., *L'impuissance
organique de la femme d'après la jurisprudence rotale récente (1970-1981)*, Luxembourg 1982.

Chapter seven

FUNCTIONAL IMPOTENCE IN WOMAN

Art. 1. Functional impotence in the female before Zacchia. — Art. 2. Doctrine of Zacchia. # 1. Frigidity and impotence. 1. Concept of frigidity. 2. The sexual response in man and woman. 3. Female frigidity and functional impotence. # 2. "Maleficium" and impotence. — Art. 3. A critique.

Over and above the organic causes of impotence, there are other anomalous conditions that cause sexual dysfunction in the female. It is to this functional impotence that we shall now turn our attention.

Art. 1. Functional impotence in the female before Zacchia.

When he came to speak about frigidity in the female, Zacchia noted that

> "sed cum plura de virorum frigiditate attulerim, vix quicquam de mulierum frigiditate me tetigisse memini".

And the reason which he gave for this lack of attention is that canonists and even doctors thought that the female cannot be rendered impotent by frigidity.[1]

Indeed, St. Thomas had already said that only man is rendered impotent by such an anomaly:

---

[1] Zacchia, P., *QML*, 3.1.5.31-32. Zacchia added: "Tamen peculiariter sciendum, voluisse Iurisconsultos, et canonistas eam (frigiditatem) non cadere in muliere... Mulier, enim quantum est ex parte sui, semper ad coitus est prompta, neque ad illum exercendum impeditur nisi uterum occlusum habeat. Itaque quoque ex medicis... Causa vero cur mulier frigida non fiat... autem est, quod cum mulier patiens in coitu sit, frigiditas passioni obstare non videtur; neque enim calor requiritur ad patiendum, quemadmodum ad agendum".

"mas est agens in generatione sed femina est patiens. Et ideo maior caliditas requiritur in viro ad opus generationis quam in muliere. Unde frigiditas, quae facit virum impotentem, non faceret mulierem impotentem. Sed in muliere potest esse impedimentum naturale ex alia causa, scilicet arctatione. Et tunc idem est iudicium de arctatione mulieris et de frigiditate viri".[2]

But this opinion that the female is sexually neutral was also shared by some doctors. Zacchia himself referred to Jerome Mercuriali who likewise held that "in mulieribus non dari morbum in defectu desiderii coitus".[3]

This was the current opinion among canonists. And in line with this position, Sánchez himself, referring to St. Thomas, claimed:

"Frigiditas enim reddens coniugem impotentem soli viro accidit. Ut egregie docet D. Thomas ab universis receptus (Comment. in Lib. IV Sententiarum, l.4, d. 34, q. unic., art. 2 ad 6) ea ductus ratione, quod mas sit agens in generatione, foemina vero solum patiatur. At frigiditas passioni non obstat, sed soli actioni reprimens membri virilis motionem".[4]

Sánchez, and like him all those who held this view, therefore retained that since the female plays only a passive role in the sexual act, she is always capable of performing the sexual copula; and consequently she can never be considered frigid. In this sense, frigidity was not considered as an absence of the libido or deficient sexual attraction. For all intents and purposes it was considered as an anomaly that prevented the erection of the male's penis.[5] From this point of view, therefore, there was no question of functional impotence in the woman.

On the other hand, however, it was commonly agreed that the female too was liable to be the victim of some "maleficium", that would render her unable to perform the sexual act, despite the fact that she had normal genital organs.[6]

Sánchez himself noted that as a case of impotence, "maleficium" "utrique sexui commune est"[7] adding that

---

[2] St. Thomas, *Supplementum*, q. 58, a. 1, ad 6; cfr. *Commentaria in quattuor libros sententiarum*, IV, d. 34, q. unic., art. 2, ad 6.
[3] Zacchia, P., *QML*, 9.3.5.1-2; cfr. 3.1.5.31.
[4] Sánchez, T., *op. cit.*, 7.92.1.
[5] *Ibid*.
[6] Cfr. Soto, D., *Commentarium in IV sententiarum, cit.*, IV d. 34, q. unic., a. 3; Pirhing, *Ius canonicum*, lib. IV, *De sponsalibus et matrimonio*, tit. 15, # 2, n. 12, Venice 1759.
[7] Sánchez, T., *op. cit.*, 7.92.1.

"non soli viri, sed etiam feminae possunt maleficiis impotentes ad copulam reddi. Quod omnes fatentur. At frequentius id malum in viros serpit. Quod plus operae, et instrumentorum in eis desideretur. Adde, quia plures sunt maleficae, quam malefici, et ideo potius viros quam feminas maleficiis laedere conantur ... Ea autem est differentia (...) quod maleficia circa viros fiunt communiter per operationem aliquam realem, aut per motum ipsius daemonis, nulla re applicata ... At femina communiter maleficiatur per solam opinionem, seu phantasiae laesionem: potest enim vir accedere nec rigor membri relaxatur; at cum conatur accedere, illa subito horret genitale viri, quasi improportionatae magnitudinis, et nulla ratione sinit se cognosci. Cum tamen re vera non ita sit, sed daemon efficit speciem in phantasia mulieris, ut membrum aliter appareat, quam revera sit. At quamvis communiter ita accidat, solet tamen quandoque daemon vas foemineum arctare".[8]

In practice, this amounted to vaginism which according to Sánchez could take either of two forms. It could close the entrance of the vagina which is normally wide enough to permit penetration or it could produce its narrowness by sudden contractions.[9]

Art. 2. Doctrine of Zacchia.

The current doctrine among canonists and some doctors at the time of our author was therefore that frigidity was not recognised as a cause of impotence in woman. On the other hand, it was common doctrine that "maleficium" could cause functional impotence in the female.

Zacchia took a completely contrary position. He held that just like the male, the female too can suffer from frigidity, which in some cases can result in her inability to perform the sexual act. But he did not admit that she could be affected by "maleficium" as such.

1. Frigidity and impotence

Zacchia confessed that he was astonished how a doctor of such fame as Jerome Mercuriali could think that

"in mulieribus non dari morbum in defectu desiderii coitus".

---

[8] *Ibid.*, 7.94.3.
[9] *Ibid.*, 7.94.3-6; cfr. Gómez López, A., *El impedimento de impotencia en Tomás Sánchez, cit.*, pp. 102-104.

This was something, said Zacchia, which experience itself contradicted[10]; and on his part he insisted that even women can be frigid:

> "Mulieres non secus ac viros, posse esse a natura frigidas, non tantum quia nullo veneris stimulo teneantur, sed neque ullum semen intra se generent, cuius stimulis ad coitum agantur, quemadmodum de viris evenire palam est".[11]

In evaluating Zacchia's opinion on this matter, which as we have seen was in contrast with that of his contemporaries, one must be very careful to take into consideration all the references which he made throughout his work.

1. *Concept of frigidity*

Both canonists and doctors considered frigidity in relation to the effects it has on man. They concluded that only man can be frigid, and this not in the sense that he shows an absence of the libido or a deficient sexual attraction, but rather because he cannot have an erection.

Zacchia, on the contrary, directly related frigidity and libido, saying that the presence of frigidity means the absence of sexual stimulus or attraction.[12]

It is in view of this fundamental premise that his opinion must be read and interpreted.

2. *The sexual response in man and woman*

As far as generation is concerned, Zacchia rightly considered the female's contribution as essential as that of the male. On the other hand, however, he noted the different reactions in man and woman that naturally accompany sexual relations. He admitted that apparently the female plays a more passive role in the act of sexual intercourse. Here, the male is much more active than his

---

[10] ZACCHIA, P., *QML*, 9.3.5.1: "Unicum impedimentum in muliere agnoverunt canonistae..."; cfr. 3.1.5.31.

[11] *Ibid.*, 9.3.5.2.

[12] Cfr. *ibid.*, 3.1.5.34: "Sed si consideremus frigiditatem, quatenus obstare possit consummationis illius actus ex parte ipsius foeminae, nempe quod cum nulla voluptate coeat, cum nulla partium tensione, cum nulla seminis emissione, mulier non secus ac vir frigida esse potest". 9.10.2.15: "Sed veram frigiditatem in mulierem cadere; non secus ac in virum iam probavi, nempe frigidam totius intemperiem, ob quam mulier intra se semen non generet, et ob id neque ullis veneris stimulis irritetur..."; cfr. 3.1.5.32-36; 9.3.5.2.

partner. "Non est par ratio — he said — viri et uxoris in reddendo debito"[13], the reason being that

> "mulier satisfacit debito matrimoniali sola patientia copulandi se cum viro".[14]

Her role consists "in simplici redditione", so that during the sexual act "magis resolvitur vir quam mulier"[15], meaning that orgasm is more intensely felt by man than by the woman.[16] However, he was aware that things are not as simple as that and he realised the importance of female sexuality. All this is referred to by Zacchia when he dealt with the consequences that can result from an incomplete sexual act. Zacchia noted that

> "quod pertinet ad virum difficile esse credo, non subesse semper spontaneae pollutionis periculum, si a copula non emisso semine desistat".[17]

The man who is already in a state of sexual arousal will sooner or later ejaculate even if he does not continue with the sexual act. On the contrary, the woman does not normally ejaculate, since she can even permit herself to participate passively in the sexual act without feeling any sexual arousal. But this only applies, said Zacchia, if she

> "venere accensa non fuerit ..., sed si iam in venerem sit accensa, periculosum etiam in ipsa erit, ut a copula desistat".[18]

He therefore insisted that just like the male, the female too has a sexual impulse which she feels the need to satisfy. He categorically rejected the opinions of those who held that during sexual intercourse the female does not experience any gratification. On the contrary he claimed that during the sexual act the female's gratification is of a longer duration than that experienced by the male, though not as intense.[19]

---

[13] *Ibid.*, 7.3.3.1.
[14] *Ibid.*, 7.3.3.3.
[15] *Ibid.*, 7.3.3.5.
[16] *Ibid.*, 7.3.3.1.
[17] *Ibid.*, 7.3.6.7.
[18] *Ibid.* For this reason, Zacchia suggested that the husband should wait for his wife to reach her orgasm, and this for two reasons: "Primo quia si debiti redditio respicere debeat generationem iam absque eo, quod mulier semen emittat, nulla sequi potest generatio ... Quod si redditio debiti respiciat extinctionem stimulorum carnis et coertionem incendii eiusdem, tantum abest, ut mulier a viro inita, et semen non emittens, ab eiusmodi stimulis vindicetur, ut potius acutiores eos experiatur, non enim cessat libido, donec semen effundatur", 7.3.6.3.
[19] *Ibid.*

3. *Female frigidity and functional impotence*

His conclusion therefore was that since the female possesses a sexual impulse, she too can be frigid. However, with regard to the effect this frigidity can have on the ability to exercise the sexual act and therefore on the very validity of marriage, one notes a very fundamental change in Zacchia's approach. When he first took up this problem in Book III (which was published in 1628), Zacchia held that since frigidity does not deprive the female of her ability to perform the sexual act, it does not affect the validity of the marriage:

> "Sciendum tamen, mulieris frigiditatem nulli rei posse esse impedimento, quoad matrimonium valide contrahendum, cum ex hoc non impediatur quin debitum reddere marito possit".[20]

Clearly, the reason behind such a stand is that Zacchia too, at least until then, was holding that the female's "patientia copulandi" was sufficient to permit her to perform the sexual act, and therefore to marry.

However, by the time he published his ninth Book of the *Quaestiones* in 1650, Zacchia had revised his opinion, and he now held that frigidity can prevent the female from performing the sexual act. He now distinguished two types or classes of frigidity. Taken in an improper and less accurate sense, frigidity is considered to be present when the woman affected by it still has the possibility to generate and even to act passively during intercourse, even though she feels no sexual stimulus: in this sense, admitted Zacchia, frigidity does not amount to an impediment of the sexual act:

> "Ego quidem non dissentio, si ita res accipiatur, quod in tantum in muliere non detur, in quantum non impedit eam ad patiendum".[21]

In practice, this would amount to a copula without orgasm.

But there exists another type of frigidity, said Zacchia, which he called "true frigidity", and which not only deprives the female of her sexual libido but also of her ability to generate:

> "sed veram frigiditatem in mulierem cadere non secus ac in virum probavi, nempe frigidam totius intemperiem, ob quam mulier intra se semen non generet, et ob id neque ulli veneris stimulis irritetur,

---

[20] *Ibid.*, 3.1.5.36.
[21] *Ibid.*, 9.10.2.15.

nec consequenter generationi ullo modo sit apta, ut in viris frigidis evenire solet".[22]

Interestingly enough, Zacchia had proved the existence of this frigidity when he first approached the problem in Book III. There he made a parallelism between the various anomalies resulting from frigidity in the male and those which result from the same cause in the female. There also, Zacchia considered the different types of frigidity, according to the nature, gravity or consequences that can result in both sexes.[23]

On that occasion, however, his conclusion still was that such frigidity does not cause any impotence in the female, but only deprives her of any sexual gratification:

> "Ergo licet mulier nunquam pene impediri possit, quin coitum admittat, impeditur tamen ex frigiditate, ne cum voluptate, et membrorum tensione coeat, ne semen excernat, aut paucum, tenuius, et aquosius quam par sit, ... immo etiam ne omnino intra se semen generet; tandemque ne ad generationem habilis sit".[24]

It is therefore evident that contrary to what other doctors and canonists were holding, Zacchia held not only that the woman too can be frigid, but also that such frigidity can, at least in some cases, be such as to cause sexual impotence in her. Under the title "de impedimento coitus ex parte mulieris", he openly accused those canonists who erroneously denied that frigidity can render the female spouse "ad coitum impotentem":

> "Et tamen, non extra possibilitatem est, ita frigidas nasci foeminas, ut virum, nequaquam admittere possit, coarctante ipsa frigiditate muliebria loca".[25]

Frigidity in the female, therefore, amounts to her congenital inability to perform the sexual act.

The presence of frigidity in women is marked practically by the same signs as in man, as for example

> "pilorum in locis consuetis omnimoda carentia, genitalium flacciditas, coitus ad venereorum stimulus nullus, et alia id genus, cum quibus alia adsunt ipsius mulieris propria".[26]

[22] *Ibid.*
[23] *Ibid.*, 3.1.5.35-36.
[24] *Ibid.*, 3.1.5.34,36.
[25] *Ibid.*, 9.3.5.1.
[26] *Ibid.*, 9.10.2.15; cfr. 9.3.5.2.

In the female, frigidity can cause sexual impotence in either of two ways. It can cause a "coarctatio uteri", and this because of certain spasms which cause the contraction of the vagina ("coarctante ipsa frigiditate muliebria loca"), thereby preventing the male from effecting penetration. In practice this amounts to vaginism, which was the only cause recognised by canonists. This condition, according to Zacchia, did render the sexual copula impossible and consequently marriage was to be declared null.

The second case of functional impotence resulting from frigidity to which Zacchia referred was in connection with the condition of those women who

> "absque ulla causa manifeste impense dolent, quin etiam animo deficiunt".[27]

In this case he made no reference to any contractions of the vagina. It seems that this was a case of dyspareunia.

In view of this, Zacchia proposed to the canonists to see

> "an probata vera frigiditate mulieris, ut in casibus propositis, licet virum admittat, tamen vir causam iustam habeat, dirimendi matrimonium".

However, he himself was very skeptical about the answer they would eventually give.[28]

2. *"Maleficium" and impotence*

On this point, Zacchia had very little to say. Once again, the impression one gets is that he personally believed very little in the devil's having a share in rendering a woman functionally unable to perform the sexual act. So much so that, following Fortunato Fidele, Zacchia noted

> "quod viri solummodo ex maleficio redduntur ad coitum impotentes, mulieres autem nequaquam; vel saltem frequentius viri quam mulieres".[29]

And the reason which he gave was that since the devil can only act through natural causes, he has very few possibilities at his disposition in the case of women.[30]

---

[27] *Ibid.*, 9.3.7.7; cfr. 7.3.5.7.
[28] *Ibid.*, 9.3.5.2; cfr. 9.10.2.15.
[29] *Ibid.*, 3.1.5.42.
[30] *Ibid.*, 3.1.5.45.

However, he did admit that certain potions, foods or herbs can adversely affect also the woman, thereby increasing her sexual desire or rendering her sterile or even unable to exercise the sexual act.[31]

Nor is there any doubt that what Zacchia said about impotence resulting from some psychological factor in man, he also intended it in the case of a woman.[32]

Art. 3. A CRITIQUE.

Zacchia's doctrine on functional impotence in woman provides two very important intuitions. The first is with respect to female sexuality. Zacchia recognised that the female too possesses a sexual impulse or appetite. Consequently her role in the sexual act cannot be simply considered as passive. Though very partial in his explanation, he has been proved fundamentally right by modern study, which has shed much light on the different sexual response of both sexes and on the complex process that takes place in the woman, for whom orgasm is very often not such a simple mechanism as it is in men.[33]

In view of this, Zacchia was therefore also right when he said that the female can be frigid; and this primarily in the sense of suffering from a deficient sexual appetite. Even today, frigidity is strictly linked with the inability of the woman to achieve orgasm in the course of a normal heterosexual intercourse or with the lack of sexual appetite if not total repugnance for the sexual act.[34]

One can perhaps also mention here Zacchia's relating frigidity to sterility, saying that the frigid woman is also sterile. It is known today that both phenomena are independent from each other. Frigidity as such does not impede intercourse so that fecundation can take place even without the active collaboration of the woman, since her sexual gratification is not required.[35]

---

[31] *Ibid.*, 3.1.5.48.

[32] In this Zacchia was very useful to subsequent jurisprudence. Cfr. e.g., Forolivien. Dissolutionis Matrimonii, 8 augusti 1761, in *Thesaurus*, vol. 30, pp. 153-156; Seinen. Matrimonii, 16 februarii 1884, *ibid.*, vol. 143, p. 155; Neopolitan. Matrimonii, 15 februarii 1888, *ibid.*, vol. 147, p. 768; Versavien. seu Luceorien. Dispen. Matrimonii, 27 augusti 1892, *ibid.*, vol. 151, p. 574; Parisien. Dispen. Matrimonii, 19 augusti 1899, *ibid.*, vol. 158, p. 725.

[33] Cfr. SANTORI, G., *Compendio di sessuologia, cit.*, p. 415; SAPONARO, A., *Vita sessuale matrimoniale*, Milan 1972, pp. 20-29.

[34] Cfr. SANTORI, G., *ibid.*, pp. 416-417; SAPONARO, A., *La vita sessuale della donna, cit.*, pp. 28-29.

[35] Cfr. SAPONARO, A., *ibid.*, pp. 31-32: "Tuttavia, è stato dimostrato che

Another point where Zacchia was understandably partial, is with regard to the causes behind frigidity. Such causes can be either organic (affecting the sexual glands, the external genital organs or organism in general), or purely psychic or psychosexual. It is the latter that are by far the most common.[36] Naturally the role which Zacchia attributed to psychological factors in impotence cannot be underestimated.

Two sexual anomalies usually associated with frigidity are *dyspareunia* and *vaginism*. According to Santori, the former represents the most common form of sexual dysfunction in the woman. In the wider sense, it includes all the morbid conditions, both anatomical and functional, which prevent the sexual act from taking its normal course:

> "Se in alcuni casi, fortunatamente rari, il dolore ed il timore del rapporto sessuale danno luogo al grave quadro del vaginismo, molto più spesso gli stessi fattori non giungono ad impedire la unione sessuale, che può ugualmente avere luogo, sebbene attraverso qualche difficoltà e suscitando sgradevoli sensazioni. È questo il vastissimo campo della DISPAREUNIA (...) che dopo la frigidità alla quale del resto abitualmente si associa, rappresenta la più comune forma di disfunzione sessuale della donna".[37]

Its causes can likewise be multiple.[38]

On the other hand, *vaginism* can be considered as a graver form of dyspareunia, in the sense that great pain and fear of the sexual act are accompanied by spasmic contractions of the vulva and the vagina at the least stimulus, thereby rendering unapproachable the genital organs:

> "Consequenter vaginismus non in *sola* hyperestesia consistit, sed fert secum etiam contractionem spasmodicam et involuntariam musculorum vaginae. Neque dolor ac difficultas in coitu, absque

---

l'orgasmo sessuale della donna può favorire il concepimento, perché uno stato di eccitazione erotica comporta fenomeni atti a rendere più facile la fecondazione dell'ovulo da parte dello spermatozoo ... Traendo pertanto le debite conclusioni, il tema dei rapporti tra frigidità e sterilità femminile si può riassumere dicendo che la fecondazione non ha bisogno dell'orgasmo sessuale, ma che tuttavia questo può favorirla. In altre parole la donna frigida non è affatto necessariamente una donna condannata alla sterilità; ma la piena partecipazione erotica della donna all'atto sessuale crea condizioni che rendono più facile e più probabile il concepimento".

[36] Cfr. *Ibid.,* pp. 33-42.

[37] SANTORI, G., *Compendio di sessuologia, cit.*, p. 432; cfr. SAPONARO, A., *La vita sessuale della donna, cit.*, pp. 67-70; BERSINI, F., *Matrimonio e anomalie sessuali e psicosessuali, cit.*, pp. 87-88.

[38] Cfr. *Ibid.*

tamen contractione defensiva musculorum vaginae, esset vaginismus, sed simplex 'dispareunia'".[39]

Although sometimes the causes of vaginism are of an organic nature yet, in the majority of cases, they are purely psychic and can vary from a morbid fear of the pain caused by the sexual act to a true and proper aversion of the sexual act itself or even of the partner.[40]

It is evident that Zacchia was aware of the presence of these two anomalous conditions behind the functional impotence of the female. There is no doubt that it was to the spasmic contractions caused by vaginism that he was referring when he spoke about the "coarctante muliebria loca"; and to dyspareunia (though he never used the term itself), in the case of the female who can only allow penetration with great pain, though without any spasms. Obviously, he was very partial in his explanation of the mechanism causing such anomalies, at least from the medical point of view. For juridically, as on other occasions, he was very clear as to the negative consequences such conditions can have on the validity or the consummation of marriage.

Even here it must be noted that in line with the criterion offered by G. Versaldi, all cases of impotence whose cause is of an organic or physiological nature should be considered as organic. All other forms of impotence should be considered as psychic, and this either primary or secondary.[41]

The other important contribution of Zacchia consists in the fact that he practically did away with "maleficium". After all, his insistence on the role of psychic factors at play in the sexual act had already supplied a valid and very real explanation of those cases of impotence which to the inexperienced eyes of many appeared "absque ulla causa manifesta".

[39] GORDON, I., *De processu super rato*, Roma 1977, pp. 121-122; cfr. SANTORI, G., *op. cit.*, pp. 427-428; BERSINI, F., *op. cit.*, pp. 187-188; SAPONARO, A., *op. cit.*, pp. 55-56; SKALABRIN, N., *De vaginismo et inconsummatione matrimonii in decisionibus rotalibus (1945-1975)*, Diacovo 1987, pp. 95-116.

[40] GORDON, I., *op. cit.*, pp. 121-124; SAPONARO, A., *op. cit.*, pp. 54-56; SANTORI, G., *op. cit.*, pp. 427-432. Today it is held that practically in all cases of vaginism, including those where the cause is an apparently organic one, there is also a psychic factor involved: cfr. SKALABRIN, N., *op. cit.*.

[41] VERSALDI, G., *L'oggettività delle prove in campo psichico, cit.*, pp. 162-163.

CONCLUSIONS

Though partial in certain respects, Paolo Zacchia's treatment of sexual impotence was indeed a very valuable contribution, not only from the medical point of view, but also for its forensic applications. Its great merit lies in the extensive and detailed presentation of the organic and functional anomalies that cause impotence both in man and in woman as well as of the accurate legal consequences which such anomalies entail. This was no small feat on the part of the author, who succeeded in gathering the available but as yet still scattered information on the subject and present it with his own critical evaluation in one single treatise. No wonder, it soon became the constant point of reference and a useful tool for judges and advocates in ecclesiastical tribunals.

Zacchia's contribution can be most clearly seen in his presentation of the following points:

1. *A personalistic view of marriage*. As a Christian doctor, he offered a very positive outlook of marriage as a "consuetudo vitae" and of the intimate conjugal acts, which he considered as an important factor in the husband — wife relationship. Marriage, he said, has other ends besides the procreation of children, not least that of the "bonum coniugum". For this very reason, the sexual act cannot be restricted to a mere biological function.

Even where procreation is not possible, the sexual act is not only licit but also praiseworthy. Thus Zacchia presented a very personalistic view of sexual relations in marriage. The "remedium concupiscentiae" itself is not a negative secondary end, but contributes to the growth of communion between the married couple.

2. *Human sexuality*. Though the sexual response varies in man and woman, yet Zacchia realised and pointed out that the female too, just like the male, possesses a sexual impulse or libido, which she feels the need to satisfy. Therefore, her role in the sexual act cannot be considered a passive one, as many of his contemporary

authors, both doctors and canonists, thought. Besides, for the purpose of generation, the physiological contribution of the female is as necessary as that of the male.

3. *The sexual copula*. The sexual copula that consummates marriage is constituted of three essential moments: erection, penetration and ejaculation. Zacchia's insistence on the necessity of penetration and ejaculation inside the vagina was a very relevant intuition and an important step forward in the true definition of consummation of marriage.

4. *"Potentia coeundi" and "verum semen"*. In view of this, potency on the part of man consists in his ability to sustain an erection long enough to penetrate inside the wife's vagina and ejaculate therein. Zacchia did not share the canonists' position that the *verum semen* is an essential element of *potentia coeundi*. In reality, we have here a doctor writing soon after Sánchez and the *Cum frequenter*, who was saying that in this regard the position of canonists was to a very great extent contradictory, and was causing confusion between *impotentia coeundi* and *impotentia generandi*; not to mention the discrimination made in the use of two different criteria applied to judge what constituted impotence in man and in woman. *Verum semen*, insisted Zacchia, is only required for generation, and a man is considered potent as long as he can ejaculate inside the wife's vagina, irrespective of the nature of the liquid.

On her part, the female is considered potent, when she possesses a vagina which is capable of permitting sufficient penetration and semination by the male inside it.

5. *Causes of impotence*. The causes that can render an individual unable to exercise the sexual act can be many and various, some being organic in nature, others purely psychic. Apart from the detailed description of the various organic conditions which result in impotence in both man and woman, Zacchia also offered a very valuable contribution with regards to the various psychological factors that lie behind the complex mechanism which sometimes results in one's incapacity to perform the sexual act. Love, fear, shyness, aversion of the sexual act and even of one's partner are important elements that every doctor must look for in cases of impotence. Furthermore, he very ably redimensioned the then-current understanding of *maleficium*, and proposed a very real explanation, one that was more in line with medical science.

6. *The role of the Expert in Court*. It was precisely in view of this complex mechanism that Zacchia insisted on the need of seeking medical expert advice in cases of impotence. The judge is

very often faced with the difficult task of deciding about the nature, gravity and curability of such causes and the resulting impotence, which are not nor can be defined by law. It is for this reason that "in particularibus ad medici iudicium recurrendum omnino est", as Zacchia very often repeated; adding that on his part, the expert must be conscious of his great responsibility which he is to fulfil with diligence. The expert's role consists in helping the judge clarify doubtful cases.

THE WORKS OF PAOLO ZACCHIA

This appendix contains a complete catalogue of all the published and unpublished works of Paolo Zacchia. L. Allacci was the first author to give such a list[1], which was in turn updated by P. Mandosio.[2] Both P. Capparoni[3] and G. Deffenu[4] made use of these previous catalogues.

It must be pointed out that many of the works of Zacchia lack the date and place of publication. Mandosio says that these writings "quae mss. remansere apud heredes, deperdita tamen fere omnia eorum incuria".[5] Capparoni is of the opinion that at least some of these works must have been integrated into the major work, to form part of the *Quaestiones medico-legales*.[6]

I. DATED WORKS

La Fenice di Lattanzio Firmiano, tr., Rome 1608.
Il vitto quaresimale, Rome 1637, 1673.
De' mali hipochondriaci, Libri due, Rome 1639, 1644; Libri tre, Rome 1651; Venice 1663, 1665; Augusta 1671. In 1771, the work was translated into Latin by A. Khonn, Vienna.
Quaestiones medico-legales, in quibus omnes eae materiae

---

[1] ALLACCI, L., (henceforth referred to as Al), *Apes Urbanae sive de viris illustribus qui ab anno 1630 per totum 1632 Romae adfuerunt, ac typis aliquid evulgarunt*, Rome 1633. The section related to Paolo Zacchia was reproduced by his nephew Lanfranco among the tributes in the 1661 Lyon edition of the *Quaestiones medico-legales*.

[2] MANDOSIO, P., (henceforth referred to as Md), *Theatron in quo maximorum Christiani orbis pontificum Archiatros Prosper Mandosius inspectandos exhibet*, in MARINI, G., *Degli Archiatri Pontifici*, vol. II, Rome 1784, pp. 119-121.

[3] CAPPARONI, P., *Profili bio-bibliografici di medici e naturalisti celebri italiani dal secolo XV al secolo XVIII*, vol. II, Rome 1926, pp. 134-136.

[4] DEFFENU, G., *Invito a Zacchia*, in *Castalia*, 3 (1953) 103-117.

[5] MANDOSIO, P., *op. cit.*, p. 121.

[6] CAPPARONI, P., *op. cit.*, p. 136.

medicae, quae ad legales facultates pertinere videntur, pertractantur et resolvuntur. Book I, Rome 1621; Book II, Rome 1625; Book III, Rome 1628; Book IV, Rome 1628: Book V, Rome 1630; Book VI, Rome 1634; Book VII, Rome 1635; Books VIII-IX, Amsterdam 1650, 1661.

The first four books were published collectively in a single volume at Leipzig in 1630 (Al also mentions Frankfurt, 1630). The complete treatise, made up of the nine Books was first published in Lyon, in 1654, to which there followed another publication at Avignon, in 1655.

After Paolo Zacchia's death, his nephew Lanfranco added the tenth book, which contained "responsa seu consilia octogintaquinque, ad materias medico-legales pertinentia; necnon decisionum Sacrae Rotae Romanae, ad easdem materias spectantium centuriam". This edition was then published at: Lyon in 1661, 1674, 1701, 1726; Avignon in 1660, 1661; Frankfurt in 1666, 1668, 1688, 1701; Nürnberg in 1726; Venice in 1737, 1751, 1771.

An abridged edition, with the title *Novus Zacchia, sive Opera celeberrimi ecc. ecc. in breve compendium redacta a D. Facundo Lozano*, was published at Cesena, in 1774.

II. UNDATED WORKS

Miscellaneorum libri tres (Al).

In Cardani librum de malo medendi usu antipracticae animadversiones (Al).

Responsorum juridicorum et consultationum medicarum (Al).

De subitis et insperatis mortis eventibus eorumque praecognitione et precautione, liber singularis (Al).

De maculis in utero a foetu contractis, quae vulgo dicuntur "le voglie" (Al).

De quiete servanda in curandis morbis, libri tres (Al).

De sacrae Scripturae miraculis physica consideratio, libri quattuor (Al).

Delle passioni dell'anima e dei mali che da esse procedono; della loro cura tanto fisica quanto morale, libri duo (Al).

Della birra o cervosa. Discorso medico (Al).

Del contagio; ove si prova il contagio essere men da temersi di quello che si teme. Discorso (Al).

Del riso e del pianto. Libri duo (Al).

Il bacio. Discorso (Al).

Poesie varie, cioè sonetti, canzoni, madrigali, etc. (Md).

La strage degli innocenti (Md).

TRIBUTES TO PAOLO ZACCHIA

The following are some of the tributes paid to Zacchia by his contemporaries and reproduced by Lanfranco in the 1661 Lyon edition of the *Quaestiones medico-legales*:

I. FROM A LETTER OF JEROME BARDI, DATED 1ST DECEMBER, 1652:

"Omniscio et politissimo iurisperitiae medicinaeque antesignano, viro clarissimo, D. Paolo Zacchiae, medico romano.
Orbis terrarum universus in te admirabundus oculos mentemque sustollit, ob insigna virtutum tuarum germina, quibus rempublicam literariam perpetuo, aeternumque duraturis maximis monumentis, ab iniuriis temporis vindicatis condecoratam exornas. Ad te enim omnium gentium typographi veluti cervi sitientes, per epistolas ad fontem limpidissimum doctrinarum, aquarumque scientificarum in-deficiens flumen sitim expleturi, facto agmine accurrunt ...
Gaudeo et gratulor studiosissime et amicissime vir, ...
Tu vero medicinam cum legumperitia ad currum humanae vitae pertrahendum, quasi ibim et ciconias et grues simul, et genio et ingenio discrepantes, coniunxisti, et sacro foedere copulasti, ut quaenam harum maior et excellentior sit non dignoscatur, quaecunque enim comparatio odiosa, a te utriusque congrua dilucidatione de medio tollitur et debacchatur ...".

II. FROM AN ODE WRITTEN BY B. TORTOLETTI:

"In libris nova, PAULE, tuis ostenta refulgent. Nascitur artes saeculis ignotae priscis. Legum consultus Apollo evasit inter phar-maca...
Tu vero reperis, quo denique jungere dextras discit facultas utraque ...
Victori oceani sociabere iamque Columbo, rerum novarum auctor-ibus:

necnon palladiis, quorum mortalia ductu crevere plurimum bona.
Ortis nempe novis pridem orbibus, insuper artes novas oriri fas fuit;
unde salus vitam melior meliorque capessat Rempublicam secur-
itas".

III. A. Nardus dedicated the following distich to Zacchia:

"Quod medica sis arte potens, legumque peritus, Paule, quid est
mirum? Talis Apollo fuit...;"

and these lines from an epigram:

"Seque inter certant, valeat quod dicere quisque; nunc dea fit
medicus, fit medicusque dea. Hisque diu assiduis Tu praeceptoribus
usus, foedere inaudito nectis utrumque decus. Felix sorte tua, cui
jungere contingit uni tam posse deum, tam bene posse deam.
Ingenio tandem quis surgere posse negabit semivirumque deum,
semideumque virum?"

IV. From a letter of L. Guidiccioni, dated 14th September, 1634.

"Exegisti monumentum aere perennius. Ad septenarium devenisti
opus, ... Mirandus es semper, quanto magis in his, quae portenta
sunt? ...
Tibi vero nequaquam ulterius procedendum immortalitatis gratia.
Nam singuli tui labores caeteros vincunt, postremus te ipsum ...
Nam universo isto tuo laudatissimo ac longe lateque extra Italiam
circumacto septem voluminum complexu, quasi compacta erudi-
tionis sphaera duobus veluti insistis polis, omnem humanae vitae
rationem omnino regentibus. Homines quippe, et animo constamus
et corpore. Corpus medicae artis beneficio servamus, animum iuris
imbutum prudentia, rebus arduis et consendis et peragendis red-
dimus parem. Tu circa utrumque versatus. Scientiam conflas medi-
co-legalem, et perficis ...
Vives geminata sorte immortalitatis. Volitabis per ora virum gemina
sublimis pluma. Non tanti fuere medico-reges vestri illi Avicenna
cum reliquis, quorum nomine Arabia superbit, seipsa felicior.
Neque tu si ipsa Phoenicis pluma nitaris, altiore volatu, ac peren-
niore insurgas. Nam calamus iste tuus, et inde sublimis, quia scite
haeret terrestribus, sive constat, tuto et cum dignitate procedit vel in
humilioribus; non praepeditus indagine, non varietate distractus.
Caetera sileo; id assero mirum de te. Plerique docti in agenda re
una, multiplicare delinquunt, variabiles sunt. Tu quicquid varieta-
tum amplecteris, quaestionem tuam semper reddis unam; et

quocunque in eadem divertas, quantumcunque deflectas, et quidem
ultro, licet multum in alieno progredi videaris, continenter tuam
causam agis (tua porro causa nostra est) unus semper idem legenti,
fixus in re, in te ipso consistens, a via declinans, sed non aberrans a
negotii constantia ..."

V. FROM A LETTER OF G. NAUDÉ, DATED 23RD DECEMBER, 1635:

"... Tuae vero Quaestiones cum subiecto sint variae, fine nobiles,
usu ipso necessariae, tantum insuper illis ornamenti ab ingenio,
tantum soliditatis a judicio, tantumque ab improbo labore erudi-
tionis conciliasti, ut superbiam, meritis tuis quaesitam, haud injuria
sumere possis, et ita de te ipso sentire, et loqui quasi monumentum
exegeris aere perennius.
    Quod non imber edax, non aquilo impotens possit diruere, aut
innumerabilis annorum series et fuga temporum...
Tandiu, Paule Zacchia, nomen tuum in immensae gloriae sudo
conquiescet, tandiu, quod nunquam alteri contingit, arbiter eris
eorum quibus de reliquis arbitria facere concessum est.
Atque erit in triplici par tibi nemo foro. Et sane, cum huius tui
laboris, quo nullum censeo vel Reipublicam a gravissimis difficulta-
tibus explicandae convenientiorem, vel illustrandis legum ac medicinae studiis, quae plurimum iam provecta sunt, aliorum industria
majorem, aut meliorem afferri potuisse, tales encomiastas nactus
sis, quibus praestantiores non in urbe, nec orbe invenias. Miror
profecto maiorem in modum vestram omnium fortunam, qui ita
simul convenistis ut, quod tu omnium optimus opus exarasti, illi
omnium optimi non probarent modo, sed lauderent ..."

VI. FROM A LETTER OF ZACUTO (KNOWN AS LUSITANUS), DATED 10TH NOVEMBER, 1635:

"Miraberis fortasse, eruditissime Zacchia, quod ad te ignotus scrip-
serim, et praesertim tanti nominis virum ...
Cum videndi Quaestiones tuas Medico-legales iam diu desiderio
exardescerem, quarum mirificam doctrinam omnis medicorum chor-
us unanimiter suscipit, et veneratur, ecce convenio bibliopolam,
qui, cum me doctorum librorum hellvonem agnoscat, in manus meas
obtulit statim opera tua ... Ea emi, vidi, legi, obstupui: nec enim
putabam in nostrae professionis hominibus tot diversarum faculta-
tum dotes eximias posse cumulari ... Verum superavit praesentia
famam: inveni siquidem non sellulariam ac trivialem in eis doctrinam, sed qualem Hippocratis, aut Ulpiani, Graecaeve antiquitatis
fuisse memorant: nam in his scientiis adusque miraculum caeteros

excellis; cum sis, mirum dictu, in auctorum lectione versatissimus, quoniam graviter dissertas, subtilissime obiicis, et ardua, atque hactenus non tentata dubia, omnium primus in argumento novo patefacis, aperis, emedullas ...
Vale iterum, Aesculapius ipse meus, et medicinae decus".

VII. Among the tributes, there is also an extract from the book of L. ALLACCI, *Apes Urbanae*. Allacci mentioned a number of authors who spoke "cum laude" of Zacchia. Mark Aurelio Severino called Zacchia "medicorum et iureconsultorum Mercurium", and "medicorum et iurisperitorum Hermes italicus".

Roderigo da Castro dedicated a number of verses "D. Paolo Zacchiae, viro praestantissimo, *Quaestionum Medicolegalium* auctori celeberrimo, in alma Urbe archiatro laudatissimo, omni literarum genere ornatissimo, cuius fama nomenque longe lateque, communi iureconsultorum medicorumque applausu pervagatum":

"Paulus erat quondam, medica qui floruit arte.
Legifer insignis Paulus et alter erat.
Mira loquor, Paulum superat nunc Paulus utrumque,
seu medicas artes, seu sacra iura colat.

Extulerat magnum iuris prudentiae Celsum;
alter erat medica Celsus in arte potens.
Dat nunc Roma virum, non Celsum nomine, sed re;
ille autem duplici nomine Celsus erit.

Gaudent iura sibi medicas connectere leges.
Qui queat hoc, medicus iure peritus erit.
Iure tibi duplex debetur, Paule, corona;
Non tamen ex facili est utraque lecta iugo".

Ludovico Settala wrote this to Zacchia in a letter from Milan, dated 21st September, 1628:

"... Laudo igitur in libris tuis duo haec, in indagandis controversis solertiam, in enodandis maturitatem. Quin illud dignius est, et non vulgares exposcit laudes, quod praestantissimas duas facultates, a quibus gubernatur et servantur homines, nempe iurisprudentiam et medicinam, olim inter se de principatu concertantes, amico, et certissimo foedere, quasi sorores inter se unieris, ut et leges statuat medicina et iurisprudentia medeatur. Iamque iudex et morborum peccata litesque concertantium humorum cognoscet, et remedia praecipiet; et ex adverso, foro et tribunali donasti medicinam; nec immerito quidem, quoniam et lex ipsa est animorum medela, ac medicina vere dixeris corporum legem. Ita et medentur utraeque, et leges ambae constituunt et iudicant".

L. Allacci himself, having read the first seven books, wrote the following lines in honour of Zacchia:

"Paulus at absolvit septem cum laude libellis artis opus medicae, iuris et egit opus.
Lex ubi corporibus, reddit medicina salutem mentibus, et varias ars obit una vices.
Mentibus an leges medicus non pandit?
An ultro laesa pari iudex non ope membra iuvat?".

Titulus III: De praegnantia, superfoetatione et mola.

Q.   I. An praegnantia ex certis quibusdam signis possi in-
fallibiliter cognosci.

      II. De signis ex quibus praegnantiae coniectura depromi
potest.

      III. An detur superfoetatio, quomodo et quanto tempore
post priorem conceptionem fieri possit.

      IV. Quid sit superfoetatio.

      V. Quid sit mola.

      VI. Utrum mola absque viri concubitu generari possit.

      VII. An molam gerens mulier ad quosdam effectus praeg-
nans dici debeat.

Titulus IV: De morte causa partus.

Q.   I. De causa exceptionis mortis violentae et mortis ex
partu et causa partus, quae fieri solet in contractibus
societatum.

      II. Quandonam mors ex partu, aut praegnantia eveniens
debeat censeri excepta.

      III. Declarantur ea verba in instrumento apposita, excep-
ta morte partus, et causa partus et praegnantiae.

      IV. Particulares casus, ac regulae exceptioni locum
facientes.

      V. Casus pro lucro facientes.

      VI. Partus et praegnantia in casibus exceptionis quomodo
debeant esse causa mortis.

      VII. Casus aliqui dubii proponuntur ac solvuntur.

      VIII. Argumenta in contrarium obiecta proponuntur ac
resolvuntur.

      IX. Eorum omnium, quae in universo hoc titulo continen-
tur, Epilogus.

Titulus V: De similitudine et dissimilitudine natorum.

Q.   I. De causis similitudinis natorum, variae auctorum
sententiae.

      II. De differentiis similitudinum, earumque causis.

      III. Quid sit simile, quid dissimile, ac de vera et adae-
quatae similitudinis causa.

      IV. Similitudo an debeat facere coniecturam filiationis.

      V. Filius mulieris, quae ab obitu prioris mariti illico alteri
nupsit, cuiusnam censendus.

LIBRI SECUNDI

Titulus I: De dementia, et rationis laesione, et morbis omnibus, qui rationem laedunt.

Q.   I. De multiplici dementia et huiusmodi nominum acceptione.
      II. De pluribus amentiae differentiis.
     III. De signis non sanae mentis.
    IV. Quaenam animi facultates, ac qua ratione, in quibusque dementiis laedantur.
     V. De rationis diminutione ex defectu aetatis et sexus.
    VI. De rationis laesione ex animi passionibus, et ex pravitate morum.
   VII. De ignorantibus, fatuis, stolidis, obliviosis, et memoria orbatis.
  VIII. De mutis et surdis.
    IX. De melancholicis.
     X. De amantibus.
    XI. De ebriis.
   XII. De dormientibus et noctambulis.
  XIII. De lethargicis, comatosis, caroticis, omnisque generis somniculosis.
  XIV. De apoplecticis, epilepticis, lunaticis, et huiusmodi.
   XV. De ictis a fulmine, attonitis, congelatis, et catalepticis.
  XVI. De phreneticis, maniacis, furiosis, ecstaticis, lycanthropicis, cynanthropicis, etc.
 XVII. De hydrophobis, seu rabiosis, ex assumpto veneno delirantibus, etc.
XVIII. De daemoniacis, fanaticis, lymphaticis, praestigiatis, enthusiasticis, engastrimythis, et similibus.
  XIX. De syncopizantibus, sensu defectis, agonizantibus, et in articulo mortis positis.
   XX. De mente alienatis ex morbis longis, seu vehementibus, ut peste et similibus.
  XXI. De paraphreneticis, hypochondriacis, et omnibus dilucida intervalla habentibus.
 XXII. De suffocatis ex utero, et ex utero furentibus.
XXIII. In quibusdam dementibus locum habeant eae conclusiones, nimirum: Semel furiosus semper praesumitur furiosus; et illa: Demens de praeterito praesumitur etiam demens de praesenti.

Titulus II: De venenis, et veneficiis, et aliis ad ea pertinentibus.

Q.   I. De veneni nomine, et appellatione.
        II. De venenorum divisione, et de variis venenorum effectibus.
       III. De venenorum divisione iuxta eorum effectus.
        IV. De qualitate et quantitate veneni.
         V. An venenum sic proprie dictum possit in nostro corpore generari.
        VI. An dentur certa signa assumpti veneni.
       VII. De signis propinati veneni, et de fallacia, et validitate eorum signorum.
      VIII. De veneni ingeniti certitudine, et de signis distinctivis inter unum et aliud nonnulla reiterantur.
        IX. An venenum veneno resistat.
         X. An detur venenum ad tempus.
        XI. Venenandi, qui modi possibles, qui non.
       XII. Quorum praecipue venenorum commercium sit inter-dicendum.
      XIII. De veneficiis, incantamentis, et fascino.

Titulus III: In. ll. aliquot, ff. de Aedilitio edicto.

Q.   I. De edicti, aedilitii causa, et de morbi conditionibus, qui locum redhibitioni facere debeant.
        II. De morbi ac vitii appellatione, et de differentia inter morbum et vitium.
       III. De animi vitiis.
        IV. De morbi gravitate et levitate et de morbo sontico.
         V. De melancholicis et fatuis.
        VI. De impetigine, prurigine et scabie.
       VII. De spadonibus et eunuchis.
      VIII. De lingua abscissa et mutitate.
        IX. De caeteris loquelae vitiis.
         X. De vitiis sensus visus.
        XI. De oris foeditate, edentulis, gutturosis, et antiadas habentibus.
       XII. De varis et vatiis, et claudis et varicosis.
      XIII. De praegnante et puerpera, de pariente mortuos: de sterili et arcta: de ea quae bis in mense purgatur.
       XIV. Sanatus quis dicatur? De convalescentibus, de recidi-vantibus, et de morbis circuitus habentibus.
        XV. De hydropico, clavum habente, polyposo, scaeva et manco, et de urinam faciente.

LIBRI TERTII

Titulus I: De impotentia coeundi et generandi.

Q.   I. De causis impotentiae tam coeundi, quam generandi.
         II. De impotentia ex defectu aetatis.
        III. De impotentia ex defectu naturali.
         IV. De impotentia ex morbis.
          V. De frigidis et maleficiatis.
         VI. De impotentia *respectiva* dicta.
        VII. De sterilitate foeminarum et de imperforatis.
       VIII. Mulier an ex semine virili concipere possit absque eius
             coniunctione, et sine totali membrorum applicatione.
         IX. De hermaphroditis, spadonibus et eunuchis.

Titulus II: De morborum simulatione.

Q.   I. Qui morbi ut plurimum, simulari soleant, qui item
             facilius, qui difficilius simulari possint.
         II. Qua ratione deprehendantur qui morbum simulant.
        III. De simulata febre, effictisque ulceribus.
         IV. De simulato dolore.
          V. De simulata insania.
         VI. De simulato morbo cum defectu animi et sensus
             amissione, ut syncope, apoplexia, epilepsia, ecstasi et
             aliis.
        VII. De simulata virginitate.
       VIII. De simulata praegnantia, et de partu supposito.
         IX. Mulierem peperisse, aut abortum fecisse, ex quibus
             coniici possit.
          X. De morbos dissimulantibus.

Titulus III: De peste et contagio.

Q.   I. Pestis quid sit, quid item epidemia, et quae sit inter
             eas differentia.
         II. Quas conditiones habere oporteat morbum epidemi-
             cum, ut pestis dicatur, et ad hoc ut pestis privilegiis
             locus detur.
        III. De signis futurae aut praesentis pestis.
         IV. De cura praeservativa a peste.
          V. Quid sit contagium, quid et quotuplex contagiosus
             morbus.

VI. Iurisconsultorum assertiones nonnullae circa contagium, et contagiosos morbos, quibus in casibus locum habeant.

LIBRI QUARTI

Titulus I: De miraculis.

Q. I. Quid sit miraculum.
II. De variis miraculorum generibus.
III. De conditionibus effectus miraculosi.
IV. Vera miracula cum raro fiant, multa tamen et frequenter facta celebrantur.
V. De prophetia, seu rerum futurarum praedictione, occultarumque cognitione.
VI. De ecstasi et raptu.
VII. De longo ieiunio.
VIII. De miraculosa infirmorum sanatione.
IX. De morte miraculosa, et de morbis divinitus immissis.
X. De cadaverum incorruptibilitate, et aliis nonnullis ad ea pertinentibus.
XI. De mortuorum resurrectione.

Titulus II: De virginitate et stupro.

Q. I. Virginitas proprie quid sit, et an ex certis signis cognosci possit.
II. De minus fallacibus notis, ac coniecturis virginitatis.
III. De signis violatae virginitatis.
IV. De tempore nubendi in virginibus.
V. Constuprati pueri signa.

LIBRI QUINTI

Titulus I: De ieiunio et quadragesima.

Q. I. Quid sit ieiunium et quotuplex, ad quem finem ab Ecclesia institutum, et quot conditiones ad illius observantiam requirantur.
II. An ieiunium et praecipue quadragesimale corporeae saluti sit noxium.

XII. Pluribus simul, eodemque casu extinctis, quis citius, quis posterius expiraverit.

Titulus III: De membris, eorumque mutilatione et debilitate.

Q.   I. Membrum quid sit, et quaenam proprie membra sint in corpore.
        II. De mutilatione, impedimento et debilitate membrorum.
      III. Mutilata membra an reparari possint.
      IV. De naso, auribus et labiis.
       V. De oculis, barba, dentibus et lingua.
      VI. De manibus, pedibus et digitis.
    VII. De pene, testibus et mammillis.

Titulus IV: De aere, aquis et locis.

Q.   I. De boni, ac mali aeris conditionibus et signis.
        II. De aquis, earumque bonitate, et vitio.
      III. Quae servitutes aquis impositae ipsarum aquarum bonitati praeiudicare possint.
      IV. De locorum salubritate, et insalubritate.
       V. Quaenam et quo tempore tuta aeris et locorum mutatio, et quae vero non tuta.
      VI. Quae incommoda sanitatis ex importunis aedificiis vicinis habitantibus immineant.
    VII. De cloacis, aquaeductibus, canalibus, horreis, hortis, pomariis, furno, fornacibus, sterquiliniis, latrinis, stabulis et de artibus, immundis.

LIBRI SEXTI

Titulus I: De medicorum erroribus a lege punibilibus.

Q.   I. Medici nomine qui veniant hic, quot modis errare medicus dicatur, et quinam errores sint a lege punibiles.
        II. In quibus casibus dolus, in quibus vero ignorantia, in quibus denique negligentia praesumi possit.
      III. De erroribus medicorum rationalium et primo de iis, qui ad mores et scientiam spectant.
      IV. De erroribus omissionis ad consilia spectantibus.

V. De erroribus commissionis ad consilia spectantibus.
VI. De erroribus omissionis circa operationem.
VII. De erroribus commissionis circa operationem.
VIII. De erroribus tam in omittendo, quam in committendo ad mercedem spectantibus.
IX. De chirurgorum, aliorumque similium artificum erroribus.
X. De aromatariorum et seplasiariorum erroribus.
XI. De empiricorum et chimicorum erroribus.
XII. De obstetricum erroribus.
XIII. De assidentium seu ministrantium erroribus.

Titulus II: De tormentis et poenis.

Q.   I. Tormentum, quaestio, tortura, poena quid. Tormentorum quot genera, quot item genera poenarum.
II. De gradibus torturae et de carceribus.
III. De tormentis in specie, et primo de tormento funis.
IV. Quaenam impedimenta in causa esse possint, ne rei chordae tormento subiiciantur.
V. De tormento vigiliae.
VI. Reos in tormentis deficere ex quibusnam signis cognosci possit.
VII. De taxillis, sibillis et ferula.
VIII. De poenis.

Titulus III: De praecedentia inter medicum et iurisperitum.

Q.   I. Quid sit honor, quid praecedentia honor maior uni, quam alteri cur debeatur in republica.
II. Obiecta in medicum et medicos.
III. Obiecta in leges et legumperitiam.
IV. Respondetur iis, quae contra medicinam et medicos obiecta sunt.
V. Satisfit ad ea, quae contra iurisprudentiam, eiusque professores obiiciuntur.
VI. Lex quomodo orta; politica unde originem traxerit, unde item jurisperitia.
VII. Vocum ac terminorum elucidatio.
VIII. Decidendae quaestionis ratio ostenditur. Obiecta in contrarium respondetur.

LIBRI SEPTIMI

Titulus I: De monstris.

Q.   I. De monstri, ostenti, portenti, prodigii appellatione.
Monstrum quid et quotuplex.
II. De causis generationis monstrorum.
III. Quae monstra ex diversis specie animalibus progigni
possint, quae non, quae item ex humana specie
possibilia, quae non.
IV. Quae monstra in humana specie rationalem animam
sortiantur, quae non.
V. Bicorpora monstra et quae principaliora membra
duplicata habent, pro unicone homine, an pro gemino
habendo.
VI. Quae monstra vitalia, quae non vitalia.
VII. De partu ex incubis suscepto.
VIII. De hermaphroditis.
IX. Novae monstrorum aliquorum historiae, et alia circa
hanc materiam scitu digna.

Titulus II: De officiis divinis.

Q.   I. Quaenam requirantur in recitandis officiis divinis,
quae item in Missa, vel dicenda, vel audienda.
II. Quinam morbi excusare possint a privata divinorum
recitatione.
III. De recitatione publica in choro facienda.
IV. Qui recitare officia divina non possunt, an teneantur
alium recitantem audire, et quaenam etiam ab audi-
tione recitanda hominem excusare possint.
V. Qui morbi Missae dicendae, quive audiendae impedimento esse possint.
VI. Medica praecepta in recitandis divinis officiis iis servanda, quibus recitatio ab aliquem morbum noxia
quoquo modo esse posset.

Titulus III: De debito coniugali.

Q.   I. Quando, quantum, quomodo debitum coniugale sit
reddendum.
II. De his, quae virum a redditione debiti excusare
possunt ex parte sui.

III. De his, quae uxorem a debito reddendo excusant ex parte sui.

IV. De his, quae vel alterum, vel utrumque coniugem prohibent exigere.

V. De his, quae coniuges a redditione debiti excusant ex parte alterius.

VI. Examinantur nonnulla, quae secundum canonistas in usu matrimonii cum peccato inter coniuges contingunt.

Titulus IV: De stigmatibus magorum.

Q.   I. Quid sint stigmata, de quibus hic, et historica eorum disquisitio.

II. Utrum eiusmodi naturae stigmata dari possint.

III. Rationes nonnullae in stigmatum defensionem producuntur, illisque occurritur.

IV. Naturane, an arte caro viventis hominis ita affici possit ut puncta dolorem non sentiat, nec sanguinem effundat.

V. Ex praecedentibus quid eliciendum.

LIBRI OCTAVI

Titulus I: De irregularitate.

Q.   I. Irreguralitas quid et quotuplex, et quaenam circa eam medicus considerare possit.

II. De irregularitate spirituali et utrum medicinae exercitium inducat irregularitatem.

III. De irregularitate ob causam morbi in genere.

IV. De morbis magis specialiter, et primo de iis qui secundum canonistas ad animum spectant.

V. De epilepsia et apoplexia.

VI. De caeteris morbis, ex quorum culpa homo evadit irregularis et primo de morbis capitis.

VII. De vitiis oculorum.

VIII. De nasi vitiis, aurium ac labiorum.

IX. De vitiis oris, palati, dentium, gingivarum, linguae.

X. De vitiis pectoris, partiumque caeterarum spiritualium.

XI. De stomachi seu oesophagi et ventriculi vitiis.

XII. De vitiis intestinorum, hepatis, lienis.
XIII. De renum, et vesicae urinariae vitiis.
XIV. De vitiis membrorum generationis.
XV. De externarum partium vitiis et primo de vitiis capillorum, cutis, capitis, colli, spondilium et vertebrarum.
XVI. De faciei et conspicuarum partium cicatricibus, maculis et defoedationibus.
XVII. De vitiis brachiorum, pedum, et manuum, ac digitorum.
XVIII. De crurum et ambulationis vitiis.
XIX. De membris superfluentibus.
XX. De podagra et arthritide.
XXI. De scabie et lepra, caeterisque cutis infectionibus.
XII. De morbo gallico.
XXIII. De febre et peste.
XXIV. De irregularitate foeminarum.

Titulus II: De remediis medicis.

Q.   I. Quaenam sint remedia medica; quaenam personae circa eorum usum errare soleant. Infirmus an et in quibus casibus teneatur medico obedire.
II. Diaetetica.
III. Pharmaceutica.
IV. Chirurgica.

Titulus III: De clausura monialium.

Q.   I. Quid sit clausura, utrum noxia, et quibus ex causis moniales possint a clausura exire.
II. Utrum praeter pestem et lepram alii morbi sint iusta causa exeundi a clausura.
III. Vigente peste, aut lepra in aliqua clausura, sanae ne, an infirmae ab ea exire permittendae.
IV. Moniales lepra, vel peste infectae, et a clausura dimissae, si sanentur quandonam reverti ad clausuram teneantur.
V. De monialibus, quae ex culpa aeris ipsius clausurae infirmantur, et in quibus casibus videatur adesse iusta causa relinquendi clausuram.

LIBRI NONI

Titulus I: De foetus humani animatione.

Q.   I. Quid semen? Quid anima?
        II. Semina quorumcunque viventium, homine excepto, propriam animam ex traduce a progenitoribus reci-pere.
        III. Animam rationalem ex traduce non esse.
        IV. Animam rationalem de novo creari et infundi.
        V. Foetum humanum nullo unquam tempore alia anima dotari nisi rationali, eamque in ipso primo concep-tionis momento a Deo creatam et infusam recipere.

Titulus II: De foetu exsecto, seu de partu caesareo.

        Quaestio unica. Appendix ad Titulum secundum libri primi *Quaestionum medico-legalium*, post quaes-tionem quintam.

Titulus III: De impedimentis coeundi et generandi.

Q.   I. De impedimentis copulae carnalis in viro: et primo de impedimento ob aetatem minorem aut maiorem.
        II. De impedimento coitus ob frigiditatem et maleficium.
        III. De impedimento copulae ob membri magnitudinem, et alia vitia praeter naturam.
        IV. De impotentia copulae ex morbis aut praesentibus aut praegressis.
        V. De impedimento coitus ex parte mulieris.
        VI. De impedimento generandi ex parte viri.
        VII. De impedimentis generandi ex parte mulieris.

Titulus IV: De resignatione beneficiorum.

        Quaestio unica, de variis causis resignandi beneficia ecclesiastica, de quibus medici consulendi sunt.

Titulus V: De terminus sumendae experientiae eorum qui de peste suspecti sunt.

        Quaestio unica, de peste et contagio. Ad ornatum tit. 3, lib. 3, *Quaestionum medico-legalium*.

Titulus VI: Ars conficiendi sericum an tempore pestis sit excluden-
da a civitate tanquam ars immunda.

Quaestio unica. Appendix ad tit. 3, lib. 3, *Quaestionum medico-legalium*.

Titulus VII: De tabacco.

Quaestio unica. De ieiunio et quadragesima: ad orna-
tum tit. 1, lib. 5, *Quaestionum medico-legalium*.

Titulus VIII: De choccolata et Aqua vitae.

Quaestio unica: de ieiunio et quadragesima, ad tit. 1,
lib. 5, *Quaestionum medico-legalium*.

Titulus IX: De morbis impedientibus Eucharistiae sumptionem.
Quaestio unica: variae morborum species consideran-
tur, ex quibus non debet parochus sacrosanctam
Eucharistiam eis laborantibus ministrare.

Titulus X: De dissolutione matrimonii, divortio, tori separatione
et solutione sponsalium.

Q.   I. Quid sit matrimonii dissolutio, quid divortium, quid
tori separatio, quid dissolutio sponsalium.
II. De dissolutione matrimonii ob impedimentum con-
summationis non amovibile.
III. De divortio.
IV. De tori separatione.
V. De dissolutione sponsalium.

Titulus XI: De semine foemineo.

Quaestio unica: Appendix ad tit. 3, lib. 7, *Quaestionum medico-legalium*.

Titulus XII: De primogenitis.

Q.   I. Quis dicatur primogenitus.
II. Priorem conceptum ultimo nasci, quae ratio persua-
dere possit.
III. Ex naturae ordine priorem conceptum, priorem nasci.

    IV. An ex accidenti evenire possit, ut posterior conceptus prior nascatur.

    V. In dubio quis ex gemellis prior natus praesumendus.

    VI. Quis ex gemellis ab utero matris exsectis praesumendus prior natus.

LIBER DECIMUS

Continet responsa seu consilia octoginta quinque, ad materias medico-legales pertinentia; necnon decisionum sacrae Rotae Romanae, ad easdem materias spectantium centuriam.

BIBLIOGRAPHY

ZACCHIA PAOLO, *Il vitto quaresimale*, Rome 1637.
ZACCHIA PAOLO, *De' mali hipochondriaci*, Rome 1639.
ZACCHIA PAOLO, *Quaestiones medico-legales*, Lyon 1661.

SOURCES AND ANCIENT WRITERS

ALLACCI, L., *Apes urbanae sive de viris illustribus qui ab anno 1630 per totum 1632 Romae adfuerunt, ac typis aliquid evulgarunt*, Rome 1644.
ANTONINUS (S.), *Summa maior*, Venice 1503.
ARISTOTLE, *Opera omnia*, ed. F. DIDOT, Paris 1854.
AVICENNA, *Canon medicinae, quo universa medendi scientia pulcherrima et brevi methodo planissime explicatur*, Venice 1595.
AZPILCUETA, M.D. (alias Dr. Navarro), *Consiliorum sive responsorum libri quinque, iuxta ordinem Decretalium dispositi*, Rome 1590.
BERNARD OF PAVIA, *Summa de matrimonio*, ed. LASPEYRES, Ratisbonne 1860.
BERNARD OF PAVIA, *Summa Decretalium*, ed. LASPEYRES, Ratisbonne 1860.
COSCI, C., *De separatione thori coniugalis*, Florence 1856.
D'ANDREA, J., *In IV Decretalium librum novella commentaria*, Venice 1581.
DE TABIA, J.C., *Summa*, Venice 1569.
DE TRANI, G., *Summa in titulos Decretalium*, Venice 1586.
FEIJE, H.J., *De impedimentis et dispensationibus matrimonii*, Louvain 1893.
GALEN, C., *Oper omnia*, in *Medicorum graecorum opera quae extant*, ed. GOTTLOB KÜHN, Leipzig 1882.
GONZALEZ-TELLEZ, E., *Commentaria perpetua in singulos textus quinque librorum Decretalium*, Lyon 1715.
GRATIAN, *Decretum Magistri Gratiani*, in *Corpus Iuris Canonici*, vol. I, ed. RITCHER & FRIEDBERG, Leipzig 1879.
GUTIÉRREZ, J., *Canonicarum quaestionum*, Frankfurt 1607.
GUTIÉRREZ, J., *Quaestiones tam ad sponsalia de futuro quam ad matrimonia eorumque impedimenta pertinentes*, Venice 1618.
HOSTIENSIS (Henry de Segusio), *Summa Aurea*, Venice 1574.

HOSTIENSIS (Henry de Segusio), *In Decretalium libros commentaria*, Venice 1581.

INNOCENT IV (Sinibaldus Fliscus), *In quinque Decretalium libros commentaria*, Venice 1610.

LEDESMA, P., *Tractatus de magno matrimonii sacramento*, Venice 1595.

LITTRÉ, *Oeuvres complètes d'Hippocrate*, Paris 1839.

MANDOSIO, P., *Theatron in quo maximorum christiani orbis pontificium archiatros Prosper Mandosius inspectandos exhibet*, Rome 1784.

MANSELLA, J., *De impedimentis matrimonium dirimentibus ac de processu iudiciali in causis matrimonialibus*, Rome 1881.

MARINI, G., *Degli archiatri pontifici*, Rome 1784.

PALUDANUS, P., *Lucubrationum opus in quartum sententiarum*, Salamanca 1552.

PANORMITANUS (Nicholas Tudeschus), *Commentaria in Decretales*, Venice 1578.

PICHLER, V., *Jus canonicum secundum quinque decretalium titulos Gregorii Papae IX explicatum*, Venice 1758.

PRAEPOSITUS (J. Antonius a S. Giorgio), *Commentaria in Decretales*, Venice 1579.

SALMANTICENSES (in coll.), *Cursus theologiae moralis*, Venice 1750.

SÁNCHEZ, T., *De sancto matrimonii sacramento disputationum*, Lyon 1654.

SCHMALZGRUEBER, F., *Jus ecclesiasticum universum*, Rome 1845.

SCHMIER, F., *Iurisprudentia canonico-civilis seu Jus canonicum universum*, Salzbourg 1729.

SILVESTER PRIERAS, *Summa*, Venice 1572.

SIXTUS V, *Cum frequenter* (27th June 1587), in *C.I.C. Fontes*, vol. I, 1923.

SOTO, D., *Commentarium in quartum sententiarum*, Venice 1575.

S.C. CONCILII, *Thesaurus Resolutionum S.C. Concilii quae consentanee ad Tridentinorum Patrum decreta aliasque canonici iuris sanctiones prodierunt in causis ab anno 1° (1718) ad annum 168° (1909-1910)*, voll. 1-5, Urbino 1739-1740; voll. 6ff., Rome 1741ff.

TANCREDI, V., *Summa de matrimonio*, ed. WUNDERLICH, Gottingen 1841.

THOMAS AQUINAS (S.), *Commentaria in quattuor libros sententiarum*, in *Opera omnia*, vol. VI-VII, 2, New York 1948.

VOLANTES, P.U.G. collection, 1640-1870.

MODERN AUTHORS

ABBO, J.A., *De quibusdam quaestionibus iuris matrimonialis iuxta rotalem iurisprudentiam*, in *Apollinaris*, 40(1967)571-590.

AGOSTINI, A., *Considerazioni sull'impotenza sessuale maschile*, in *Sessuologia*, 2(1961)48-57.

AGUIRRE, Ph., *De impotentia viri iuxta jurisprudentiam rotalem*, in *Periodica*, 36(1947)5-23.

ALPI, M., *De viri coeundi impotentia sive organica sive psicogena. Ad usum privatum*. Rome 1979.

ALVAREZ-MENÉNDEZ, S., *De matrimonio rato et non consummato ac probationibus tum communibus tum speciali in casu afferendis*, in *L'Année Canonique*, 15(1971)23-58.

AMERIO, A., *La preminenza della medicina sul diritto nel pensiero di Paolo Zacchia*, in *Medicina nei Secoli*, 8 (1971)4:51ff.

ANTONELLI, J., *De conceptu impotentiae et sterilitatis relate ad matrimonium*, Rome 1900.

ANTONELLI, J., *Pro conceptu impotentiae et sterilitatis relate ad matrimonium. Animadversiones in opus P. Eschbach, Disputationes*, Rome 1901.

ANTONELLI, J., *De mulieris excisae impotentia ad matrimonium*, Rome 1903.

ANTONELLI, J., *Brevis synopsis historica circa evolutionem doctrinae de impotentia et sterilitate apud veteres doctores*, Rome 1932.

ARENDT, G., *Relectio analitica super controversia de impotentia feminae ad generandum*, Rome 1913.

ARENDT, G., *Circa controversiam validitatis matrimonii feminae excisae*, Rome 1923.

ARENDT, G., *De absoluta habilitate sterilium ad matrimonium*, in *Ius Pontificium*, 5(1925)77-93.

ARENDT, G., *De recentissima disquisitoria circa impotentiam mulieris*, ibid., pp. 94-100.

ARENDT, G., *Num mulier occlusa possit consummare matrimonium*, in *Periodica*, 16(1927)70-78.

ARENDT, G., *De genuina ratione impedimenti impotentiae*, in *Ephemerides Theologicae Lovanienses*, 9(1932)28-69, 442-450.

AZZOLINI, L., *De impedimento impotentiae in viro. Disceptatio de Ep. "Cum frequenter" Sixti V*, in *Studi di Scienze Ecclesiastiche*, vol. II, Napoli 1961, pp. 235-244.

BAFFONI, A., *Il pensiero medico e biologico di Platone e quello di Ippocrate*, in *Pagine di Storia della Medicina*, 4 (1960) 3-14.

BALLESTER, L.G., *Aproximación genetica a la obra anatómica de Galeno*, in *Asclepio*, 23 (1971) 191-210.

BALLESTER, L.G., *Galeno. En la sociedad y en la ciencia de su tiempo*, Madrid 1972.

BAMBERG, A., *L'impuissance organique de la femme d'après la jurisprudence rotale récente (1970-1981)*, Luxembourg 1982.

BARILLARO, *Nullità di matrimonio per mancanza di organi necessari per la generazione*, in *Il Diritto Ecclesiastico*, 58 (1947) 319 ff.

BERGH, E., *Impotentia ob defectum seminis testicularis*, in *Nouvelle Revue Théologique*, 78 (1946) 338-346.

BERSINI, F., *Un aspetto dell'impotenza virile nella concezione personalistica della sessualità*, in *Studi di Diritto Canonico in onore di Marcello Magliocchetti*, vol. I, Rome 1974, pp. 149-196.

BERSINI, F., *De muliere excisa et de vagina occlusa in ordine ad validitatem matrimonii*, in *Monitor Ecclesiasticus*, 99 (1974) 232-254.

BERSINI, F., *La dibattuta questione del "verum semen"*, in *Monitor Ecclesiasticus*, 101 (1976) 256-278.

BERSINI, F., *Validità del matrimonio e impotenza maschile. In un recente Decreto della Sacra Congregazione per la Dottrina della Fede*, in *La Civiltà Cattolica*, 1977/4:234-247.

BERSINI, F., *Il decreto circa l'impotenza che dirime il matrimonio e la problematica da esso suscitata*, in *Il Diritto Ecclesiastico*, 90 (1978/II) 228-241.

BERSINI, F., *In margine al decreto circa l'impotenza che dirime il matrimonio*, in *Monitor Ecclesiasticus*, 104 (1979) 338-351.

BERSINI, F., *Matrimonio e anomalie sessuali e psicosessuali*, Rome 1980.

BOGANELLI, *De coacta sterilitate*, in *Apollinaris*, 9 (1936) 58 ff.

BRIZON, J., *Malformations de l'appareil genital musculin et azoospermies*, in *Cahiers Laennec*, 16 (1956) 3-11.

CAMPBELL, F.-HARRISON, J., *Urology*, Philadelphia, London, Toronto 1970.

CANDOR, *De aequa extensione conceptus impotentiae prout est impedimentum dirimens. Sterilitas non est impotentia generandi*, in *Jus Pontificium*, 7 (1927) 90-96.

CAPALTI, L., *Per un nuovo indirizzo nello studio dell'impedimentum impotentiae*, in *Il Diritto Ecclesiastico*, 40 (1929) 360-370.

CAPALTI, L., *Fisiologi e canonisti nello studio dell'impedimentum impotentiae*, in *Il Diritto Ecclesiastico*, 59 (1948) 26-33.

CAPPARONI, P., *Profili bio-bibliografici di medici e naturalisti celebri italiani dal secolo XV al secolo XVIII*, Rome 1926.

CAPPELLO, F., *La sterilità maschile e l'impedimento d'impotenza*, in *Archivio di Diritto Ecclesiastico*, 4 (1942) 237-250.

CAPPELLO, F., *Tractatus canonico-moralis de sacramentis*, tom. V, *De matrimonio*, Rome 1961.

CAPPONI, N., *Impotenza maschile e decreto del 13 maggio 1977 della S. Congregazione per la Dottrina della Fede*, in *Il Diritto Ecclesiastico*, 89 (1978/II) 53-65.

CASORIA, J., *De matrimonio rato et non consummato*, Roma 1959.

CASTAÑEDA DELGADO, E., *Una sentencia española en el siglo XVI. La validez del matrimonio de los eunucos y espadones*, in *Revista Española de Derecho Canónico*, 12 (1957) 259-287.

CASTELLANI, C., *Intuizioni endocrinologiche nelle opere di alcuni autori italiani del '600*, in *Castalia*, 18 (1962) 15 ff.

CASTELLANI, C., *Il problema della generazione da Ippocrate al XX secolo*, in *Bollettino delle Riunioni Medico-chirurgiche*, 46 (1963) 1-23.

CASTIGLIONI, A., *A history of medicine*, New York 1947.

CERAFOLI, G.E., *De periti interventu iudicisque decisione in vaginismi casibus*, in *Studi di Diritto Canonico in onore di Marcello Magliocchetti*, vol. I, Rome 1974, pp. 279-295.

CERATO, P., *La controversa impotenza femminile al matrimonio*, Padova 1949.

CERCHIARI, E., *Cappellani Papae et Apostolicae Sedis Auditores causarum sacri palatii apostolici seu Sacra Romana Rota*, Rome 1921.

CHAPUT, R., *Opérations chirurgicales et impuissance*, in *Studia Canonica*, 1 (1967) 37-43.

CHARTIER, M., *Malformations de l'appareil génital féminin et vaginisme*, in *Cahiers Laennec*, 16 (1965) 12-17.

CIAMPOLINI, A., *Sessualità e medicina legale*, Milan 1936.

CIRINEI, F., *La fisiologia di Galeno*, in *Scientia Veterum*, 23 (1961) 53-65.

CONSTANTINI, F., *De sexuali impotentia functionali viri in Decretalibus Gregorii IX et in neuropsychiatria hodierna*. Appendix in *Actorum Congressus Iuridici Internationalis*, Rome 1936.

CONSTANTINI, F., *De vaginismo ut causa impotentiae mulieris*, in *Apollinaris*, 11 (1938) 377-380.

CORNAGGIA-MEDICI, L., *Dell'essenza del matrimonio e di due recenti scritti sull'impedimento dell'impotenza*, in *Il Diritto Ecclesiastico*, 39 (1928) 398-442.

CORNAGGIA-MEDICI, L., *I capaci alla copula che si conoscono incapaci alla generazione*, in *Il Diritto Ecclesiastico*, 41 (1930) 3-10.

CORNAGGIA-MEDICI, L., *L'impotenza a generare si può produrre come causa di annullamento del matrimonio*, in *Il Diritto Ecclesiastico*, 43 (1932) 417 ff.

CORSINI, A. (dir.), *Vita dei medici e naturalisti illustri*, Florence 1928.

CRISCUOLO LIMIDO, M., *Fecondazione artificiale e matrimonio canonico*, in *La Scuola Cattolica*, CXV (1987) 1:32-47.

DAMIZIA, G., *Vasectomia e matrimonio*, in *Apollinaris*, 51 (1978) 146-193.

D'AVACK, P.A., *L'impotenza generativa maschile nel diritto matrimoniale canonico*, in *Il Diritto Ecclesiastico*, 62 (1951) 36 ff.

D'AVACK, P.A., *Cause di nullità e di divorzio nel diritto matrimoniale canonico*, vol. I, Florence 1952.

D'AVACK, P.A., *Corso di diritto canonico*, vol. I, *Il matrimonio*, Milan 1961.

D'AVACK, P.A., *Sul recente decreto della S. Congregazione per la Dottrina della Fede in tema d'impotenza maschile*, in *Rassegna di Teologia*, 19 (1978) 43-48.

DEFFENU, G., *Invito a Zacchia*, in *Castalia*, 9 (1953) 101-117.

DEL AMO PACHÓN, L., *La impotencia que dirime el matrimonio. Comentario al Decreto de 13 de mayo de 1977*, in *Revista Española de Derecho Canónico*, 33 (1977) 445-480.

DE MARTINI, V., *Considerazioni sulla dottrina dello pneuma in Galeno*, in *Pagine di Storia della Medicina*, 8 (1964) 41-48.

DE REINA, V., *Impotencia y esterilidad*, in *Ius Populi Dei*, vol. III, Rome 1972, pp. 441-465.

ECK, M., *L'impuissance psychique*, in *Cahiers Laennec*, 16 (1956) 23-50.

ESCHBACH, E., *Casus de feminae impotentia*, Rome 1899.

ESCHBACH, E., *Disputationes physiologico-theologicae*, Rome 1901.

ESCHBACH, E., *De novo quodam sterilitatis conceptu*, Rome 1902.

ESMEIN, A.-GENESTAL, R., *Le mariage en droit canonique*, Paris 1929.

FEDELE, P., *Punti controversi in tema di impotenza nella più recente giurisprudenza della Sacra Romana Rota*, in *Zacchia*, Serie 2a, XIV (1951) 204-213.

FEDELE, P., *L'Impotenza*, Rome 1962.

FEDELE, P., (Dir.), *Nuova nozione d'impotenza dell'uomo*. Quaderni romani di Diritto Canonico, vol. II, Rome 1978.

FERNÁNDEZ ALLER, P., *La impotencia en el matrimonio*. Salamanca 1960.

FERRERES, J.B., *De vasectomia duplici necnon de matrimonio mulieris excisae*, Madrid 1913.

FERRIO, C., *Trattato di psichiatria clinica e forense*, Torino 1970.

FORD, C.J., *Double vasectomy and the impediment of impotence*, in *Theological Studies*, 1955, pp. 533-557.

FRACHE, G., *Elementi di medicina legale della assicurazione vita negli scritti di Paolo Zacchia*, in *Atti del III Congresso Internazionale di medicina dell'Assicurazione Vita*, Rome 1949.

FRACHE, G., *Orientamenti giurisprudenziali in tema di impotenza generandi*, in *Zacchia*, Serie 2a, XIV (1951) 213-217.

FRANCESCHINI, P., *Il secolo di Galileo e il problema della generazione*, in *Physis*, 4

(1964) 141-204.

FRANCHINI, A., *Medicina legale in materia legale*, 2 ed., Naples 1968.

FRATTIN, P.L., *The matrimonial impediment of impotence; occlusion of the spermatic ducts and vaginismus*, Washington DC 1958.

GARCÍA FAILDE, J.J., *Nulidad de un matrimonio por impotencia funcional coeundi y por incapacidad, derivada de esa impotencia de concedar — aceptar el derecho — obligación a los actos por su naturaleza actos para la procreación*, in *Revista Española de Derecho Canónico*, 28 (1972) 127-234.

GASPARRI, P., *Tractatus canonicus de matrimonio*, Vatican City 1932.

GEMELLI, A., *De conceptus "impotentiae coeundi". Definitione sub respectu medicinae pastoralis*, in *Studi dedicati alla memoria di Paolo Zanzucchi della Facoltà di Giurisprudenza*, Milan 1927, pp. 411-458.

GERIN, C., *La medicina legale nei suoi momenti storici e nel suo sistema*, in *Zacchia*, Serie 2a, XII (1949) 1 ff.

GHERRO, S., *Il problema del "verum semen" nel "Breve" "Cum frequenter" di Sisto V*, in *Il Diritto Ecclesiastico*, 77 (1966) 98-117.

GIROLA, A., *De vero semine*, in *La sterilità nel matrimonio*, Milan 1966, pp. 177-199.

GOLDLEWSKI, S., *Les impuissances d'ordre neurologique*, in *Cahiers Laennec*, 4 (1956) 18-22.

GÓMEZ LÓPEZ, A., *El impedimento de impotencia en Tomás Sánchez*, Pamplona 1980.

GÓMEZ LÓPEZ, R., *Revisión del concepto de impotencia a la luz del Decreto de la Sagrada Congregación para la Doctrina de la Fe de 13.V.77*, in *Ius Canonicum*, 17 (1977) 159-205.

GORDON, I., *De processu super rato*, Rome 1977.

GORDON, I., *Adnotationes quaedam de valore matrimonii virorum qui ex toto secti sunt a tempore Gratiani usque ad Breve "Cum frequenter"*, in *Periodica*, 66 (1977) 171-247.

GORDON, I., *Decisio Signaturae Iustitiae diei 19 iunii 1834 qua nova forma contentiosi-administrativi in statu Pontificio introducta est*, in *Investigationes Theologico-Canonicae*, Rome 1978, pp. 185-210.

GRAZIANI, E., *Il caso limite della impotenza muliebre*, in *Il Diritto Ecclesiastico*, 57 (1946) 98 ff.

GRAZIANI, E., *L'impotenza maschile per mancanza dei didimi e per blocco delle vie spermatiche*, in *Il Diritto Ecclesiastico*, 58 (1947) 365-378.

GUTIÉRREZ, A., *Il matrimonio. Essenza, fine, amore coniugale con particolare riferimento alla donna recisa*, Naples 1974.

GUTIÉRREZ, A., *Mulier excisa potesne contrahere valide matrimonium?*, in *Ephemerides Iuris Canonici*, 33 (1977) 89-114.

GUTIÉRREZ, A., *In "de muliere excisa. Animadversiones in opus recens editum" contra animadersiones*, in *Periodica*, 64 (1975) 661-667.

HABERLINGER-HUBOTTER-VIERORDT, *Biographisches lexikon der hervorragenden Ärzte alle Zeiten und Volker*, vol. 5, Berlin-Wien 1934.

HARRINGTON, P., *The impediment of impotence and the notion of male impotency*, in *The Jurist*, 19 (1959) 29-66; 187-211; 309-351; 465-497.

HERVADA XIBERTA, F.J., *La impotencia de varon en el derecho matrimonial canónico*, Pamplona 1959.

HERVADA XIBERTA, F.J., *Sobre el hermafrodismo y la capacidad para el matrimonio*, in *Revista Española de Derecho Canónico*, 13 (1958) 100 ff.

KAHN, F., *La vita sessuale*, Rome 1973.

KAPLAN, H., *Nuove terapie sessuali*, Milan 1976.

KARPLUS, H., *Medical ethics in Paolo Zacchia's «Quaestiones medico-legales»*, in H. KAPLUS, ed., *International Symposium on Society, Medicine and Law, Jerusalem, March 1972*, Amsterdam 1973, pp. 125-134.

KELLY, W., *Pope Gregory II on Divorce and Remarriage*, Analecta Gregoriana 203, Rome 1975.

KNOX, J.R., *De copula coniugali inconsummativa matrimonii iuxta doctrinam et praxim S. Congregationis pro Sacramentis et Cultu Divino*. Ad usum privatum, Rome 1972.

LAIGNEL LAVASTINE, M., *Histoire générale de la médicine*, Paris 1938.

LANVERSIN, B. DE, *Decouvertes medicales recentes et impuissance masculine au sens canonique du terme*, in *Ius Populi Dei*, vol. III, Rome 1972, pp. 467-489.

LANVERSIN, B. DE, *Évolution de la chirurgie moderne et ses répercussions sur les cas d'impuissance masculin d'origine excrétoire*, in *L'Année Canonique*, 14 (1969) 93-122.

LAZZARATO, D., *Jurisprudentia Pontificia*, Naples 1963.

LEFEBVRE, C., *L'impuissance: science médicale, et jurisprudence rotale*, in *l'Année Canonique*, 15 (1970) 415-428.

LEFEBVRE, C., *Impotentia mulieris occlusae, impotentia viri*, in *Periodica*, 62 (1973) 403-412.

LEFEBVRE, C., *L'évolution actuelle de la jurisprudence matrimoniale*, in *Révue de Droit Canonique*, 24 (1974) 350-375.

LEFEBVRE, C., *De Joanne Gutiérrez deque constitutione "Cum frequenter" quoad verum semen*, in *Études de Droit et d'Histoire*, Mélanges Mgr. H. Wagnon, Louvain 1976, pp. 591-601.

LEFEBVRE, C., *La questione del "verum semen": evoluzione della dottrina e della prassi*, in *Monitor Ecclesiasticus*, 102 (1977) 356-362.

LESAGE, G., *Psychic impotence, a defect of consent*, in *Studia Canonica*, 4 (1970) 61-78.

LUCA, M. DE, *Summa praelectionum in libris Decretalium*, Prati 1904.

LUTRARIO, C., *De mulieris impotentia sive organica sive functionali*. Ad usum privatum. Rome 1977.

MAJOR, R.H., *A history of medicine*, Illinois 1954.

MARCHETTA, N., *Scioglimento del matrimonio canonico per l'inconsumazione*, Padova 1981.

MARRUBINI, G., *Il vaginismo nella matrimonialità forense*, in *Zacchia*, 32 (1957) 9-19.

MARRUBINI, G., *Aplasia congenita dei condotti. Impotenza. Nullità di matrimonio*, in *Rivista del Diritto Matrimoniale e dello Stato delle Persone*, 1966, pp. 12-24.

MARTÍN DE CASTRO, M., *La vagina artificial. Estudio jurídico-canónico*, Madrid 1971.

MASTERS, W.-JOHNSON, V.E., *Human sexual inadequacy*, Boston 1971.

MASTERS, W.-JOHNSON, V.E., *L'atto sessuale nell'uomo e nella donna*, It. tr., Milan 1978.

McCarthy, J., *The marriage capacity of the "mulier excisa"*, in *Ephemerides Iuris Canonici*, 1947, pp. 261 ff.

Mc Carthy, J., *Traditional concept of impotence*, in *Irish Theological Quarterly*, 18 (1951) 72-76; 19 (1952) 223-233.

McGrath, A., *A controversy concerning male impotence*. Analecta Gregoriana, vol. 247, Rome 1988.

Meineri, P.A., *Le correlazioni fra ghiandole genitali ed organismo nelle opere di Ippocrate, Aristotele e Galeno*, in *Minerva Medica*, 7 (1927) 1-20.

Meyerhof, M.-Joannides, D., *La gynécologie et l'obstétrique chez Avicenne (Ibn Sina) et leurs rapports avec celles des grecs*, Le Caire, 1938.

Millione, A., *Il problema del "verum semen" nelle cause di nullità matrimoniale della S.R. Rota*, in *Ephemerides Iuris Canonici*, 16 (1960) 92-101.

Minghetti, R., *Il Concetto di menstruazione nel '600 alla luce delle nuove acquisizioni nel campo della generazione*, in *Pagine di Storia della Medicina*, 4 (1960) 46-57.

Minghetti, R., *Endocrinologia, ginecologia e menopausa*, ibid., pp. 29-45.

Misuraca, S., *Alcune considerazioni in medicina legale canonistica in tema di impotenza*, in *Il Diritto Ecclesiastico*, 68 (1957) 405-419.

Misuraca, S., *L'impotenza canonica dal lato urologico*, in *Ephemerides Iuris Canonici*, 17 (1961) 258-303.

Misuraca, S., *Alcune precisazioni nel "verum semen"*, in *Ephemerides Iuris Canonici*, 21 (1965) 185-191.

Molieni, *Il tema di impotenza congiuntiva psichica*, in *Rivista del Diritto Matrimoniale e dello Stato delle Persone*, 1967, pp. 416 ff.

Montalenti, G., *Il sistema aristotelico della generazione degli animali*, in *Quaderni di Storia della Scienza*, Rome 1926, pp. 5-31.

Montserrat, A., *Le espina bífida oculta en las causas de nulidad de matrimonio por impotencia funcional*, in *La Ciencia*, 82 (1955) 449-461.

Money, Y.-Musaph, H., *Sessuologia*, Rome 1978.

Nangeroni, A.-Saponaro, A., *La vita sessuale dell'uomo*, Milan 1971.

Nardi, M.G., *Il problema della generazione umana nel pensiero di alcuni medici e fisiologi medievali*, in *Castalia*, 15 (1959) 101-106.

Navarrete, U., *De notione et effectibus consummationis matrimonii*, in *Periodica*, 59 (1970) 627-635.

Navarrete, U., *De muliere excisa. Animadversiones in opus recens editum*, in *Periodica*, 64 (1975) 678-681.

Navarrete, U., *De natura et de applicatione Decreti S. Congregationis pro Doctrina Fidei diei 13 maii 1977 circa impotentiam viri*, in *Periodica*, 68 (1979) 309-326.

Needham, J., *History of embriology*, Cambridge 1934.

Noonan, J.T., *Power to dissolve: lawyers and marriages in the Courts of the Roman Curia*, Massachusettes 1972.

Nowland, E., *Double vasectomy and marital impotence*, in *Theological Studies*, 1945, pp. 392-427.

Oesterle, G., *De hermaphrodismo in sua relatione ad canonem 1068 CIC*, in *Il Diritto Ecclesiastico*, 59 (1948) 5-25.

Oesterle, G., *Vera impotentia a parte mulieris?*, in *Il Diritto Ecclesiastico*, 63 (1952) 43 ff.

OESTERLE, G., *Impuissance*, in *Dictionnaire de Droit Canonique*, Paris 1953, tom. 5, coll. 1262-1292.

OESTERLE, G., *Von der psychischen impotenz*, in *Ephemerides Iuris Canonici*, 1955, pp. 133-155.

ORLANDI, G., *I "Casi Difficili" nel processo super rato*, Padova 1984.

OTTOLENGHI, S., *Il nuovo Istituto di medicina legale della R. Università di Roma: Discorso Inaugurale*, in *Zacchia*, 3 (1924) 1 ff.

PALAZZINI, A., *Storia della medicina*, Milan 1949.

PALAZZINI, A., *Elogio di Paolo Zacchia*, in *Pagine di Storia della Medicina*, 4 (1960) 130 ff.

PALMIERI, V.M., *Sterilità maschile ed impedimento d'impotenza*, in *Zacchia*, Serie 2a, 6 (1942) 137-152.

PALMIERI, V.M., *Medicina legale canonistica*, Naples 1955.

PALMIERI, V.M., *Medicina forense*, Naples 1964.

PAZZINI, A., *Paolo Zacchia e l'opera sua massima*, in *Zacchia*, Serie 2a, 23 (1960) 527-532.

PAZZINI, A., *Storia della medicina*, Milan 1964.

PAZZINI, A., *L'Opera medico-sociale di Paolo Zacchia*. Commemorazione tenuta presso l'Istituto di Medicina sociale in Roma, 18.5.1964.

PELLEGRINI, R., *Il "verum semen" in medicina legale ecclesiastica*, in *Morgagni*, 14 (1926) 417-423.

PESCETTO, G.-DE CECCO, L.-PECORARI, D., *Manuale di clinica ostetrica e ginecologica*, Rome 1981.

PEZZI, G., *Il pensiero filosofico e scientifico del seicento e gli albori della medicina moderna*, in *Atti e Memorie dell'Accademia di Storia dell'Arte Sanitaria*, Serie II, 43 (1963) 84-95.

PRUMMER, *De genuina notione impedimenti impotentiae*, in *Jus Pontificium*, 9 (1929) 214-218.

RAAD, I., *Prima e dopo il decreto del 13 maggio 1977 della S.C. per la Dottrina della Fede circa l'impotenza virile*, in *Ephemerides Iuris Canonici*, 36 (1980) 70-96.

RANDONE, M., *Le origini della medicina legale*, in *Minerva Medica*, 57 (1966) 1530-1532.

RAVÁ, A., *50 anni di giurisprudenza rotale sull'inconsumazione*, in *Il Diritto Ecclesiastico*, 1957, pp. 130 ff.

REGATILLO, E.F., *Matrimonium eorum qui vasectomiam passi sunt*, in *Sal Terrae*, 47 (1959) 292-295.

RITTY, C.J., *Possible invalidity of marriage by reason of sexual anomalies*, in *The Jurist*, 23 (1963) 394-442.

RIVAS, J.M., *Impotencia femenina por carencia de vagina*, in *Ius Canonicum*, 8 (1968) 589-597.

ROCCATAGLIATA, G., *Un capitolo di storia della medicina legale: la simulazione di malattia mentale per Paolo Zacchia*, in *Zacchia*, 49 (1974) 1-7.

RUSSO, *Incapacità dell'uomo alla copula*, in *Il Diritto Ecclesiastico*, 59 (1948) 303 ff.

SABATTANI, A., *L'évolution de la jurisprudence dans les causes de nullité de mariage pour incapacité psychique*, in *Studia Canonica*, 1 (1967) 143-161.

SANTORI, G., *Azoospermia escretoria funzionale*, in *Sessuologia*, 10 (1969) 52-55.

SANTORI, G., *I disturbi dell'eiaculazione*, in *Sessuologia*, ibid., pp. 117-120.

SANTORI, G., *La questione del "verum semen"*, in *Il Diritto Ecclesiastico*, 82 (1971) 67-78.

SANTORI, G., *Compendio di sessuologia*, Saluzzo 1972.

SAPONARO, A., *I problemi sessuali nel matrimonio*, Milan 1966.

SAPONARO, A., *Vita sessuale matrimoniale*, Milan 1972.

SAPONARO, A., *La vita sessuale della donna*, Milan 1972.

SHEEHY, G., *Male psychic impotence proceedings*, in *The Jurist*, 20 (1960) 253-294.

SILVESTRELLI, C., *Circa l'impotenza e l'inconsumazione nella giurisprudenza canonica anche del S. Ufficio*, in *Monitor Ecclesiasticus*, 98 (1973) 112-130.

ŠKALABRIN, N., *De vaginismo et inconsummatione matrimonii in decisionibus rotalibus (1945-1975)*, Diacovo 1987.

STAFFA, D., *De impotentia et inconsummatione matrimonii*, in *Apollinaris*, 28 (1955) 391-398.

STRADELLA, P.-GIAROLA, A., *Problemi medici e morali inerenti alla neoformazione artificiale della vagina*, in *Sessuologia*, 5 (1964) 17-37.

STROPPIANA, L., *Il concetto di generazione nel "Corpus Hippocraticum"*, in *Atti e Memorie della Accademia di Storia dell'Arte Sanitaria*, 4 (1964) 122-129.

SZENWIC, R., *L'impotenza nella recente giurisprudenza rotale*, in *Il Diritto Ecclesiastico*, 65 (1954) 41-142.

TAYLOR, S., (ed.), *Harlow's modern surgery for nurses*, London 1979.

TESSON, E., *L'empêchement canonique d'impuissance*, in *Cahiers Laennec*, 16 (1956) 51-67.

THARY, *L'impuissance masculine a la lumière de decisions recentes*, in *L'Année Canonique*, 9 (1965) 53-60.

THERIAULT, M., *Neovagin et impuissance*, in *Studia Canonica*, 2 (1968) 25-76.

TOCANEL, P., *Decretum circa impotentiam quae matrimonium dirimit. Adnotationes*, in *Apollinaris*, 50 (1977) 338-340.

TOPAI, F., *De necessitate uteri in generatione et in matrimonio*, Rome 1903.

TOSO, A., *De aequa extensione conceptus impotentiae prout est impedimentum dirimens*, in *Jus Pontificium*, 7 (1927) 90-96.

TOSO, A., *Animadversiones quaedam*, ibid., pp. 97-102.

CARRARA, M.-ROMANESE, R.-CANUTO, G.-TOVO, C., *Manuale di medicina legale*, Turin 1937.

VALENTINI, G., *È mutato il concetto di impotenza?*, in *Monitor Ecclesiasticus*, 104 (1979) 498-505.

VAN DUIN, A., *De impedimento impotentiae psychicae in matrimonio*, in *Apollinaris*, 23 (1950) 114-175.

VANNICELLI, L., *Rassegna delle più recenti sentenze rotali sull'impotenza*, in *Il Diritto Ecclesiastico*, 77 (1966) 450-489.

VANNICELLI, L., *Spunti per uno studio sul "verum semen" e concetti connessi*, in *Il Diritto Ecclesiastico*, 78 (1967) 13-37.

VERMEERSCH, A., *De vasectomia duplici*, in *Periodica*, 24 (1935) 43-45.

VERSALDI, G., *L'oggettività delle prove in campo psichico*, Brescia 1981.

VIGLINO, C., *Un curioso equivoco sull'impotenza al matrimonio in diritto canoni-*

co, in *Il Diritto Ecclesiastico*, 34 (1923) 1-26; 54-85.

VIGLINO, C., *Un'interessante sentenza della S.R. Rota sull'impotenza*, in *Il Diritto Ecclesiastico*, 38 (1927) 272-275.

VIGLINO, C., *In che consiste l'una caro oggetto del matrimonio*, in *Il Diritto ecclesiastico*, 38 (1927) 387-395.

VIGLINO, C., *Fondamento dell'indissolubilità del matrimonio è il valore morale dell'unione sessuale?*, in *Il Diritto Ecclesiastico*, 39 (1928) 313-322.

VIGLINO, C., *Oggetto e fine primario del matrimonio*, in *Il Diritto Ecclesiastico*, 40 (1929) 142-149.

WEGAN, M., *La jurisprudence rotale et le decrét du 13 mai 1977*, in *Revue de Droit Canonique*, 31 (1981) 226-245.

WERNZ, F.X.-VIDAL, P., *Ius Canonicum*, tom. V, *Ius matrimoniale*, Rome 1946.

WRENN, L.G., *Annulments*, Washington 1983.

ZALBA, M., *De capacitate mulieris excisae et de impotentia viri vasectomiam duplicem passi ad matrimonium valide contrahendum*, in *Revista Española de Derecho Canónico*, 2 (1947) 171-207.

ZALBA, M., *Decretum circa impotentiam quae matrimonium dirimit et Breve "Cum frequenter" Sixti V*, in *Periodica* 68 (1979) 5-58.

ZIINO, G., *Medicina legale e giurisprudenza medica*, Milan 1906.

INDEX OF PROPER NAMES

Thomas Aquinas (S.), 62, 83, 107, 149, 150.
Topai, F., 65.
Tortoletti, B., 167.
Tovo, C., 31.
Trosch, F., 62.

Ulpian, 169.

Vallesio, 50.
Van Baer, K.E., 56.
Vannet, 40.
Vatican Council II, 19, 65, 71.
Vereecke, L., 62.
Vermeersch, A., 17.
Verospio, 35.

Verrusti, 50.
Versaldi, G., 79, 126, 159.
Vesalio, A., 50.
Vesling, 137.
Vidal, P., 13, 70, 130.
Vlaming, T.M., 17.

Wernz, F.X., 13, 70, 130.
Wrenn, L.G., 126.
Wynen, 17.

Zacchia, Lanfranco, 26, 165, 166, 167.
Zacuto, Lusitanus, 169.
Zarate, 39, 80.
Ziino, G., 27.

TIPOGRAFIA POLIGLOTTA DELLA PONTIFICIA UNIVERSITÀ GREGORIANA
PIAZZA DELLA PILOTTA, 4 - ROMA